LOS
CABOS

JENNIFER KRAMER

CONTENTS

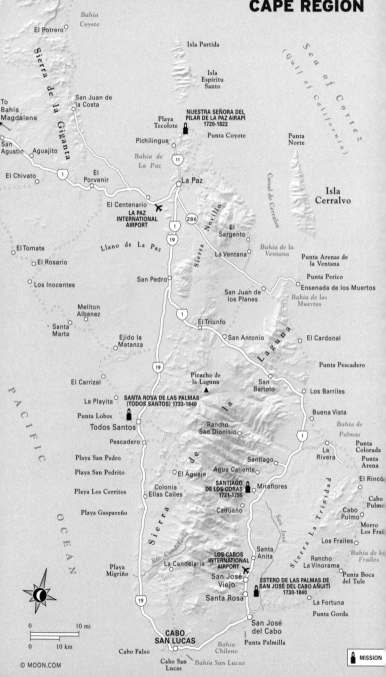

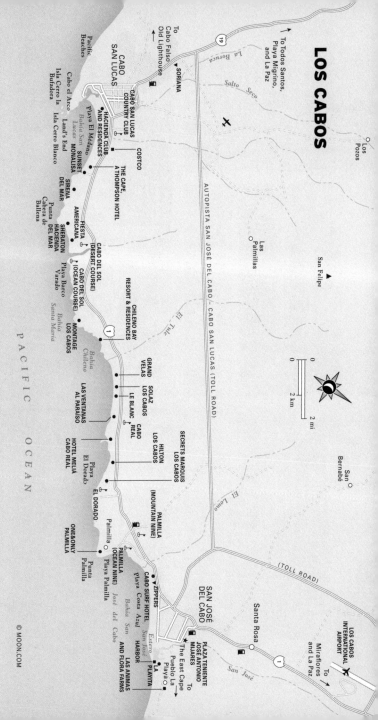

1   dolphins jumping near La Paz

2   Rancho Leonero in Buena Vista, on the East Cape

3   Mexican crafts for sale in downtown Todos Santos

4   view of the marina promenade in Cabo San Lucas

5   Catedral de La Paz

6   views along the East Cape coastal road, Camino Cabo Este

7   kayaking at Isla Espíritu Santo

DISCOVER
LOS CABOS

Here at the end of the Baja peninsula, you can choose the perfect getaway for you.

Los Cabos is synonymous with relaxation, luxury, and indulgence. Beautiful beaches beckon with sunbathing possibilities. Spas offer lavish treatments and yachts fill the marinas, while world-famous golf courses give picturesque ocean views. All-inclusive beachfront resorts call to jet-setters. Spring breakers flock here to party on the beach all day and dance at clubs all night.

Just outside Los Cabos, travelers will find a different world. Within an hour's drive, the West and East Capes offer humbler, more authentic experiences, with mountain ranges, waterfalls, near-empty beaches, and one of the few coral reefs in North America.

Two hours north, the state capital of La Paz has museums and restaurants alongside still more stunning beaches, wildlife such as sea lions and whale sharks, and abundant recreational opportunities.

It may not be an easy one, but the choice is yours.

8 TOP
EXPERIENCES

1 **Boat out to El Arco:** Take a ride to the southern tip of the Baja peninsula to see this famous rock archway up close (page 26).

2 **Hit the beach:** You'll find some of Baja's most stunning beaches here, perfect for swimming, snorkeling, and soaking up the sun (page 20).

3 **Explore underwater:** Dive coral reefs and snorkel with sea lions in the waters of the Pacific Ocean and the Sea of Cortez (page 19).

4 **Ride the waves:** The breaks here lure adventurous surfers, from novices to experts (page 21).

5 **Go gallery-hopping:** Peruse the galleries and discover the vibrant creative scenes in San José del Cabo's Historic Art District (page 57) and Todos Santos (page 158).

>>>

6 **Cast a fishing line:** Anglers come for the thrill of catching marlin, dorado, roosterfish, and more (pages 92 and 126).

<<<

7 **Party all night:** Spring breakers and the young at heart enjoy clubs where the shots never run out and the party goes until early morning (page 35).

>>>

8 **Catch a spectacular sunset:** Take a seat on the beach or at an open-air restaurant and watch as the sun sinks into the water (page 22).

PLANNING YOUR TRIP

WHERE TO GO

LOS CABOS

The most-recognized and most-visited location in all of Baja, Los Cabos refers to the region comprising the two cities of San José del Cabo and Cabo San Lucas, and the corridor that connects them. This is a Baja completely different from the rest of the peninsula. Luxury, relaxation, and fun are the focus here. Yachts fill the marinas, and all-inclusive resorts line the beaches. Dance clubs and bars are busy until the wee hours of the morning.

THE EAST CAPE AND THE SIERRA DE LA LAGUNA

The East Cape is home to beaches, world-class diving, offshore fishing, charming towns, and the lush peaks of the Sierra de la Laguna. Los Barriles attracts kiteboarders and windsurfers, while the off-the-grid town of Cabo Pulmo draws divers and snorkelers with its coral reef teeming with marinelife.

LA PAZ

La Paz centers on the beautiful malecón that wraps around the bay, where strolling locals and tourists enjoy the views, restaurants, hotels,

diving in Cabo Pulmo with a school of yellow groupers

IF YOU HAVE...

FOUR DAYS
Los Cabos can be a perfect escape for a long weekend. Pick one hotel as your base and spend the days exploring some of the highlights.

SEVEN DAYS
With a full week, add on day trips to surrounding areas. Or split your time between Los Cabos and one other destination—the East Cape, La Paz, or Todos Santos.

TWO WEEKS
With two weeks, explore the whole region. The best way to is to fly into Los Cabos and make a loop.

and shops. But its main draws are the **beaches** and the **islands. Snorkel** with **sea lions,** swim with **whale sharks,** or enjoy deserted beaches.

TODOS SANTOS AND THE WEST CAPE
Up the coast from Los Cabos, Todos Santos is a charming colonial town of **bohemian art galleries, upscale** **restaurants,** and **chic boutique hotels.** Surf spots, beautiful beaches, and the nearby **El Pescadero** community draw tourists looking for a more authentic **alternative to Cabo.**

BEFORE YOU GO

HIGH AND LOW SEASONS
Winter is the **high season** for visiting Los Cabos, with the weeks around Christmas and New Year's Day being some of the busiest of the year. Expect to pay the most for accommodations at this time, and make arrangements in advance. **Spring break** in Los Cabos now spans March-April, ending around Easter, drawing a younger, more rambunctious crowd.

Summer is **low season** in Baja Sur as temperatures and **humidity** are very high during the months of July, August, and September. Los Cabos has become such a popular destination that many hotels and restaurants here are open year-round, but smaller businesses outside the area are likely to shutter during the hottest months, including restaurants and attractions in towns like La Paz, Los Barriles, and Todos Santos. Hotels that stay open will likely offer cheaper rates. Anglers, divers, and surfers still flock to Los Cabos and surrounding areas in the summer because the fish are plentiful, the waters are warm, and the surf is good.

Baja California Sur has a hurricane season June-October, so travelers should be aware of the risk of tropical storms.

PASSPORTS AND VISAS

Passports are required to visit Baja California. Non-Mexican citizens must also obtain a *forma migratoria múltiple* (FMM) tourist permit in order to travel in Mexico. If you are flying into Los Cabos from outside of Mexico, this will be included in your ticket. If crossing by land, you can obtain your permit at the border crossing.

TRANSPORTATION

Unless you plan on spending most of your time at a resort in Los Cabos, it's best to reserve a rental car for use during your trip if you are flying in. Mexican auto insurance is required by law, so don't forget to purchase it before you leave on your trip.

ocean views from a hammock at Villa Santa Cruz in Todos Santos

WHICH CABO IS FOR ME?

Cabo San Lucas

Each area of Cabo has its own distinct personality:

- **Cabo San Lucas:** Tourist areas teem with restaurants, souvenir shops, and nightlife. This is where cruise ship passengers disembark and spring breakers stay.

- **The Corridor:** The most expensive and exclusive resorts are here, as are the most beautiful beaches.

- **San José del Cabo:** There's a more authentic Mexican feel here, with a town plaza and the Historic Art District. The vibe is relaxed and quiet, but with more and more beachfront resorts and timeshares. You can still find fairly affordable accommodations near the historic district.

EXPLORE
LOS CABOS

FOUR-DAY GETAWAY

DAY 1

Fly into the Los Cabos International Airport and drop your luggage off at your hotel before heading out to explore Cabo San Lucas. Take a quick water taxi to get a close-up view of Cabo's iconic El Arco before disembarking at Lover's Beach. Spend the afternoon sunbathing and snorkeling. When you return to town, grab a traditional Mexican dinner downtown at Mi Casa or Pancho's. Then enjoy some of Cabo's infamous nightlife with a margarita or two at Cabo Wabo Cantina or The Giggling Marlin.

DAY 2

Get in touch with the local food movement in Los Cabos by heading to the rural Las Animas Bajas area, just outside of San José del Cabo. If it's Saturday, you can check out the San José Mercado Organico, an organic farmers market. Eat brunch at one of the gorgeous farm-to-table restaurants, like Flora's Field Kitchen or Acre. On the way back to town, stop in the Historic Art District in San José del Cabo to check out the colonial architecture, bustling town plaza, and art galleries.

Playa Chileno

DAY 3

Spend a day enjoying some of the beautiful beaches in Los Cabos. Divers may want to take an organized tour to access some of the best dive spots. Snorkelers can visit Playa Chileno or Bahía Santa Maria along the corridor, where swimming is also possible. At Playa El Médano, beachgoers will find an array of activities to choose from, like kayaking or Jet Skiing. When you've had enough sun and sand for the day, enjoy a sunset beach dinner at a spot like The Office on Playa El Médano or Sunset MonaLisa along the corridor.

El Arco

DAY 4

Spend your last day truly relaxing at one of Los Cabos' incredible spas, such as Somma Wine Spa or Spa Marquis, indulging in a facial, a massage, or an entire day of treatments. Or schedule a tee time at one of the area's famous golf courses, such as Diamante or Cabo del Sol Golf Course, where you can enjoy beautiful ocean views on the greens.

THE CABO LOOP

For those who visit the Los Cabos area but want to see and experience more of the natural beauty and adventure of Baja California, this fun road trip explores the Cape area of Baja California Sur.

DAY 1

Fly into Los Cabos International Airport and rent a car at one of the stands in the airport. Drive the 15 minutes south from the airport to the town of San José del Cabo and check into one of the hotels along the beach or in the historic town center. Walk around town to take in the plaza, historic district, and art galleries. Bird-watchers will want to check out the nearby Estero San José. For dinner, check out La Revolución Comedor de Baja California, just off the plaza, for a gourmet meal featuring local ingredients.

DAY 2
89 KM (55 MI)
1.5 HOURS

Head over to the East Cape town of Cabo Pulmo where divers and snorkelers will enjoy exploring the coral reef just offshore. Snorkelers can swim out from the beach at Los Arbolitos or Los Frailes, and divers will enjoy taking a boat out to get to remoter spots. Enjoy dinner and drinks at the casual La Palapa restaurant looking out at the water. Stay in one of Cabo Pulmo's casual eco-lodging accommodations.

ALTERNATE TRIP
56 KM (35 MI)
45 MINUTES

For those not interested in diving or snorkeling, explore more of what the East Cape has to offer with the Santa Rita Hot Springs and the Cañon de la Zorra waterfall, both accessed

Baja Sur is home to a number of great diving and snorkeling sites. August-November brings the warmest waters and best visibility. Tour operators lead dive and snorkel trips out of Cabo San Lucas, San José del Cabo, and Cabo Pulmo. Many snorkeling spots along the East Cape, Cabo Pulmo, and Los Cabos can easily be accessed from the beach.

tropical fish and coral reef

- **Land's End:** A great spot for snorkeling or diving, Land's End lets you experience both the Pacific Ocean and Sea of Cortez simultaneously. You might see barracuda, tuna, or baitfish, or swim with sea lions—the site is host to a colony (page 31).

- **Sand Falls:** One of Cabo's most famous and unique dive sites, Sand Falls is a river of sand that flows between rocks and over the edge of a canyon 30 meters (98 feet) below the water's surface. Marinelife such as rays and zebra eels abound here (page 32).

- **Chileno Bay:** This shallow, protected reef offshore from Playa Chileno is a good spot for beginning divers and snorkelers to spot manta rays, sea turtles, and nurse sharks (page 49).

- **Gavilanes:** Both beginners and advanced divers will enjoy spotting rays and whitetip reef sharks in this small bay with one of the best coral reefs in Los Cabos (page 49).

- **The Blowhole:** Offshore from the shallow reef of Bahía Santa Maria, advanced divers can see large schools of fish, manta rays, and sea turtles (page 49).

- **Parque Nacional Cabo Pulmo:** This national park, one of the most popular destinations on the peninsula for scuba divers and snorkelers, has a living coral reef and abundant marinelife including tropical fish, moray eels, octopus, lobsters, and sea lions (pages 82 and 83).

sunbathing at Cañon de la Zorra

from the town of **Santiago.** Spend the night in **Los Barriles** or **Buena Vista** on the coast.

DAY 3
150 KM (93 MI)
2.5 HOURS

Get an early start driving north on Mexico 1 to La Paz. Spend a few hours in the small old mining town of **El Triunfo,** where you can walk along the mine ruins and grab some baked goods at **Caffé El Triunfo.** When you

BEST BEACHES

Playa Balandra

LOS CABOS
Cabo San Lucas, San José del Cabo, and the corridor in between are all home to some of the most beautiful beaches in Baja. Be careful, as swimming is not safe at many of the beaches. At popular tourist beaches like **Lover's Beach** (near the Land's End arch) and **Playa Chileno** (on the corridor), swimming and snorkeling are allowed and encouraged.

LA PAZ
La Paz is home to a number of beautiful Sea of Cortez beaches. Just south of town, visitors can drive to **Playa Balandra** and **Playa El Tecolote.** Both have shallow, clear waters and white sand beaches. Even more fun is to take a boat ride out to explore the beaches of the islands offshore, where you'll get to enjoy deserted stretches with bright turquoise waters.

TODOS SANTOS AND THE WEST CAPE
Todos Santos has a number of stunning beaches, but the currents and waves are strong and make most of them great for surfing, not safe for swimming. **Playa Los Cerritos,** south of Todos Santos in El Pescadero, was once touted as one of the best beaches in Baja, though some complain it's become too busy and commercial in recent years.

get to La Paz, drive out to the scenic beaches at Playa Balandra or Playa El Tecolote. Enjoy ceviche and beers with your toes in the sand at restaurant-bar Palapa Azul.

DAY 4
Take a break from driving today and book a boat excursion out to the La Paz islands, especially Isla Espíritu Santo. Dive with sea lions, swim with whale sharks, or just enjoy the beautiful island and beach views from

the boat. When you get back to La Paz, enjoy a stroll along the lively *malecón*.

DAY 5
79 KM (49 MI)
1 HOUR
Head southwest on Mexico 1 to Mexico 19 for the West Cape and its colonial artist town of Todos Santos. Check into the charming Villa Santa Cruz or La Bohemia Baja Hotel Pequeño. Spend some time walking around the historic center of town to

the historic architecture of Todos Santos

DAY 6
74 KM (46 MI)
1 HOUR

Drive south on Mexico 19 to Cabo San Lucas and hop on a water taxi to check out the famous El Arco, the Land's End arch, and to go to Lover's Beach. Spend the afternoon here snorkeling, swimming, and sunbathing. At night, head out to Cabo Wabo Cantina or somewhere else along the strip to take in a bit of Cabo's legendary nightlife.

DAY 7

Spend your last morning enjoying one of Cabo's indulgent treats—a round of golf, a massage at the spa, a morning surf, or a poolside margarita.

check out the colonial architecture, shops, and restaurants. Splurge for an incredible meal of fish carpaccio and lobster ravioli at Café Santa Fe.

BEST SURFING
LOS CABOS

South swells in summer bring consistent surf breaks in Los Cabos.

THE CORRIDOR

Breaks in the corridor are generally for seasoned surfers, but surf lessons for beginners and board rentals are also available.

- Monuments is a rocky left point that's great on south swells.
- Las Conchas access can be difficult because of the Cabo Real resort, but those who get through to the beach will find a right break with good shape.
- El Tule, farther east, is a solid right reef break and one of the few spots along the corridor where you can still camp on the beach.

SAN JOSÉ DEL CABO

Playa Costa Azul is one of the premier surfing beaches in the region, where surfers of all experience levels can find waves. It has three breaks:

- Acapulquito (Old Man's) has good waves for beginners and longboarders.

surfer at Playa Costa Azul

BEST SUNSETS

LOS CABOS

Restaurant **Sunset MonaLisa** and its bar, **Sunset Point,** are famed and aptly named spots for sunsets over the ocean and El Arco. On the west side of El Arco, along **Playa Solmar,** fine dining establishments **El Farallon** and **La Roca** have near-unobstructed views of the sun setting over the ocean.

LA PAZ

Although located on the eastern side of the peninsula, La Paz is a rare spot along the Sea of Cortez that gets gorgeous sunsets with water views because of the way the city is situated along the bay and Pichilingue Peninsula. The *malecón* is a lovely spot for watching sunsets from one of the many benches or open-air restaurants and bars along the boardwalk. Another option

sunset in Todos Santos

is **Playa Pichilingue,** which provides a beautiful beach setting along with your sunset.

TODOS SANTOS AND THE WEST CAPE

Because of the location of Todos Santos and El Pescadero along the West Cape, ocean sunsets are stunning from nearly every beach, particularly **Playa Los Cerritos.** The **El Mirador** restaurant on Punta Lobos beach is also known for splendid sunset views.

THE EAST CAPE

While the **East Cape** doesn't get ocean sunsets, early risers will enjoy colorful **sunrises** over the Sea of Cortez.

- **La Roca (The Rock)** is a right reef break, best surfed at high tide.
- **Zippers** is Los Cabos' most famous break, where the annual Los Cabos Open of Surf takes place.

TODOS SANTOS AND THE WEST CAPE

The West Cape has drawn adventurous surfers for decades with its big breaks and uncrowded waves.

TODOS SANTOS

Experienced surfers with their own boards head to this area.

- **Playa La Pastora** is known for bigger rights on northwest swells, as

well as an exposed point break with right and left breaks.
- **Punta Márquez** and **Punta Conejo** require off-road exploration as well as self-sufficient camping; the payoff is near-empty waves.
- **Playa San Pedrito** is a solid beach break notable for west and north swells.

EL PESCADERO

Surf lessons and board rentals can be found here.

- **Playa Los Cerritos** is popular with beginners, with its easy waves and sandy bottom. A break at the point offers more experienced surfers some fun as well.

LOS CABOS

The iconic rock archway El Arco

at the tip of the peninsula marks land's end. This is Los Cabos, the most-recognized destination in Baja.

Los Cabos refers to the region comprising the two cities of San José del Cabo and Cabo San Lucas, and the corridor that connects them. This is a Baja completely different from the rest of the peninsula. Yachts fill the marinas and all-inclusive mega-resorts with thousands of rooms line the beaches. Spring breakers flock here for the beach scene and nightlife. Dance clubs and

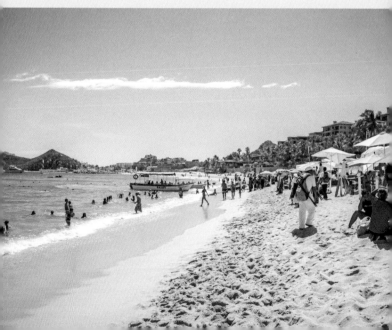

HIGHLIGHTS

✪ **EL ARCO:** The signature landmark of Cabo San Lucas is its famous rock archway at the very southern tip of the Baja peninsula, where the Pacific Ocean and the Sea of Cortez meet. Take a boat out to see it up close (page 26).

✪ **LOVER'S BEACH:** This gorgeous sandy beach on the protected Bahía de Cabo San Lucas is accessible only by boat (page 30).

✪ **GOLF:** With beautiful ocean views and a margarita waiting at the clubhouse afterward, golfing has never been more spectacular (page 34).

✪ **NIGHTLIFE:** Spring breakers and the young at heart enjoy clubs where the tequila shots never run out and the party goes until early morning (page 35).

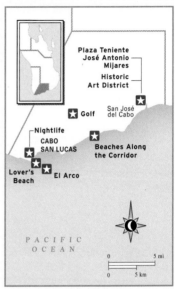

✪ **BEACHES ALONG THE CORRIDOR:** The stretch between the two towns of Cabo San Lucas and San José del Cabo is home to some of the most pristine beaches in the area. Enjoy swimming, sunbathing, snorkeling, and just relaxing (page 48).

✪ **PLAZA TENIENTE JOSÉ ANTONIO MIJARES:** The plaza is the heart of San José del Cabo, surrounded by art galleries, shops, restaurants, boutique hotels, and the mission (page 57).

✪ **SAN JOSÉ DEL CABO'S HISTORIC ART DISTRICT:** Art galleries abound in historic downtown San José del Cabo. On Thursday evenings November-June, they stay open late for the "Gallery Art Walk" (page 57).

bars are busy until the wee hours of the morning. It's hard to walk down the street in Cabo San Lucas without being prodded to take a boat trip, book a ziplining tour, or buy a T-shirt about tequila shots.

Luxury, relaxation, and fun are the focus here, and Los Cabos does all three things exceptionally well. On the extravagant and lavish side of Los Cabos, jet-setters and celebrities come to escape and play. Rooms at some of the most exclusive resorts can cost at least US$2,000 a night. Golf courses have sweeping views of the Sea of Cortez, spas specialize in indulgent services, and dining can be world-class.

Love it or hate it, this is one of the most popular spots on the Baja peninsula. Because of its worldwide attention, there's no stopping the growth in this region. More and more luxury resorts are planned to open. While it's difficult to call a trip to the area an authentic Mexican experience, it's hard to deny the unique draw that lures over two million visitors each year.

PLANNING YOUR TIME

Most people visit Cabo to enjoy the beaches and take advantage of the all-inclusive resorts. Some tourists don't even leave their hotels during their stay. Depending on how long you need to decompress and relax, a long weekend or a week is plenty. It's easy to explore all of Los Cabos—Cabo San Lucas, the corridor, and San José del Cabo—by staying in any of the three areas. It only takes 40 minutes to drive from downtown Cabo San Lucas to downtown San José del Cabo (a taxi costs about US$40). Staying in Los Cabos, you can also explore surrounding areas like the East Cape or Todos Santos on day trips; budget at least a week in Los Cabos if you'd like to take advantage of this.

Cruise ships coming into the Los Cabos area anchor just out from the marina in Cabo San Lucas and tender passengers to shore (there's no cruise ship port). The drop-off location for passengers is the marina near Soloman's Landing restaurant.

Many cruise lines only offer a half day in port at Cabo. Excursion companies are well aware of their time parameters, and many plan activities to meet the cruise ship timeline. Some cruise lines offer two days in port at Cabo, which means that passengers have the ability to stay out until 9pm on their first evening in port.

Los Cabos

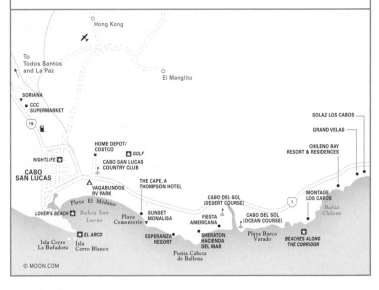

© MOON.COM

Cabo San Lucas

Cabo San Lucas anchors the region, with a variety of activities, shops, restaurants, nightlife options, and hotels. Its famous El Arco rock archway is the most-photographed landmark in Baja. Water sports and activities are taken to a new extreme here with hydroboarding, ziplining, and camel rides available in addition to the usual diving, snorkeling, fishing, and boating. There are plenty of beaches to enjoy, with Lover's Beach, accessible only by boat, the most famous.

Cabo's marina and downtown are the busy tourist spots, especially when a cruise ship is in town. Nightlife in Cabo is legendary, with large nightclubs and bars living up to stereotypical expectations: Tequila shots abound and music and dancing continue until the wee hours.

The downtown and marina area of Cabo are very walkable. A car or taxi (US$8) is necessary to reach areas such as Playa Solmar and Playa El Médano.

SIGHTS

TOP EXPERIENCE

✪ EL ARCO

As the most prominent feature of the entire peninsula, **El Arco** (also sometimes called *La Finisterra,* for Land's End) is Cabo's famous landmark. The natural rock arch dramatically singles out the tip of the peninsula and the point where the Pacific Ocean and the Sea of Cortez collide. The arch is visible from points along Playa Médano and the corridor, but

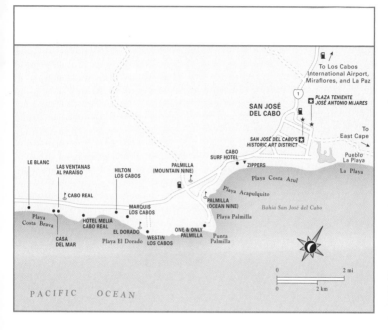

one of the best ways to experience it is to take a glass-bottom boat out to see it up close. A walk along the marina brings you to a number of companies offering glass-bottom boat trips for US$15. You could also book a private tour with a company like Roger's (www.rogerstourboatcabomexico.com). Go in the morning when waters are calmer.

Glass-bottom boats take tourists out to see El Arco.

CABO SAN LUCAS MARINA

Cabo's lively marina is conveniently located in downtown and lined with shops, restaurants, bars, and hotels. The marina is a hub for tourist activity, with snorkeling and diving tours, fishing charters, and boats out to El Arco and Lover's Beach departing from here. There's no cruise ship pier in Cabo, so cruise ships anchor away from land and tender passengers to shore, dropping them off here at the marina. At the north end of the harbor is the Puerto Paraíso Mall, a large shopping center with a movie theater, stores, and restaurants.

PLAZA AMELIA WILKES

Visitors looking for some peace and quiet in Cabo San Lucas will find it at Plaza Amelia Wilkes (Lázaro Cárdenas between Calle Cabo San Lucas and Calle Miguel Hidalgo). Set a few blocks up from the tourist area,

Cabo San Lucas

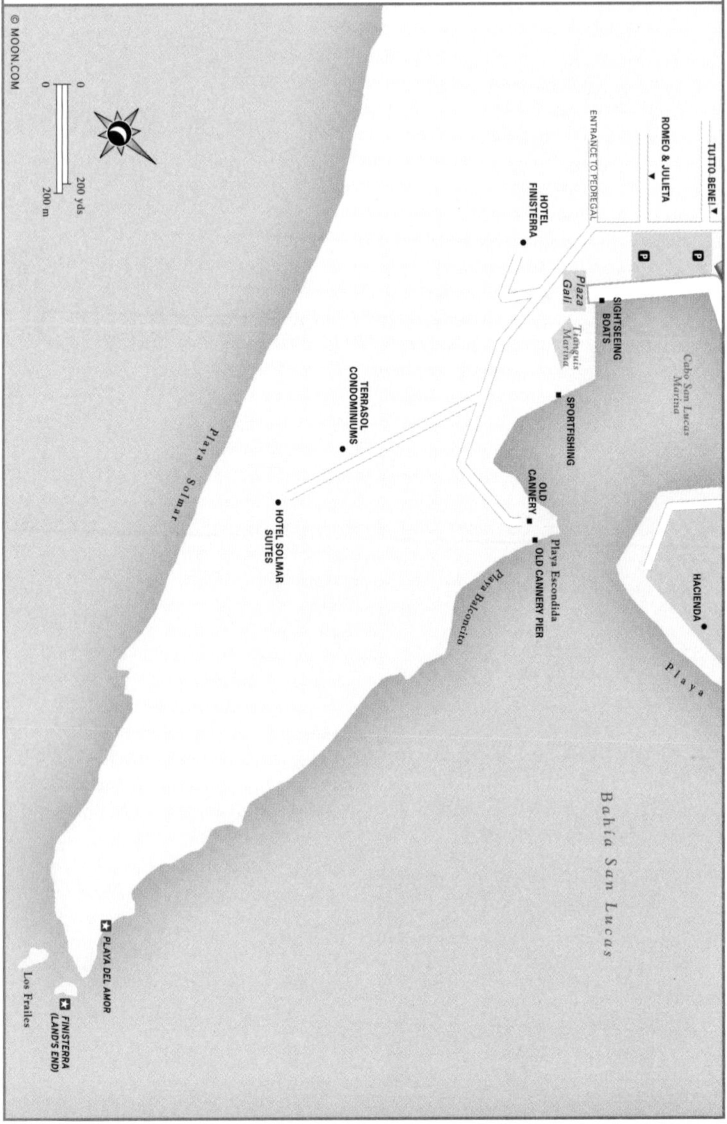

© MOON.COM

0
0
200 yds
200 m

ENTRANCE TO PEDREGAL

TUTTO BENE!
ROMEO & JULIETA

P
P

HOTEL
FINISTERRA

Plaza
Galí

Tianguis
Marina

Cabo San Lucas
Marina

SIGHTSEEING
BOATS

TERRASOL
CONDOMINIUMS

SPORTFISHING

OLD
CANNERY

HOTEL SOLMAR
SUITES

Playa Escondida
OLD CANNERY PIER

HACIENDA

Playa
Solmar

Playa Balconcita

Playa

Bahía San Lucas

PLAYA DEL AMOR

Los Frailes

FINISTERRA
(LAND'S END)

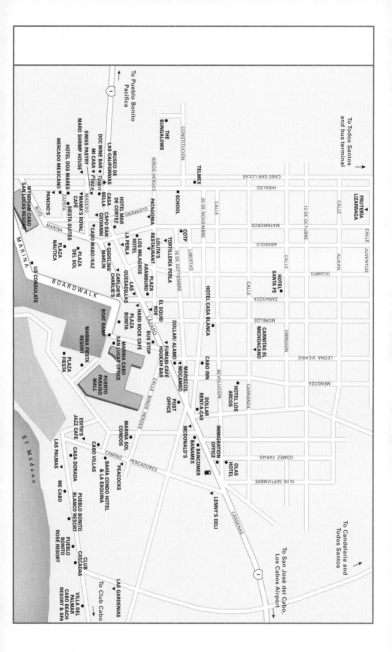

there's a gazebo with benches where visitors can sit to relax for a bit. Lining the plaza is a small natural history museum, **Museo de Historia Natural Cabo San Lucas** (tel. 624/105-0661, 10am-3pm Tues.-Fri., 10am-2pm Sat.-Sun., US$1) that covers the history, archaeology, geology, and biodiversity of the region.

BEACHES

✪ LOVER'S BEACH

Accessed almost purely by boat, **Lover's Beach** is a unique two-sided beach out near El Arco. One side of the beach is lined by the Bahía de Cabo San Lucas where swimmers and snorkelers enjoy the calm waters. The other side faces the Pacific Ocean, where the water is too rough for swimming. This rough side of the beach is affectionately called "Divorce Beach."

Water taxis leaving from the marina go to Lover's Beach for US$15

the Bahía de Cabo San Lucas

every 45 minutes, granting you the flexibility to return to town whenever you're ready. There are no services (including bathrooms) or shade at the beach. As one of Cabo's highlight activities, it can get very crowded, and even more so in the afternoons.

PLAYA SOLMAR

The relatively uncrowded **Playa Solmar** is a beautiful, long beach perfect for taking a walk or sunbathing.

El Arco is one of the most iconic symbols of the peninsula.

Because of its location on the Pacific, the waves and currents here are very strong, making it unsafe for swimming. Many of Cabo's large hotels are located along Playa Solmar because of the beautiful views and tranquility of the area.

Unless you're staying at one of the hotels along the beach here, there are no services. Access to the beach is on the road to Solmar Resort.

Playa El Médano

PLAYA EL MÉDANO

Buzzing with people and activities, Playa El Médano is one of the only safe swimming beaches in Cabo San Lucas, but don't expect a relaxing float or beach day at this wild and loud beach. Spring breakers taking shots, families enjoying water sports, and vendors selling jewelry and knickknacks all crowd together here. Any kind of water activity can be booked on this beach, from kayaking to hydroboarding. Swimming is only permitted in the roped-in area. Beachfront *palapa* restaurants and bars are close by, including Mango Deck, which anchors the spring break scene. Playa El Médano is the closest beach to town and stretches from the east side of the harbor entrance to Villa del Palmar.

If walking from downtown, walk around the marina to the end and go left at the channel entrance. There's also access via Avenida del Pescador or Camino Hotel Hacienda. Follow the blue signs for "Médano Beach." There's no parking lot and street parking can be hard to find, especially on weekends or during spring break, so walking or taking a cab is often the best solution.

SPORTS AND RECREATION

There's no lack of tour operators in Cabo for a seemingly unlimited number of activities.

EXTREME ADVENTURES

Whether you want to mountain bike, hydroboard, fly in a small plane, zipline, or sail, Cabo Adventures (tel. 624/173-9500, www.cabo-adventures. com) can make your activity dreams come true. It has a large booking office in downtown Cabo on Paseo de la Marina and offers discounts when you book more than one activity.

Wild Canyon (tel. 624/144-4433, www.wildcanyon.com.mx) takes tourists outside Cabo to the "Wild Canyon," where the company has set up a large park with ziplines, ATVing, camel rides, bungee jumping, and even a small zoo.

DIVING AND SNORKELING
Dive and Snorkel Sites
The Bahía de Cabo San Lucas was designated a protected underwater national marine park in 1973, marking it as an area abundant with sealife. The bay provides relatively calm waters for diving.

Lover's Beach and Land's End are the best spots for snorkeling in Cabo San Lucas. You can snorkel off the

31

beach at Lover's Beach on your own or with a guide. The waters won't be perfectly calm, but they should be clear enough to spot some tropical fish. Winds typically pick up later in the afternoon. For snorkeling off Land's End, a number of boat and tour operators can take you out to swim with the sea lions and fish near El Arco. Many of the outfitters out of Cabo San Lucas will take snorkelers over to Bahía Chileno and Bahía Santa Maria along the corridor, where the waters are calmer.

Sand Falls is one of Cabo's most famous and unique dive sites. Close to Lover's Beach, 30 meters (98 feet) below the surface, is a river of sand that flows between rocks and over the edge of a canyon, creating an unusual sand fall. The sand rivers are not always flowing, and are usually the most active when stormy weather makes the seas more turbulent (the opposite of normal optimal diving conditions). Even if the falls aren't active, there's still abundant sealife around the site, such as rays, zebra eels, and grouper.

For diving, Land's End is also a great option. This is a unique site because it allows divers to experience both the Pacific Ocean and the Sea of Cortez at the same time. Barracuda, tuna, baitfish, and rays can be spotted. The site is also home to a colony of sea lions that love to swim and play with divers. Nearby **Pelican Rock** is a reef that drops off a deep wall down to 150 meters (492 feet). There are devil rays, moray eels, porcupine fish, and puffer fish. There are two coral reefs at **Neptune's Finger,** which is also home to one of the largest sand falls. Tropical fish, sea turtles, and manta rays can be seen here.

Outfitters

Most hotels and resorts can arrange for a dive or snorkel trip and equipment rental. Morning outings are the most popular, as that's when the seas are calmer and better for diving.

Dive Cabo (tel. 624/105-1793, www.divecabo.com, US$75-85) offers full-day snorkel and dive trips daily. Its small groups are guided by experienced leaders. PADI courses and free 30-minute "scuba refreshers" are provided prior to your dive. Dive Cabo also provides a free underwater photography service so you can take home a memento from your dive. All tours depart from its location at the Cabo San Lucas marina (no hotel pickup).

Aqua Los Cabos (tel. 624/143-9286, www.aqualoscabos.com, US$40-100) hosts snorkel and dive trips around the Los Cabos region, as well as excursions up to Parque Nacional Cabo Pulmo. It has courses and trips for all levels of divers. Tours range 3-5 hours. Depending on the tour, your trip will depart from the company's ship in Cabo San Lucas, or else you'll be picked up from your hotel.

FISHING

Cabo was initially a small fishing village, and sportfishing remains a popular draw for the region today. A number of fishing charters and services in the area will take you out for a day. Marlin, billfish, red snapper, yellowtail, grouper, sierra, and roosterfish are all common in the region. Marlin and sailfish are caught on an optional catch-and-release program in Los Cabos to support local conservation efforts. One species is permitted per boat. Ask ahead to see if your fishing charter includes the fee for cleaning your fish, or if you'll

AUTHENTIC AND AFFORDABLE CABO

Anyone familiar with Cabo 30 years ago will tell you about the good old days when the town was nothing but a quaint fishing village surrounded by beautiful beaches. That was before the highway was paved, the commercial airport opened, the cruise ships came to visit, and the endless string of mega-resorts sprang up. But the beauty of the region is undeniable, and there are still ways to enjoy authentic Mexican charm; you just have to work harder to find it.

Stay small and in town. Stay in the downtown areas of San José or Cabo San Lucas, where you'll find boutique hotels, bed-and-breakfasts, and budget accommodations with plenty of Mexican soul, such as **Cabo Inn Hotel** or **Los Milagros.** This will also put you within walking distance of historic plazas, shops, and restaurants—helping you feel more of the local culture. Conveniently enough, these smaller accommodations are often also more authentic and the cheapest choices when compared to the large hotels and all-inclusive resorts. You'll give up staying right on the beach, but some of the hotels in town still have swimming pools.

Eat like a local. You'll notice that local Mexicans eat most of their meals at taco stands and hole-in-the-wall spots. This is where you'll find the cheapest prices and usually the most delicious and authentic food. Don't be afraid to ask the locals for their favorite places to eat. This may direct you to restaurants outside of the main tourist areas where you'll find cheaper prices and a truer Mexican experience.

Take advantage of public beaches. All the beaches in Los Cabos (and the rest of the peninsula, for that matter) are public property. That means you don't have to stay at an expensive resort to access its beach. The properties are legally required to provide public access to the beach, so even if a resort hasn't allowed for access along the side of the hotel, most will let you go through the resort to get to the beach.

Get off the beaten path. Get out of the heavy tourist areas to avoid the big crowds and find affordable and more authentic restaurants and shops. Even venturing just one block off of the main tourist areas can make a big difference.

Avoid peak hours. The marina and downtown area of Cabo San Lucas become mayhem during the day when cruise ship passengers are on shore. The area becomes much more relaxed after 5pm when they're back on the ship.

Get out of town. Day trips to explore the peninsula will give you a less-touristy experience (page 73). Quaint colonial towns, vast deserted beaches, cascading waterfalls, natural hot springs, and premier coral reef diving are all just an hour or so away.

need to pay it yourself when back on shore (US$2-30 depending on the size of the fish). Fishing licenses are required when angling from a boat in Mexico, and fishing charters usually provide one for you, but check ahead of time to make sure it's included.

A reputable and long-established fishing charter in the region is **Pisces Sportfishing** (tel. 624/143-1288, toll-free U.S. tel. 877/286-7938, www.piscessportfishing.com). It's located on the Cabo marina and has a huge fleet with a wide variety of options for charters. Also located at the marina is **Picante Sportfishing** (tel. 624/143-2474, www.picantesportfishing.com) with a large fleet of yachts and experienced charter captains.

Cabo Fishing and Tours (toll-free U.S. tel. 866/261-3872, www.cabofishings.com) can arrange fishing charters for first-time anglers, families, and serious anglers. It has party packages that start at US$450.

Offering a variety of packages that include lunch, transportation, fishing licenses, and live bait, **Sushi Time Sport Fishing** (tel. 624/147-5162, www.sushitimefishing.com) has a fleet of six super *pangas*. All reservations must be made through the website.

BOATING

Cabo Sails (tel. 624/355-6386, www.cabosails.com) is a sailing charter company specializing in private sailboat charters that can accommodate 2-20 guests. It also offers snorkeling, whale-watching, and sunset tours. Another option for sailing and boating is **Cabo Sailing Ocean Adventures** (tel. 624/143-8485, www.cabosailing.com). From sunset cruises to whale-watching to snorkel tours, it can arrange for private or group excursions.

In addition to the usual whale-watching and snorkeling trips, **Pez Gato** (tel. 624/143-3797, U.S. tel. 619/446-6339, www.pezgato.com) also offers sunset cruises like the "jazz and wine cruise" and a "fiesta dinner cruise" with open bar.

WHALE-WATCHING

Whale-watching is a popular activity in Cabo, as visitors have the opportunity to see humpbacks, blue whales, fin whales, sperm whales, and dolphins.

Whale Watch Cabo (Plaza Bonita, tel. 624/105-9336, www.whalewatchcabo.com) takes people out in smaller groups (10-12 people) and lets you get closer to the whales. The guides are marine biologists, and the company has a 100 percent sightings guarantee. Customers can choose from either Zodiac-style or covered boats. The 2.5-hour tours depart three times daily December 15-April 15, and start at US$89 for adults.

Cabo Trek (Paseo de la Marina, tel. 624/143-6242, www.cabodivetrek.com) also leads 2.5-hour whale-watching tours, starting at US$85 for adults and offered three times daily December 15-April 15. Multiday trips to visit the gray whales in Bahía Magdalena are also available.

✪ GOLF

Several world-class courses in Cabo attract golfers from all over the world. The courses wind through beautiful desert and mountain terrain with stunning ocean views. November-May is ideal for golfing because the temperatures are mild and there's very little rain. Summer months can be too hot and bring tropical storms but, given this, prices are discounted and budget golfers are lured to the region during this time. Greens fees can be around US$300 during peak time. Teeing off during twilight hours costs close to half the regular price.

The **Cabo San Lucas Country Club** (tel. 624/143-4654, www.cabocountry.com) features a Dye-designed 18-hole golf course. Set among cacti and bougainvillea, this is the only golf course in the area that has views of Cabo's famous El Arco.

For an exclusive golfing experience, **Diamante** (tel. 624/172-5812, www.diamantecabosanlucas.com) offers two courses. The Dunes course meanders through untouched sand dunes and was ranked 38th in *Golf Magazine*'s Top 100 Courses in the World. The new El Cardonal course was designed by Tiger Woods and offers long-range views of the Pacific Ocean.

With a stunning setting, **Quivira Golf Club** (toll-free U.S. tel. 800/990-8250, www.quiviragolfclub.com) has dramatic ocean views set among granite cliffs and sand dunes.

HORSEBACK AND CAMEL RIDES

It's possible to do both horseback riding and camel riding on the beach in Cabo. If you want to go horseback riding and get off the beaten path, **Cuadra**

San Francisco (Mexico 1 Km 19.5, tel. 624/144-0160, www.loscaboshorses.com) is a world-class equestrian center where travelers can go for longer horseback rides along the beach as well as on the trails of nearby hills and canyons. It can accommodate riders of all levels. Camel riding is offered through a couple of tour companies in the region, such as Cabo Adventures (tel. 624/173-9500, www.cabo-adventures.com) and Wild Canyon (tel. 624/144-4433, www.wildcanyon.com.mx).

SPAS

With affordable prices, Eden's Spa (Calle Camino Real, tel. 624/143-0311, www.edenspacabo.com, 8am-8pm daily) is a full-service facility offering services like massages, facials, manicures, pedicures, and hot stones. With its location near Playa Médano, one of its popular services is a beach massage.

Located in Villa del Arco, The Desert Spa (Camino Viejo Km 0.5, tel. 624/145-7202) is popular because of the array of services it offers. The European-inspired spa has dozens of treatments like massages, facials, hydrotherapy, body wraps, and couples experiences. The large facility also has an adjacent fitness center.

On Playa Solmar, there are four different spa experiences run by Solmar Spa Collection (tel. 624/145-7575, www.solmarspacollection.com), ranging from serene indoor services to outdoor beach cabanas. It offers an extensive selection of high-end services. Treatments such as the couples moonlight oceanfront massage are meant to luxuriously pamper clients and deliver a uniquely memorable experience. Services and features vary between the spas but all bookings can be made on the website.

ENTERTAINMENT AND EVENTS

TOP EXPERIENCE

✪ NIGHTLIFE

The unofficial Cabo spring break headquarters is Mango Deck (tel. 624/144-4919 or 624/143-0901, www.mangodeckcabo.com, 7am-11pm daily), the happening place on Playa Médano for entertainment and drinks. Get there early in the day to grab a deck chair and listen to the emcee, who will guide you through a day's worth of entertainment and contests. When you're thirsty, there are two-for-one drink specials, or flag down "Big Johnson," the tequila man, with a holster full of tequila and shot glasses. Mango Deck serves breakfast, lunch, and dinner in case you need to soak up some of the alcohol. Also on Playa Médano, and located at ME Cabo, is beach club Blue Marlin Ibiza (tel. 624/145-7800, www.bluemarlinibizaloscabos.com, 10am-midnight daily), formerly Nikki Beach Club, where the party takes place all day long around the pool and outdoor bar. Spring breakers will love this daytime poolside scene, as well as the DJs and parties at night.

A standard on the Cabo bar scene for over 30 years is The Giggling Marlin (Paseo de la Marina, tel. 624/143-0606, www.gigglingmarlin.com, 9am-1am daily). It's most famous for its gimmick of allowing visitors to hang upside down by their feet, like a caught fish, next to a large marlin for a shot and a unique photo op. A fun and friendly staff serves decent food, including salsa made tableside.

Probably the most popular and classic late-night Cabo spot is El

Squid Roe (Lázaro Cárdenas, tel. 624/226-7130, www.elsquidroe.com, 10am-4am daily), located on the main strip. If you're looking for dancing, loud music, drinking, and fun, this is your place.

For an evening of live music, drinks, and food, head to Sammy Hagar's Cabo Wabo Cantina (Vicente Guerrero, tel. 624/143-1188, www.cabowabo.com, 9am-3am daily). It makes its own blue agave tequila and serves Mexican food (US$19-30). It's one of the liveliest spots in Cabo, day or night.

Near the marina, Monkey's Cave Bar (Blvd. Marina Plaza Marlin, tel. 624/143-6799, 9am-midnight daily), formerly Monkey Business, is a funky little hole-in-the-wall bar for patrons of all ages. Its margaritas are extremely popular and made with freshly squeezed limes.

Nearby, outdoor *palapa* bar Uno Mas? (Paseo de la Marina, tel. 624/105-1877, www.unomascabo.com, 11am-midnight daily) is popular for its cheap drinks and fun, casual atmosphere. The friendly staff makes drinks using fresh juices and real fruits.

Located in downtown Cabo is what's advertised to be the "world's smallest bar," Slim's Elbow Room (Paseo de la Marina, tel. 624/172-5576, www.slimscabo.com, noon-10pm daily). Dollar bills plaster the walls of this dive bar. Grab one of the few stools, or sidle up to the bar along the sidewalk and enjoy a beer or shot of tequila.

For those who enjoy a more subdued scene away from the large clubs and spring breakers, Bar Esquina (Av. El Pescador, tel. 624/143-1890, www.bahiacabo.mx, 8am-11pm daily) offers a more elegant and sophisticated

El Squid Roe

ambience. Located in the Bahia Hotel & Beach Club, it features live music, such as jazz or Spanish guitar, almost every night. This is also a favorite dinner spot with a full menu featuring Mediterranean and Mexican fusion.

For beer drinkers, Rámuri Cerveza Artesanal Mexicana (Lázaro Cárdenas, tel. 624/105-0163, www.cervezaramuri.com, 1pm-10pm Tues.-Sat., 1pm-9pm Sun.) is a microbrewery serving its own Belgium and German-influenced craft beers. Visitors can take a tour of the brewery or enjoy pub-style food like burgers, wings, and gourmet pizzas at the restaurant. If the weather is nice, patrons can savor their beer and food outside on the rooftop beer garden, where there are a number of flat-screen televisions. Other options for craft beer are the two Cabo San Lucas locations of Baja Brewing Co. (www.bajabrewingcompany.com), at the Cabo Villas Rooftop and along the marina in Puerto Paraíso Mall.

SHOPPING

There's no lack of souvenir shopping in Cabo. Across the street from The Giggling Marlin, Plaza de los Mariachis y de la Salsa (Paseo de la Marina, tel. 624/143-4596, 8am-4pm daily) has a smattering of souvenir shops as well as open-air bars. Silver, colorful Talavera pottery, beaded jewelry, and other typical Mexican souvenirs can be found in the small shops here.

Mega souvenir shop **Hacienda Tequila** (Paseo de la Marina, 9am-9pm daily) sells sombreros, shot glasses, T-shirts, and, as the name suggests, a large selection of tequila. There's a large **"flea market"** on Melchor Ocampo, a few blocks up from the marina, where visitors will find a large market of stalls full of souvenirs and curios (but don't expect any vintage or antique finds here, as the name may suggest).

For more authentic shopping, **Zen-Mar Mask Store** (Lázaro Cárdenas, tel. 624/143-0661, 9am-6pm daily) sells a large selection of masks, rugs, Catrina figurines, and other decor from Oaxaca and other areas of mainland Mexico. The store has been here for 35 years.

Edith Jimenez (the owner of The Office and Edith's restaurants) turned her hacienda-style home into a unique shop, **La Coyota** (Leona Vicario, tel. 624/143-0714, 9am-5pm Mon.-Sat.) where everything you see is for sale. It's not in a touristy neighborhood, but those looking for hand-blown glassware, pottery, crosses and sacred hearts, and other authentic decor from mainland Mexico will find it's worth the trip.

Interior decorators and in-the-know design aficionados go to **Artesano's** (Mexico 1 Km. 4.1, El Tezal neighborhood, tel. 624/143-3850, 9am-2pm Mon.-Sat.) to find a giant warehouse full of rows of colorful pottery, glassware, outdoor furniture, handwoven baskets, and more.

Specializing in blown-glass items, **The Glass Factory** (Calle General Juan Álvarez, tel. 624/143-0255, www.glassfactory.com.mx, 9am-5pm Mon.-Fri., 10am-4pm Sat.-Sun.) has a

There are plenty of options for souvenir shopping in Cabo San Lucas.

✪ **EL FARALLON:** Fine dining, impeccable service, and a champagne bar accompany incredible views and crashing waves below (page 41).

✪ **SUNSET MONALISA:** Get a reservation for sunset and bask in the show over El Arco and the ocean (page 52).

✪ **LA REVOLUCIÓN COMEDOR DE BAJA CALIFORNIA:** Delicious food and craft cocktails come together in a sleek setting at this hip restaurant in San José del Cabo's historic district (page 65).

✪ **LA LUPITA:** Offering unique tacos (like lamb and octopus) and a mezcal menu, this hip restaurant pleases visiting foodies and locals alike (page 66).

✪ **FLORA'S FIELD KITCHEN:** For a unique experience, visit this garden restaurant where food is made with only the freshest homegrown ingredients (page 69).

✪ **HUERTA LOS TAMARINDOS:** Enjoy picturesque farm-to-table outdoor dining surrounded by the gardens that provide most of the produce on the menu (page 70).

large selection of home decor items, kitchen and serving ware, stained-glass windows, figurines, and decorative pieces.

In downtown Cabo near the marina, **Puerto Paraíso Mall** (Lázaro Cárdenas 1501, tel. 624/144-3000, www.puertoparaiso.mx, 9am-10pm daily) is a large, modern mall with stores like Kenneth Cole, Sunglass Hut, and Tommy Bahama.

There are plenty of large grocery stores for those staying at condos. There's also a **Costco** (San José del Cabo 1659, tel. 624/146-7180, 9am-9pm Mon.-Sat., 9am-8pm Sun.).

FOOD
DOWNTOWN AND MARINA
Mexican

For authentic Mexican food in a charming courtyard setting, **Mi Casa** (Av. Cabo San Lucas, tel. 624/143-1933, www.micasarestaurant.com.mx, 11:30am-10:30pm Mon.-Sat.,

5:30pm-10:30pm Sun., US$12-25) is right on Plaza Amelia Wilkes. It serves traditional Mexican dishes from the heart of the mainland, like rich moles, *chile en nogada,* and seafood cocktails. It also has a second location in San José del Cabo.

Traditional Mexican food is served in large portions at the family-owned and operated **Maria Jimenez Restaurante Mexicano** (Calle Narcizo Mendoza, tel. 624/105-1254, 3pm-10pm Tues.-Sun., US$10-14). There's a casual but festive atmosphere with mariachi bands. The restaurant currently only accepts cash.

With almost 200 options available, patrons head to **Pancho's** (Hidalgo and Emiliano Zapata, tel. 624/143-0973, www.panchos.com, 8am-10pm daily, US$11-14) for the tequila tastings as much as the Mexican food. The service is friendly, the portions are large, and the restaurant is conveniently located in downtown.

At **Maria Corona** (16 de Septiembre, tel. 624/143-1111, www.mariacoronarestaurant.com, 5pm-11pm daily, US$9-14), every Tuesday patrons enjoy a live show featuring traditional dancers and music. Traditional Mexican dishes are served with a spectacle that tourists enjoy—such as guacamole made tableside and Mexican coffee lit on fire.

For signature moles and authentic traditional Mexican dishes that have been passed down for generations, head to **Los Tres Gallos** (20 de Noviembre, tel. 624/164-5869, www.lostresgallos.com, 8am-10pm daily, US$12-14). There's a cozy atmosphere with a charming outdoor patio as well as an open kitchen.

The place to go for breakfast is **Mama's Royal Café** (Calle Hidalgo, tel. 624/143-4290, www.mamasroyalcafeloscabos.com, 7am-2pm Mon.-Sat., US$6-9). From *huevos charros* (a deluxe version of huevos rancheros) to eggs Benedict and a large selection of omelets, the dishes are rich and savory. The bright and colorful setting is casual, with plenty of Mexican charm.

Seafood

The seafood dishes are what keep patrons coming back to **Misiones de Kino** (Vicente Guerrero 5 de Mayo, tel. 624/105-1408, www.misionesdekino.com, 3:30pm-11pm Mon.-Sat., US$10-14). There's indoor seating as well as a small and intimate courtyard with romantic outdoor lighting. The seafood pastas are a favorite, and shrimp lovers won't want to miss the shrimp served in a special garlic sauce.

Don't let the very casual, no-frills setting at **Mariscos las Tres Islas** (Revolución de 1910, tel. 624/143-3247, 8am-10pm daily, US$8-12) fool you—

it offers some of the best and freshest seafood around. The catch of the day is always fantastic at this locals' spot. Wash it down with a mango margarita.

The eclectic and quirky **Maro's Shrimp House** (Av. Hidalgo, tel. 624/143-4966, noon-10pm daily, US$14-17) is decorated with college sports team pennants and the signatures of patrons. As the restaurant's name suggests, it's known for its shrimp, and the lobster comes in a close second. For being a tourist restaurant downtown, the prices are reasonable for the value.

Don't miss the seafood combination platter at **Las Mariscadas** (Calle Cabo San Lucas, tel. 624/105-1563, 1pm-10pm daily, US$7-11), where you'll enjoy casual dining under a large open-air *palapa*. From coconut mango shrimp to ceviche to grilled octopus, the food is delicious at reasonable prices, and the staff is friendly and welcoming.

Taco Stands

Tacos Guss (Lázaro Cárdenas, tel. 624/105-1961, US$5-7) serves classic Mexican street food (*huaraches,*

Tacos Guss

tortas, tacos, and quesadillas) in a casual sit-down restaurant. This is a popular place, so the lines can be long and it can be difficult to get a table after you've ordered, but most patrons think it's worth the wait. You can always take the food to go.

For *carnitas,* the best place to go in the area is Carnitas Los Michoacanos (Mexico 19, tel. 624/146-3565, 7:30am-6pm daily, US$4). You can order *carnitas* by the kilo, which comes with tortillas and all the salsas and fixings. Don't miss the *chicharrón* as well. Carnitas Los Michoacanos has four locations throughout Los Cabos, but the main location is on the highway on the road to Todos Santos, across from the Soriana grocery store.

International

Solomon's Landing (Paseo de la Marina, tel. 624/154-3050, 7am-11pm daily, US$18-25) is a popular spot for expats, tourists, and cruise ship passengers. It's conveniently located on the marina, with well-prepared food (the extensive menu has sushi, seafood, pastas, and more) and a fun and lively atmosphere.

For Italian dining featuring huge portions and friendly service, locals and tourists head to Salvatore's (Emiliano Zapata, tel. 624/105-1044, 11am-3pm and 6pm-10pm daily, US$13-16). The pork shank is slow-cooked, tender, and savory, served with a side of alfredo. The lasagna is famous here because it's delicious and large enough for two people to share.

Mediterranean specialties like stuffed tenderloin scaloppini and pasta carbonara are served up at Alcaravea (Calle Ignacio Zaragoza and 16 de Septiembre, tel. 624/143-3730, 11am-11pm Mon.-Sat., US$9-16). It has a French chef who makes rich and savory sauces that top items like filet mignon and the catch of the day.

You can find an eclectic assortment of international fare such as barbecue ribs, Argentinian steak, and tuna tartare at El Peregrino (Calle Ignacio Zaragoza, tel. 624/688-4872, 1pm-10:30pm daily, US$10-14). The delicious food, casual atmosphere, and friendly staff make this a pleasurable dining experience. Make a reservation if you have a large group.

PLAYA EL MÉDANO
Mexican

For elegant outdoor dining at Playa Médano, Hacienda Cocina y Cantina (tel. 624/163-3144, www.haciendacocina.mx, 8am-10pm daily, US$16-24) is a casual but sophisticated option. Views look out at El Arco, and the menu features Mexican specialties from mainland regions such as Oaxaca, Puebla, Guerrero, and Veracruz. Tequilas, local craft beers, handcrafted cocktails, and wine top off the selection.

From the same owners as The Office, Edith's (Camino a la Playa El Médano, tel. 624/143-0801, www.edithscabo.com, 5pm-11pm daily, US$17-36) serves Baja California cuisine with a Guerreran influence, creating a fusion of steaks and seafood along with local flavors and ingredients. Owner Edith has been with this restaurant since arriving in Cabo from Jalapa in 1977 when she was 15 and working as a waiter (she changed the name to Edith's in 1994). Serving Mexican fare in a fun atmosphere, La Catrina (Playa del Pescador, tel. 624/143-9561, 8am-11pm daily, US$12-20) has an extensive menu offering many traditional Mexican dishes. Chiles rellenos, moles, fresh seafood, and fajitas are all on the menu. Don't miss the guacamole, which is made tableside. The open-air restaurant has a friendly staff and is a favorite among travelers and local expats.

Taco Stands

With a convenient location downtown, seafood lovers will want to head to Tacos Gardenias (Paseo de la Marina, tel. 624/143-4295, www.tacosgardenias.com, 8am-10pm daily), featuring fish tacos, shrimp *molcajetes,* and seafood cocktails.

If you follow celebrity and TV chefs, you'll definitely want to head to Asi y Asado (Mexico 1 Km. 3.8, tel. 624/105-9500, www.asiyasado.com, 10am-9pm daily), which Guy Fieri visited on his show *Diners, Drive-ins and Dives.* He called the octopus taco "so fresh, it tastes like the sea." Asi y Asado has an extensive toppings bar with cucumbers, salsas, radishes, and coleslaw.

International

Eat with your toes in the sand at casual beach restaurant The Office (Playa El Médano, access to Av. del Pescador, tel. 624/143-3464, www.theofficeonthebeach.com, 7am-11pm daily, US$8-14), which has become a Cabo staple for most tourists. The prices are reasonable and the atmosphere is fun with live music, lively crowds, and flowing drinks. From burritos and coconut shrimp to burgers and steak, the menu is diverse, and the spot is great for hanging out during the day, drinking, eating, and watching people go by. It's also nice for a sunset dinner.

For indoor or outdoor fine dining, La Casona (Villa la Estancia, Camino Viejo a San José del Cabo Km. 05, tel. 624/145-6900, 7am-11pm daily, US$18-23) is a popular steakhouse.

The Office restaurant on Playa El Médano

Breakfast, lunch, and dinner are served daily. Friendly staff, savory food, and excellent steaks make this restaurant a favorite among tourists.

For Asian fusion, Panazia (Paseo de la Gaviota, tel. 624/688-2302, 2:30pm-10:30pm Tues.-Wed., 2:30pm-11:30pm Thurs.-Sat., 2:30pm-9pm Sun., US$12-16) is an enjoyable spot where the service, food, drinks, and stylish ambience are all impeccable. From sea urchin to foie gras, the menu features delicately delicious flavors crafted with fresh ingredients.

PLAYA SOLMAR

International

On the property of The Resort at Pedregal, ✪ El Farallon (Camino del Mar 1, tel. 624/163-4300, 5pm-11pm daily, US$30-75) provides guests with an exquisite dining experience. Fresh fish, shrimp, lobster, and steak are all on the menu for main courses, in addition to the set family-style appetizers served beforehand. Built right into the side of the mountain, with the crashing waves below, the atmosphere and views are spectacularly memorable, especially at sunset. There's also a champagne terrace carved out of rock where diners can choose from over 15 types of champagne to try with a selection of salts.

Located at the Grand Solmar, **La Roca** (Av. Solmar 1A, tel. 624/144-2500, 7am-10pm daily, US$16-31) is a wonderful option for an elegant meal. The menu features authentic Baja cuisine, seafood, steak, and American dishes. Indoor or outdoor dining is available, all with stunning views of Playa Solmar. Arrive to take advantage of the sunset over the ocean. Reservations are required, and a dress code is enforced.

ACCOMMODATIONS

For those looking for a more authentic and intimate experience than the resorts, there are a few options for boutique hotels and budget accommodations in the downtown and marina area. Only resorts and large hotels will be found along the beaches and water's edge. To get beachfront, you'll need to head out of downtown to Playa Médano or Playa Solmar. The beach at Playa Médano is buzzing with energy, people, and activities, since it's one of the few swimmable beaches in Cabo San Lucas. Playa Solmar, in contrast, is a beautiful and more deserted beach on the Pacific Ocean side. The expansive beach is great for enjoying a peaceful walk, but the sand is coarse and the strong waves and currents here make it unsafe for swimming.

Many of the large resorts in Cabo will let you book room and airfare at the same time.

DOWNTOWN AND MARINA

For budget accommodations, **Baja Cactus Hotel & Hostel** (Lázaro Cárdenas, tel. 624/143-5247, US$28-50) offers both shared dorm rooms and private suites. There's wireless access throughout, a common area with games, a communal kitchen, and a rooftop terrace. Continental breakfast is provided.

For boutique hotel accommodations in a resort town, head to ✪ **Casa Bella** (Hidalgo 10, tel. 624/143-6400, www.casabellahotel.com, US$160-200). This 14-room hotel has plenty of Spanish character with arched windows and rooms centered around a lovely lush courtyard with a small pool. A stay here evokes a more authentic old-world Mexican charm than you'll get at any of the typical Cabo resorts. A free continental breakfast of fruits, pastries, coffee, and tea is included in your stay. The staff is friendly and helpful and can make arrangements for excursions like fishing trips, golfing, and whale-watching. The prime location is quiet and relaxed, just off the plaza and walking distance to the lively downtown and marina area.

Off the beaten path, **Norman Diego's The Mexican Inn** (16 de Septiembre and Abasolo, tel. 624/143-4987, www.themexicaninn.com, US$120-160) has six basic rooms decorated with Mexican accents. Rooms have TVs and DVD players (DVDs are available to borrow at the front office). There's a common area where free continental breakfast is served in the mornings (cooked breakfast available for an extra price).

With plenty of charm, **Los Milagros** (Matamoros 3738, tel. 624/143-4566, www.losmilagros.com.mx, US$85-125) features a calming colonial courtyard with Talavera tiles, wrought-iron tables with mosaic work, and overgrowing bougainvillea. There are plenty of spots to sit and

BEST ACCOMMODATIONS IN LOS CABOS

✪ **CASA BELLA:** This charming hacienda-style boutique hotel in Cabo San Lucas has a prime location near the bustle of town, but offers a serene escape (page 42).

✪ **THE CAPE, A THOMPSON HOTEL:** This resort is making a splash with its sleek urban design, luxurious feel, world-class restaurant, and chic rooftop bar (page 53).

✪ **CASA NATALIA:** Offering luxury with chic decor, this boutique hotel is just off the San José del Cabo plaza and has a pool and restaurant on-site (page 71).

✪ **EL DELFIN BLANCO:** Enjoy personal attention, Swedish pancakes, and comfy accommodations for the right price (page 73).

✪ **HOTEL EL GANZO:** The understated but hip El Ganzo draws artists, musicians, and trendsetters with its relaxed vibe and chic setting (page 73).

relax around the gardens and courtyard, and even a small dipping pool. Additionally, there's a sun terrace on the upper level. The rooms are basic but clean and feature Mexican accents with Saltillo floors and colorful Talavera tiles.

Cabo Inn Hotel (20 de Noviembre and Leona Vicario, tel. 624/143-0819, www.caboinnhotel.com, $55) has a wide range of rooms available, from standard rooms with twin beds to rooftop *palapa* suites. Originally built in 1955, this historic property was one of Baja's first brothels. The colorful and funky property has a courtyard, rooftop patio, small dipping pool, and full communal kitchen and barbecue.

With affordable prices and a location in the heart of the action downtown, **Siesta Suites** (Emiliano Zapata between Guerrero and Hidalgo, tel. 624/143-2773, toll-free U.S. tel. 866/271-0952, www.cabosiestasuites. com, US$65) is walking distance to nearly everything in Cabo. Rooms are large and clean, and the property is pet-friendly. There's a great deck

where guests can mingle and enjoy happy hour Wednesday-Friday.

The colonial-style **Hotel Mar de Cortez** (Lázaro Cárdenas 140, tel. 624/143-0032, toll-free U.S. tel. 800/347-8821, www.mardecortez. com, US$85) is a budget hotel in a historic building in downtown Cabo. The rooms are basic (no TV or minifridge), but the location is ideal and there's a nice pool in the courtyard. American-style breakfast is included in the stay. The restaurant is also open for lunch, and there's a sports bar with happy hour 1pm-2pm and again at 5pm-6pm daily.

With a great location right on the marina, **Marina Fiesta Resort & Spa** (Paseo de la Marina, tel. 624/145-6020, www.marinafiestaresort.com, US$180-220) is walking distance to everything in downtown. There are now two ways to book—bed-and-breakfast (with just breakfast included with your room) or all-inclusive, which requires a four-night minimum stay. The swimming pool has a large *palapa* swim-up bar. The friendly staff pay a lot of attention to detail and customer satisfaction.

For an authentic Mexican experience, El Nido at Hacienda Escondida (Libertad and Miguel Angel Herrera, tel. 624/143-2053, www.cabobedbreakfast.com, US$160-180) is a bed-and-breakfast nestled in a charming hacienda building. There are six rooms in total—two are on the ground floor and the other four are "*palapa* rooms," with *palapa* roofs that are open on one side to the mountains. There's a rooftop deck, Jacuzzi, and restaurant and cantina on the property.

At The Bungalows Hotel (Miguel Angel Herrera, www.thebungalowshotel.com, US$165-185), all rooms have kitchenettes, air-conditioning, pillow-top mattresses, handmade desert soaps, and bathroom amenities. A delicious, full gourmet breakfast is served in the morning. The hotel is happy to help arrange activities and rental cars or recommend restaurants and things to see. The location is great, out of the touristy area but close enough to walk to downtown and the marina.

PLAYA EL MÉDANO

The high-end, family-friendly resort Villa del Arco Beach Resort and Spa (Camino Viejo a San José Km. 0.5, tel. 624/145-7200, toll-free U.S. tel. 800/062-1658, www.villadelarco.com, US$885-1,085) has 217 suites, all with kitchenettes or full kitchens, air-conditioning, and private balconies. There are two outdoor pools with waterfalls, right on Médano beach with views of El Arco. One is home to a full-size replica of a Spanish galleon that serves as a bar. Two room packages are available when booking—all-inclusive or room only.

The ultramodern ME Cabo by Meliá (Playa El Médano, tel. 624/145-7800, toll-free U.S. tel. 888/956-3542, www.melia.com, US$290-325) is a popular place for 20- and 30-somethings who want a nice hotel on the beach close to the nightlife of downtown. The pool area has numerous cabana lounges and a DJ playing music. Weekends can be rowdy with music coming from the bar areas until late at night.

All-inclusive Casa Dorada (Av. Pescador, tel. 624/163-5757, www.casadorada.com, US$715) has a number of restaurants on the property, with 12 Tribes being a favorite among guests. Médano beach and two large pools provide plenty of space for sunning and relaxing. Casa Dorada tends to draw an older clientele, and the property is relatively quiet at night, so you'll need to go into town nearby if you're looking for a nightlife scene.

Boutique Bahia Hotel & Beach Club (Av. El Pescador, tel. 866/224-4234, www.bahiacabo.com, US$310) is set a block away from Médano beach and two blocks away from the marina. There's a pool area and poolside bar. Bar Esquina on the property is a popular spot for both locals and tourists and serves handcrafted food and cocktails.

For an all-inclusive experience, Hotel Riu Palace (Camino Viejo a San José del Cabo Km. 4.5, tel. 624/146-7160, toll-free U.S. tel. 888/748-4990, www.riu.com, US$1,040 for three nights, all-inclusive double occupancy) provides 24/7 service in a relaxing environment right on the beach. A three-night minimum is required. There are two freshwater swimming pools, a spa and wellness center, and plenty of organized activities like volleyball, gymnastics, windsurfing, kayaking, and golf. Restaurants, bars, and clubs on the property offer entertainment in the evenings. You'll need to get up early (before 7am) if you want to get a pool lounge facing the ocean. No "spring breakers" are allowed at Riu Palace any time of year, but right next door is the Riu Santa Fe (Camino Viejo a San José del Cabo Km. 4.5, tel. 624/163-6150, www.riu.com, US$688 three nights, all-inclusive double occupancy), which attracts a lot of 20-somethings with more of a party vibe.

In the middle of the action on Médano beach is Cachet Beach Los Cabos (Callejón del Pescador, tel. 624/143-9166, www.cachethotels. com, US$234-325). The hotel features luxury touches like an infinity pool with a bar, mobile check-in, and a 24-hour gym with on-demand spa services. The Beach Restaurant and Beach Club are popular spots even for travelers not staying in the hotel, as is the rooftop terrace, which is home to the Cabo San Lucas location of Baja Brewing Company.

Set back from the beach on the other side of the highway from Playa El Médano in a neighborhood called El Tezal is Los Patios Hotel (Mexico 1 Km. 4.5, tel. 624/145-6070, www. lospatioshotel.com, US$50). This affordable option has nicely appointed rooms with air-conditioning, in-room safes, hair dryers, coffeemakers, and private terraces with hammocks. The hotel still has plenty of Mexican charm with bright colors and Mexican decor accents. There's a heated pool, a Jacuzzi, and a restaurant on-site. The downfall is that you'll need to take a taxi or bus to get to the beach or other parts of town.

Also in El Tezal is Casa Contenta (Calle Modelo, tel. 624/143-6038, www.cabocasacontenta.com, US$200-225), a bed-and-breakfast situated in the house of a former mayor of Cabo. This beautiful residence has been turned into a comfortable and spacious luxury hotel where guests can enjoy personal attention and a relaxing and rejuvenating stay.

PLAYA SOLMAR

Playa Solmar is a more secluded and empty beach than the busy Playa Médano. Swimming here is not advised because of strong surf and currents.

A luxurious stay at The Resort at Pedregal (Camino del Mar 1, tel. 624/163-4300, www. theresortatpedregal.com, US$990) will provide you with all the standard upscale resort amenities. The staff are genuine and welcoming, offering outstanding service. Daily guacamole, salsa, and Coronitas are delivered to your room between 4pm and 5pm, making a perfect pre-dinner snack. The famous El Farallon restaurant is on the property, where guests can enjoy exquisite seafood dishes with waves crashing in the background. Although the resort is private and secluded, the entrance of the property (you can take a golf cart, as you'll need to go through the signature tunnel) is just a short walking distance to the marina.

There are five Solmar properties in Cabo: Solmar Resort (Av. Solmar 1, toll-free U.S. tel. 800/344-3349, www. solmarcabosanlucas.com, US$164 for B&B, $274 for all-inclusive double occupancy) is one of the intimate oceanfront resorts. Guests can book either an all-inclusive plan (which includes all food, drinks, and activities) or a B&B plan that just includes breakfast. From the property guests can hike to Lover's and Divorce Beach (only reachable by boat for most travelers). For a more exclusive experience, Solmar offers its **Grand Solmar Land's End Resort & Spa** (Av. Solmar 1-A, tel. 624/144-2500, www.grandsolmarresort.com, US$450). This property features the highly acclaimed **La Roca** restaurant. The new **Grand Solmar at Rancho San Lucas Resort** (Mexico 19 Km. 120, tel. 624/143-0900, www.grandsolmarranchosanlucas.solmar.com, US$650) features all luxury oceanfront suites on 834 acres of private property.

Once the legendary Hotel Finisterra, **Sandos Finisterra Los Cabos** (Paseo de la Marina, toll-free U.S. tel. 888/774-0040, www.sandosloscabosresort.com, US$340) is now a renovated all-inclusive resort. There are beautiful beach views and a large pool area, anchored by the hotel's famous tall *palapa* pool bar in the middle. There's no swimming on the beach here, as the waves of the Pacific are too fierce, but the resort has *palapas* and lounges on the beach to enjoy the views. Unlike at many other resorts in the Los Cabos area, finding a chair near the pool or on the beach is not a problem here.

Opened in 2019, **Hard Rock Los Cabos** (Fraccionamiento Diamante, toll-free U.S. tel. 855/695-6679, www.hardrockhotelloscabos.com) is an all-inclusive resort with 639 rooms, six restaurants, and multiple pools. There are both family-friendly and adults-only sections. Live music performances, a full-service spa, and a workout facility round out the services offered at the resort.

Also opened in 2019 is the 200-room, beachfront **Nobu Hotel** (Blvd. Diamantes N., tel. 624/689-0160, www.nobuhotels.com, US$580). The luxury accommodations have a contemporary and elegant style with inspiration coming from the local beach as well as Japan. The resort features a signature **Nobu Restaurant and Bar** as well as a spa and wellness center.

CAMPING AND RV PARKS

Set in a gated residential community, **Villa Serena RV Park** (Mexico 1 Km. 7.5, tel. 624/145-8244, www.villaserenacabo.net, US$23) offers access to the pool, restaurant, lounge, and other services in the community. There are 60 spaces, all with full hookups.

INFORMATION AND SERVICES

MEDICAL SERVICES

There are plenty of clinics in the area with English-speaking doctors. Open 24/7, **AMC American Medical Center** (Lázaro Cárdenas 911, tel. 624/143-4911, www.amchospitals.com) is located in El Médano and is equipped to handle emergency services, has a bilingual staff, and accepts insurance policies. Dial 911 for emergencies.

TRANSPORTATION

GETTING THERE
From Los Cabos International Airport
Ruta del Desierto (tel. 624/128-3760) is a bus service that takes you from Los Cabos International Airport in San José del Cabo to Cabo San Lucas for US$5. You can collect the bus from Terminal 1 at the airport, and it will drop you in downtown Cabo San Lucas near the marina on Lázaro

Cárdenas at Acuario. The bus makes numerous stops along the route, so it will take an hour.

Many of the larger hotels in Cabo San Lucas offer a free or paid shuttle service that can be arranged prior to arrival. It takes about 40 minutes to reach Cabo San Lucas by taxi and costs about US$80.

Although Cabo San Lucas has car rental companies, note that the cheapest options are at the Los Cabos International Airport.

Car

It's a 30-kilometer (19-mile) drive to Cabo San Lucas from the Los Cabos airport. Travelers can either take the faster and more direct route on the Autopista San José del Cabo/Cabo San Lucas toll road (US$4), which takes 30 minutes, or drive closer to the coast along Mexico 1, which takes 15 minutes longer.

Most large hotels in Cabo San Lucas have parking lots.

Bus

Aguila (toll-free Mex. tel. 800/026-8931, www.autobusesaguila.com) and **Autobuses de la Baja California** (ABC, tel. 664/104-7400, www.abc.com.mx) run buses to and from La Paz and Todos Santos, with similar schedules and prices. From La Paz, the bus ride to Cabo San Lucas takes three hours and costs US$22, with buses running about every hour. From Todos Santos, the two-hour bus ride costs US$9, with buses departing every hour.

The bus terminal in Cabo San Lucas is located on Avenue Hidalgo near Avenue Reforma, 2.5 kilometers (1.6 miles) northwest of the marina and downtown. It's a 30-minute walk to the downtown marina area from the bus station, or a taxi costs US$6.

GETTING AROUND

Most visitors who stay in Cabo San Lucas get around by walking or taking a taxi because driving a car can be challenging due to narrow one-way streets, unmarked stop signs, and a lack of parking around town.

Taxi

Most taxis in Los Cabos are large vans that can fit 10 passengers or more. A taxi around town should cost under US$8, but always ask about the fare before getting in. Larger hotels and resorts will have taxis waiting outside the lobbies.

Ridesharing service **Uber** (www.uber.com) is now available in Los Cabos. Uber is not currently available for rides to or from the Los Cabos International Airport.

Bus

Aguila (toll-free Mex. tel. 800/026-8931, www.autobusesaguila.com) and **Autobuses de la Baja California** (ABC, tel. 664/104-7400, www.abc.com.mx) run bus services between Cabo San Lucas and San José del Cabo, with similar schedules and prices. The bus ride to San José del Cabo takes 30 minutes and costs US$3. Buses run every half hour.

The Corridor

Mexico 1 (also called the Carretera Transpeninsular, or Transpeninsular Highway) runs along the 30-kilometer (19-mile) coastal corridor between Cabo San Lucas (Km. 0) and San José del Cabo (Km. 30), a sprawling stretch of beautiful beaches populated with posh resorts. This constantly growing area provides a seamless connection between the two Cabos, with an endless belt of hotels, restaurants, and shops.

There's no city center here in the corridor. Many of the area's restaurants are those found at the hotels. Visitors stay in this region to relax and enjoy the resort life. Major accommodations and beaches are just off the highway, and signs and kilometers are well marked so it's easy to find your way around.

✪ BEACHES

The corridor is home to some of the most beautiful beaches in Los Cabos. Whether you're looking for activities such as snorkeling, swimming, and Jet Skiing or just want to relax, the corridor has a beach for you.

BAHÍA SANTA MARIA

A good spot for snorkeling is Bahía Santa Maria (Mexico 1 Km. 12), where you can rent a snorkel and mask from a vendor on the beach if you didn't bring your own. It's best to go in the morning when waters are calm and you have the best chance at reserving one of the beach *palapas*. There are new public showers and clean restrooms. The sand here is very coarse, more like little pebbles, so plan on wearing water shoes if you

resorts along the corridor

have sensitive feet. Watch for beach access signs to get to the dirt parking lot.

PLAYA CHILENO

One of the most picturesque and swimmable beaches in the region is **Playa Chileno** (Mexico 1 Km. 14). The protected bay provides a calm area for swimming, and the coral reef out near the point provides one of Cabo's most popular spots for snorkeling from shore. This family-friendly beach is located adjacent to the new Auberge Chileno Bay Resort, but public access is still easily available. Just follow the signs from Mexico 1. There's a dirt parking lot and porta-potties.

PLAYA BLEDITO (TEQUILA COVE)

An artificial breakwater makes swimming possible at **Playa Bledito** (Mexico 1 Km. 19.5), also known as **Tequila Cove.** You can rent a Jet Ski or WaveRunner on the beach here. There's public access through the arroyo at kilometer 19.5 or through the Hilton or Meliá Cabo Real hotels.

PLAYA PALMILLA

Even though **Playa Palmilla** (Mexico 1 Km. 27) serves as the beach for many upscale resorts, it's open for anyone to enjoy. This beach is protected enough for swimming and snorkeling, which makes it a popular spot for families. There are no facilities here other than a few *palapas* for shade on either side of the fishing fleet. Take the Palmilla exit off the highway and follow signs to the main beach.

SPORTS AND RECREATION

SURFING

South swells in summer bring consistent breaks in the corridor at spots like **Monuments** (Mexico 1 Km. 5.5), which is great on south swells; **El Tule** (Mexico 1 Km. 16.2), a right reef break; and **Las Conchas** (Mexico 1 between Km. 19 and 20), with a right break. There are a few surfing schools for beginners and for board rentals.

Surf in Cabo (tel. 624/117-9495, www.surfincabo.com) can handle everything from beginner lessons to weeklong surf trips to Scorpion Bay for advanced surfers. It can also customize special surf events or multiday trips.

DIVING AND SNORKELING

There are five great dive sites in the corridor. **Whales Head** is a shallow dive site (ranging 1.5-15 m/5-50 ft) with a coral reef and marinelife such as sea turtles, octopus, eels, and rays. **Chileno Bay** is a protected reef that starts 91 meters (100 yards) offshore from Playa Chileno and is a good spot for beginning divers and snorkelers with its shallow, calm waters. The reef here is home to manta rays, sea turtles, and nurse sharks. **Gavilanes** is a small bay with one of the best coral reefs in Los Cabos. Both beginner and advanced divers will enjoy seeing rays, whitetip reef sharks, angelfish, and lobsters. **Bahía Santa Maria** has a shallow reef (ranging 3-14 m/10-45 ft) with a variety of fish and rays, good for both snorkelers and beginning divers. Offshore from Bahía Santa Maria is **The Blowhole,** where more advanced divers will see larger schools of fish, manta rays, and sea turtles.

Divers can take trips to any of the five corridor dive sites with **Dive Cabo** (tel. 624/105-1793, www. divecabo.com). Sites are a 10- to 30-minute boat ride from the Cabo San Lucas marina, where corridor tours depart (no hotel pickup) three

palm trees on a beach along the corridor

times a week. A trip costs US$95 for a two-tank dive. **Manta Scuba Diving** (tel. 624/144-3871, www.caboscuba.com) offers daily dive trips departing at 8am from its facility at the Cabo San Lucas marina (no hotel pickup) to sites along the corridor; the 5-hour tour's pricing starts at US$115. It also offers a 5-hour snorkeling trip daily to spots along the corridor, departing at 8am, for US$70 per person. Offering private scuba trips to dive sites along the corridor is **Cabo Trek** (tel. 624/143-6242, www.cabodivetrek.com). Tours depart daily from the Tesoro hotel on the Cabo San Lucas marina (no hotel pickup), with flexible start times and tours lasting 4-8 hours. Prices start at US$145. Cabo Trek also offers snorkeling tours to sites along the corridor, which cost US$70 for a 4-hour trip.

GOLF

Opened in 1994, **Cabo Del Sol Golf Course** (Mexico 1 Km. 10.3, toll-free U.S. tel. 866/231-4677, www.cabodelsol.com, US$175-365) is a Nicklaus Design course. There are two 18-hole courses here—the ocean

course has incredible views but is more expensive than the desert course.

The multi-themed target-style **Cabo Real Golf Club** (Mexico 1 Km. 19.5, tel. 624/173-9400, www.questrogolf.com, US$245) was designed by Robert Trent Jones Jr. and has some beautiful views and great staff.

Palmilla Golf Club (Mexico 1 Km. 27.5, tel. 624/144-5250, www.palmillagc.com, US$145-175) has three nine-hole courses with an interesting layout on the desert and hills as well as some ocean views.

The 18-hole Nicklaus Design **Club Campestre San Jose Golf Club** (free road to the airport, Km. 119, tel. 624/173-9400, toll-free U.S. tel. 877/795-8727, www.clubcampestresanjose.com) is laid out in the foothills of the Sierra de la Laguna with views of the Sea of Cortez.

SPAS

Spas along the corridor are located in the resorts. Reservations are required.

Sheraton Hacienda del Mar's **Cactus Spa** (Mexico 1 Km. 10, tel. 624/145-8000, www.sheratonhaciendadelmar.com, 7am-9pm daily) has an authentic Mexican hacienda feel and offers single treatments or a full day of pampering.

With a peaceful and modern ambience, Grand Fiesta Americana's **Somma Wine Spa** (Mexico 1 Km. 10.3, tel. 624/145-6287, spa2falc@posadas.com) infuses wine and other natural ingredients like chocolate, olive oil, lavender, and avocado into various treatments. Facilities include outdoor oceanview massage cabanas, a sauna, a steam room, a hydro-massage pool, and hot and cold plunge pools.

With a beautiful indoor/outdoor

design, **The Spa at Las Ventanas** (Mexico 1 Km. 19.5, tel. 624/144-2800, lasventanas.spa@rosewoodhotels.com, 8am-8pm daily) offers a Four Elements menu tapping into the powers of earth, air, fire, and water, and inspired by the ancient healers of Baja. Las Ventanas al Paraíso's spa offers a wide range of services, including treatments geared specifically for kids, expectant mothers, and bridal parties.

At 13,000 square feet and located at the Marquis Los Cabos, **Spa Marquis** (Mexico 1 Km. 21.5, tel. 624/144-2000, www.marquisloscabos.com, spa@marquisloscabos.com) is of the largest and most comprehensive spa and fitness centers on the entire peninsula. It features oceanview rooms and a full range of holistic face and body treatments.

With 13 private treatment villas, luxury is what you'll get at the **One&Only Palmilla Spa** (Mexico 1 Km. 27.6, tel. 624/146-7000, spa.reservations@oneandonlypalmilla.com). The plush and serene spa facilities include hot and cold rock pools, steam rooms, saunas, outdoor relaxation areas, day beds, cabanas, a salon, and a fitness center.

NIGHTLIFE

For a lively nightlife scene, travelers will need to head to Cabo San Lucas, or even San José del Cabo. However, some resorts along the corridor do have their own bars, making for a more relaxed and elegant scene.

The Rooftop (Mexico 1 Km. 5, tel. 624/163-0000, 5pm-11pm Sun.-Thurs., 5pm-1am Fri.-Sat.) at The Cape, a Thompson Hotel features, aptly, a rooftop lounge and beer garden. You'll enjoy crafted cocktails and local artisan beers as you enjoy the stunning views of Cabo San Lucas and El Arco.

Also with beautiful views, particularly at sunset, as you might guess, is **Sunset Point** (Mexico 1 Km. 6.5, tel. 624/145-8160, www.sunsetmonalisa.com, 4pm-10pm daily), located at the Sunset MonaLisa restaurant. The lively wine bar serves tapas in addition to gourmet pizza.

With specialty cocktails and a large selection of appetizers, **The Lounge Bar** (Mexico 1 Km. 7, tel. 624/145-6400, http://esperanza.aubergeresorts.com, 11:30am-midnight daily), located in Esperanza, an Auberge Resort, features beautiful ocean views, a cigar and tequila menu, and live entertainment in the evenings.

SHOPPING

Shopping options in the corridor are not as plentiful as those found in either Cabo San Lucas or San José del Cabo. For artisan goods or art galleries, it's best to head to the towns.

The Shoppes at Palmilla (Mexico 1 Km. 27.5, www.theshoppesatpalmilla.com) is an international shopping and dining center, and the only area of the Palmilla property open to the general public. Boutiques, fine jewelry stores, and cigar shops can be found among the restaurants, which serve everything from Chinese to pizza to seafood. Casa Vieja is a clothing store that carries a number of Latin American designers, and Regalito Gifts showcases Mexican souvenirs and locally made products.

FOOD

Many of the resorts along the corridor have restaurants on their properties, so many guests prefer to remain on-site for meals or explore neighboring resorts. Most restaurants have views of the ocean, and many feature outdoor seating.

Manta (Mexico 1 Km. 5, tel. 624/163-0000, www.mantarestaurant.com, 6pm-11pm daily, plates US$19-28) is the signature restaurant at The Cape, a Thompson Hotel. Chef Enrique Olvera is one of Mexico's top chefs (his Pujol restaurant in Mexico City is consistently near the top of San Pellegrino's Top 50 Best Restaurants in Latin America). The sleek space features walls of windows looking out at El Arco. The menu focuses on smaller plates such as octopus *anticucho,* beef yakitori, sea bass ceviche, and black miso fish tacos that can be shared or eaten alone. A four-course tasting meal is available.

For modern Mexican with an Asian twist, head to Toro Cabo (Mexico 1 Km. 6, tel. 624/104-3184, www.richardsandoval.com/toro-cabo, 5pm-midnight Sun.-Thurs., 5pm-2am Fri.-Sat., US $20-30). The menu includes an extensive ceviche bar and chef's specialties such as grilled fish and steaks from the wood-burning grill.

Make a reservation for sunset if you go to ✪ Sunset MonaLisa (Mexico 1 Km. 6.5, tel. 624/145-8160, www.sunsetmonalisa.com, 4:30pm-10pm daily, US$24-32). The sprawling outdoor patios are perched on the cliffs and offer sweeping views of the ocean and El Arco. Seafood and Italian specialties make up the menu. There are two other areas on the property in addition to the main restaurant: Sunset Point, a wine and pizza lounge, and Taittinger Terrace, an oyster and champagne bar.

At Esperanza, Cocina del Mar (Mexico 1 Km. 7, tel. 624/145-6400, four courses US$88) offers outdoor fine dining featuring fresh seafood dishes inspired by North, Central, and South American cuisines. Many diners create their own three- or four-course meal from items on the menu.

For oceanfront fine dining at the Sheraton Hacienda del Mar, De Cortez Grill and Restaurant (Mexico 1 Km. 10, tel. 624/145-6113, www.decortezrestaurant.com, 5pm-10:30pm daily, US$27-42) serves steak, salmon, shrimp, and other grilled specialties. It also has wine-tastings on Thursday 5:30pm-6:30pm. Also at the Sheraton is Pitahayas Restaurant (tel. 624/145-8010, www.pitahayas.com, 5pm-10:30pm daily) serving Asian fusion cuisine in an enormous *palapa* and outdoor patio. It has over 400 wines from around the world.

Located at Chileno Bay Resort and Residences, Comal (Mexico 1 Km. 15, tel. 624/104-9751, www.comalcabo.com, 7am-2pm and 6:30pm-10:30pm daily, US$15-20) features traditional Mexican dishes with a modern twist. With unobstructed Sea of Cortez views and a lovely outdoor setting, evening is particularly romantic with candles and strung lights adding to the ambience. Make a reservation for one of the tables closest to the water. There's live music on Friday and Saturday evenings, and on Sunday brunch is served.

El Merkado (Mexico 1 Km. 24.5, tel. 624/137-9834, www.elmerkado.mx, 8am-11pm daily, US$8-12) is a collection of food stalls located inside a large warehouse. Foodies will enjoy the two-story space featuring food offerings such as gyros, pizza, sushi, barbecue, burgers, and tacos. Wash it all down with a craft beer, glass of wine, or cocktail. While you'll find more international fare than Mexican food here, with so many options, this is an easy crowd-pleaser.

In The Shoppes at Palmilla, Blue Fish (Mexico 1 Km. 27.5, tel.

El Merkado

624/172-6652, US$9-12) serves seafood with fresh ingredients and local flavors. The casual menu features tacos, tostadas, ceviche, and seafood cocktails.

ACCOMMODATIONS

Many of the most luxurious resorts in Los Cabos are found along the corridor. This is an area where all-inclusive resorts and large hotels are the standard. Travelers looking for smaller or more basic accommodations should look in Cabo San Lucas or San José del Cabo.

✪ **The Cape, a Thompson Hotel** (Mexico 1 Km. 5, tel. 624/163-0000, toll-free U.S. tel. 877/793-8527, www. thompsonhotels.com, US$400-875) offers guests a stay with style and impeccable service. This 161-room luxury resort mixes the urban aesthetic of Thompson with a modern mid-century Baja vibe. There are two pools with cabanas and a popular rooftop bar with lounge areas. Three eateries are on the property, with the signature restaurant being **Manta.** Panoramic corner suites come with breathtakingly impressive views of El Arco, balconies with private plunge pools, and a complimentary bottle of tequila. Rooms on the 5th and 6th floors can be subject to noise from the rooftop

bar during the weekend when there's a DJ and the rooftop turns into a club.

The exclusive **Esperanza, an Auberge Resort** (Mexico 1 Km. 7, tel. 624/145-6400, toll-free U.S. tel. 855/331-2226, http://esperanza. aubergeresorts.com, US$800-1,700) has rooms that come with a personal concierge and suites with private infinity-edge Jacuzzis on the balconies. The resort is à la carte in terms of food (not all-inclusive), with nothing but breakfast included in the room rate. A number of restaurants are on the property. Along with a spa, there are complimentary yoga and fitness classes daily, as well as activities like painting lessons and cooking classes.

Located on 39 acres of beachfront property on Bahía Santa Maria is **Montage los Cabos** (Mexico 1 Km. 12.5, toll-free U.S. tel. 800/772-2226, www.montagehotels.com/loscabos, US$850), which opened in 2018. All of the 122 rooms have ocean views and large terraces to fully enjoy the outdoors. The property has three pools, three restaurants, a large spa, and an immersive children's program.

Located on prime property at Playa Chileno, **Chileno Bay Resort & Residences** (Mexico 1 Km. 15, toll-free U.S. tel. 844/207-9354, http:// chilenobay.aubergeresorts.com, US$625), a property by Auberge, opened in 2017. The modern boutique hotel has 29 rooms and amenities including two dining venues, a full-service spa, a fitness center, kids' and teen clubs, a theater, a pool, and private pool cabanas. It's also building 32 residential beach villas on the 9-hectare (22-acre) property.

Grand Velas (Mexico 1 Km. 17.3, toll-free U.S. tel. 888/505-8406, www.loscabos.grandvelas.com,

US$970-1,100 for 4 people) was remodeled into a luxury all-inclusive resort in 2016. The 304 modern suites are spacious and generously appointed with goose-down bedding, stocked mini-bars, and ocean views, and some come with their own private plunge pools. Resort amenities include three pools, a world-class spa, a fitness center, a 24-hour personal concierge, eight restaurants, and four premium bars. A yacht cruise is also included.

Opened in 2018, five-star resort **Solaz Los Cabos** (Mexico 1 Km. 18.5, tel. 624/144-2108, www.solazloscabos.com, US$670) has 128 luxury rooms, multiple restaurants, a spa, and a private beach club. Each room has a private entrance and private terrace. It offers a variety of high-end experiences, like private helicopter trips to explore some of Baja's cave paintings.

The all-inclusive **Le Blanc** (Mexico 1 Km. 18.4, toll-free U.S. tel. 888/702-0913, www.leblancsparesorts.com/los-cabos, US$1,200), also opened in 2018, is an adults-only property. All the details radiate luxury, from the lavish decor to personal butlers. There are 373 luxury suites with ocean views, four beachfront pools, numerous restaurants, and a state-of-the-art spa.

Golfers will rejoice in a stay at **Casa del Mar Golf Resort & Spa** (Mexico 1 Km. 19.5, tel. 624/145-7700, toll-free U.S. tel. 888/227-9621, www.casadelmar.com.mx, US$200), where seven courses are located within minutes of the resort. Run by Zoëtry Resorts, this boutique property has 32 suites, multiple swimming pools (including one with a swim-up bar), tennis courts, two restaurants on the property, and the Sueños del Mar Spa.

Over-the-top service is what sets apart **Las Ventanas al Paraíso, a Rosewood Resort** (Mexico 1 Km. 19.5, tel. 624/144-2800, toll-free U.S. tel. 888/767-3966, www.rosewoodhotels.com, US$1,470-1,680). Personal butlers will arrange meals and activities for you (both on and off the property). Spa staff will stop by for a 10-minute foot massage on the beach. Complimentary neck massages and signature foam margaritas will be waiting for you upon check-in. Suites and villas are available for rent, and most rooms have rooftop terraces and private hot tubs on the balconies. The food on-site is good with three restaurants to choose from (the tequila and ceviche bar is a favorite among many guests). There's a spa, salon, and state-of-the-art workout facility.

The adults-only **Marquis Los Cabos** (Mexico 1 Km. 21.5, tel. 624/144-2000, www.marquisloscabos.com, US$580-660) is an all-inclusive resort with five restaurants on the property as well as two bars. Resort activities include dance lessons, live entertainment each night, and weekly themed parties. Expect to be welcomed with watermelon mojitos, attentive service, and beautiful suites.

A great option for those looking for affordable accommodations in the region is the **Hampton Inn & Suites by Hilton Los Cabos** (Mexico 1 Km. 24.8, tel. 624/105-4000, US$85). The accommodations are nice and modern, and breakfast is served every morning in the lobby. You won't get beachfront here, but the rooftop pool deck and bar offer some ocean views and a nice relaxing place to hang out.

If you want to be pampered at one of the most exclusive (and expensive) resorts in the region, **One&Only Palmilla** (Mexico 1

Km. 27.6, tel. 624/146-7000, toll-free U.S. tel. 855/878-5831, www. oneandonlyresorts.com, US$1,400-3,800) will grant you the luxury of having a butler and personalized service. The historic property is not only one of the most upscale in the region, it's also the oldest. It was started by Abelardo Luis Rodríguez (son of a former Mexican president), who also owned Rancho las Cruces. He opened the One&Only in 1956, and it was a popular spot for Hollywood celebrities like John Wayne, Lucille Ball, and former U.S. president Dwight D. Eisenhower. There are two infinity-edge pools—one for adults only and one for families. Foot and head pillows are available for your pool lounge. A number of restaurants and bars are on the property, including **SEARED,** a steak and seafood restaurant from Michelin-starred chef Jean-Georges Vongerichten. The **One&Only Palmilla Golf Club** is a 27-hole course designed by Jack Nicklaus. For those who would like to enjoy some of the activities that Cabo has to offer, private whale-watching tours are available on the One&Only Palmilla yacht, and desert off-roading is offered in a chauffeured all-terrain Hummer. For those traveling with children, there's a kids' club, and in-room babysitters are also available.

TRANSPORTATION

Because the corridor is very spread out with no city center, it's nearly impossible to walk anywhere. Many resorts provide shuttles into Cabo San Lucas or San José del Cabo or will be happy to arrange for a taxi.

Mexico 1 runs parallel to the coast along the 30-kilometer (19-mile) corridor, and the major resorts and beaches are just off the highway. Signs

and kilometers are well marked, so it's easy to drive around the area.

GETTING THERE
From Los Cabos International Airport
Shuttles and taxis run from the airport to hotels for those who don't plan on renting a car. It takes about 30-45 minutes to get to the corridor, depending on where you're staying, and the fare will be about US$30-40. Many of the hotels along the corridor offer a free or paid shuttle service, so make sure to check before your arrival. If you want to rent a car, the cheapest options are at the Los Cabos International Airport.

GETTING AROUND
Car
It takes about 30 minutes to drive on Mexico 1 along the corridor between San José del Cabo and Cabo San Lucas. Resorts and most beaches have parking lots.

Bus
Ruta del Desierto (tel. 624/128-3760) is a bus service that has three stops along the corridor: **Cabo del Sol Golf Course** (Mexico 1 Km. 10.3), **Melia Cabo Real hotel** (Mexico 1 Km. 19.5), and the **One&Only Palmilla** (Mexico 1 Km. 27.6). It costs about US$2 to take the shuttle between the corridor and either Cabo San Lucas or San José del Cabo.

Taxi
Taxis from San José del Cabo or Cabo San Lucas to spots along the corridor cost approximately US$20-30.

Ridesharing service **Uber** (www. uber.com) is now available in Los Cabos. Uber is not currently available for rides to or from the Los Cabos International Airport.

San José del Cabo

For years, San José del Cabo has played the part of low-key counterpart to Cabo San Lucas. The smaller and more laid-back town has a decidedly authentic Mexican feel. While San José has the beaches, resorts, spas, and golfing, it's less developed and more relaxed when compared to its showier and more touristy neighbor. Local life centers around the town plaza and the surrounding streets full of colonial buildings that make up the Historic Art District. Here travelers will find plenty of renowned restaurants, artisanal shops, and art galleries to enjoy. While there are a few small bars, you won't find any large dance clubs here. Families and couples often prefer this area, where the tranquil town provides a nice dose of culture and the beaches are emptier and more relaxed.

Fishing, golfing, surfing, diving, and snorkeling can be enjoyed nearby. There's also a new marina, Puerto Los Cabos, which is the largest in Mexico and home to a developing and vibrant community with hotels, restaurants, and plenty of activity options.

SIGHTS

Many of the main attractions of San José del Cabo are centered around the historic downtown area, which is easy to explore on foot and includes a variety of galleries, shops, and restaurants. The estuary and marina are just a five-minute drive or taxi ride away.

Misión San José del Cabo Añuiti is located on the town plaza of San José del Cabo.

✪ PLAZA TENIENTE JOSÉ ANTONIO MIJARES

The heart and pulse of San José is the Plaza Teniente José Antonio Mijares. In the center of downtown historic San José, hotels, restaurants, and shops line the plaza and the surrounding streets. A large Mexican flag flies above the expansive plaza, which serves as a gathering place for tourists and locals. Town events like music festivals and holiday celebrations take place here, and on a daily basis, the plaza fills with families in the afternoons. Parents bring their children to play, enjoy ice cream, and eat tostadas and tamales from small food carts. Just off the plaza is the large Boulevard Mijares, where many restaurants, bars, and shops are located. Dine or drink on the 2nd floor of any of the restaurants or bars lining the boulevard to take in the lively town. The church on the plaza is on the site of the original mission for the area.

MISIÓN SAN JOSÉ DEL CABO AÑUITI

In 1730, Jesuit Padre Nicolás Tamaral traveled south from the La Purísima mission and started converting the local Pericú. Originally basing his operations on the estuary, Tamaral later moved more inland to a place known as Añuiti. Tamaral worked hard to abolish the practice of polygamy then prevalent among the Pericú. He was unpopular with the locals for this reason, and he lost his life in the Pericú Revolt of 1734. The church that now stands in the plaza was built in 1940 on the old mission site. There's a mosaic over the main entrance that depicts the murder of Tamaral. The church is still actively used today by the San José community. There are daily services in the evening and a mass in English on Sunday at noon. Visitors are welcome, but please be respectful if mass is in progress.

TOP EXPERIENCE

✪ HISTORIC ART DISTRICT

Many of the old historic colonial buildings in downtown San José del Cabo have been renovated into fine art studios and galleries. The vibrant creative scene of the Historic Art District includes original paintings, photography, sculptures, and prints from local and international artists. On Thursday nights November-June, galleries stay open 5pm-9pm for the Gallery Art Walk (www.artcabo.com). The art walk has become a don't-miss activity in San José, with some galleries offering wine or tequila, or the opportunity to see artists working in their studios. In addition to the galleries, a number of local artists who aren't represented set up booths in the plaza so patrons have the opportunity to buy affordable art from up-and-comers. The entire town comes alive, so even those who don't follow the art scene will still enjoy getting out and walking around pre- or post-dinner. If you're having a difficult time finding parking, try Avenida Centenario, just one block east of the plaza.

ESTERO SAN JOSÉ

Río San José meets the saltwater of the Sea of Cortez at the Estero San José. The estuary is a free attraction, a great place to go for a walk anytime to take in the natural habitat left in the area. Birders will enjoy catching sight of the waterbirds that inhabit the estuary, like egrets, herons, waterfowl, and osprey. To find the estuary, look for the dirt road turnoff from Boulevard Mijares just inland from the beach.

San José del Cabo

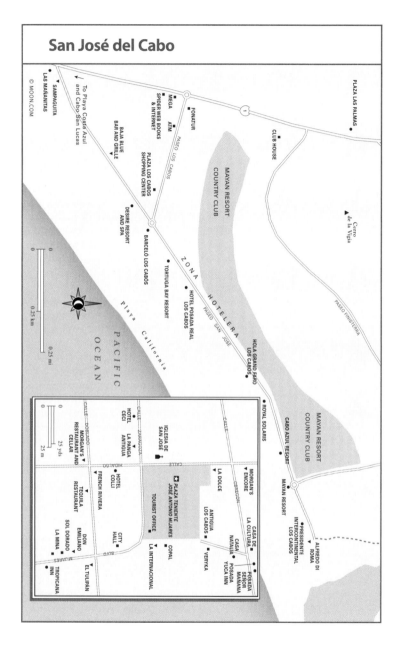

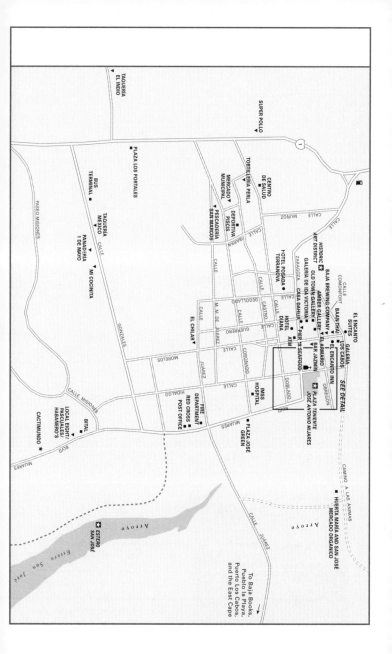

TAQUERIA EL INDIO ▲

SUPER POLLO ■

PLAZA LOS PORTALES ■

TORTILLERIA PERLA ▼

CENTRO DE SALUD ✚

MERCADO MUNICIPAL ▼

DEPORTIVA PISCIS ▼

PESCADERIA SAN MARCOS ▼

BUS TERMINAL ■

TAQUERIA MEXICO ▼

PANADERIA 1 DE MAYO ■

MI COCINITA ▼

HOTEL POSADA TERRANOVA ●

HISTORIC ✚
ART DISTRICT
AMBER GALLERY ▼
OLD TOWN GALLERY ▼
GALERIA DE IDA VICTORIA ▼
CASA DAHLIA ▼

BAJA BREWING COMPANY ▼
BAAN THAI ▼
EL ARMARIO ▼
EL ENCANTO INN ●

EL ENCANTO SUITES ●

GALERIA DOS CABOS ▼

EL CHILAR ▼

HOTEL DIANA ●

ATM ■

BAR JAZMIN ▼
PIER 19 SEAFOOD ▼

PLAZA TENIENTE JOSÉ ANTONIO MIJARES ✚

SEE DETAIL

FIRE DEPARTMENT ■
RED CROSS ✚
POST OFFICE ■

IMSS HOSPITAL ✚

PLAZA JOSÉ GREEN ■

CACTIMUNDO ■

LOCAL EIGHT/ PASCUALES/ HABANERO'S ■

BITAL ■

HUERTA MARIA AND SAN JOSÉ ■
MERCADO ORGANICO ■

ESTERO SAN JOSÉ ✚

Arroyo

Estero San José

Arroyo

CALLE MISIONES

PASEO MISIONES

GONZALES

MORELOS

JUAREZ

CALLE M.M. DE JUAREZ

CALLE IBARRA

CALLE DEGOLLADO

CALLE CASTRO

CALLE GUERRERO

CALLE CORONADO

HIDALGO

MIJARES

BLVD MIJARES

CALLE MUÑOZ

CALLE COMONFORT

ZARAGOZA

CALLE OBREGON

DOBLADO

UNO

CALLE JUAREZ

CAMINO A LAS ANIMAS

To Baja Books, Pueblo la Playa, Puerto Los Cabos, and the East Cape →

Puerto Los Cabos

To
Flora's Field Kitchen,
Huertoa los Tamarindos,
and Acre

BAJA BOOKS
AND MAPS

Puerto
Los Cabos

EL MARINERO
BORRACHO

EL DELFÍN
BLANCO

LA MARINA INN/
GEORGE'S RESTAURANT

HOTEL
EL GANZO

THE
CONTAINER

To
San José del Cabo

BRIDGE

SPORTFISHING
PANGAS

WIRIKUTA DESERT
BOTANICAL GARDEN

SWIMMING
AREA

0   400 yds

0   400 m

PACIFIC

OCEAN

© MOON.COM

PUERTO LOS CABOS MARINA
Opened in 2010, the impressive
Puerto Los Cabos Marina (www.
puertoloscabos.com) in San José del

Puerto Los Cabos Marina

Cabo is the home-away-from-home
to many of the yachts and boats that
come to the Los Cabos region. The
200 slips can hold boats up to 122 meters (400 feet) in length. As Mexico's
largest private marina, Puerto Los
Cabos is a destination that's home to
so much more than just boats. The
marina attracts tourists with a plethora of activities such as Hydro fly-
boarding, a dolphin experience, an
activity center, and a number of restaurants, including The Container
Restaurant & Bar. Hotels like the Ritz-
Carlton and El Ganzo operate here in
Puerto Los Cabos, in addition to Jack
Nicklaus- and Greg Norman-designed
golf courses.

WIRIKUTA DESERT BOTANICAL GARDEN

Just outside the marina, the **Wirikuta Desert Botanical Garden** (tel. 624/131-3131, 8am-4pm Mon.-Sat., US$8) is home to over 1,500 varieties of desert plants from around the world. The cacti and plants are arranged in serene geometric patterns that make for beautiful photos. A guide, whom you'll pick up at the entrance, will walk you through the gardens to explain about the plants, and then you're free to wander around on your own. There's a stone sculpture area as well.

BEACHES

San José del Cabo's beaches tend to be less crowded than beaches in other areas of Los Cabos. The tranquil stretches are great for enjoying long walks and sunbathing, but most are not suitable for swimming because of strong currents. Unless you're staying in a hotel on the beach along the *zona hotelera,* you will need to drive or take a taxi to reach the beaches as all of them are 2 kilometers (1.2 miles) or more from downtown. On the western end of San José del Cabo, surfers will find some of the best surf spots on the peninsula. For snorkeling and other activities, many visitors head to the beaches along the corridor.

LA PLAYITA

Now a part of the Puerto Los Cabos development, **La Playita** is a peaceful beach with a beautiful setting. It's great for families because there's a safe area inside the harbor entrance that's good for swimming or snorkeling since it's protected from waves. Near the entrance to the marina are nice

palapas and restrooms, but the restrooms are often locked. If you want to spend the entire day at the beach, there are nearby restaurants and markets to grab food.

La Playita

PLAYA COSTA AZUL

On the outskirts of San José is **Playa Costa Azul** (Mexico 1 Km. 28.5), one of the premier surfing beaches on the peninsula. It's home to three well-known surf breaks: Zippers, The Rock, and Acapulquito (Old Man's). The Los Cabos Open of Surf is held at Zippers every summer. A few restaurants and small hotels are located here as well as **Costa Azul Surf Shop** (Mexico 1 Km. 28, tel. 624/142-2771, www.costa-azul.com.mx), offering board rentals (US$25/day) and surf lessons (US$85). Swimming isn't advised here, but the beach is popular with joggers and walkers.

PLAYA CALIFORNIA

Playa California is also called Playa Hotelera because it's the beach along the *zona hotelera* in San José del Cabo. Stretching between Zippers surf point to the west and the estuary to the east, this is a large sandy beach, great for walking, observing whales and other marinelife, or activities like horseback riding and ultralight plane rides. Because of strong currents, it's not suitable for swimming. Even with all the hotels and condominiums lining the beach, it often feels relatively empty due to its vast size, even during peak times.

SPORTS AND RECREATION

DIVING AND SNORKELING

There are no snorkeling sites in San José del Cabo that can be reached by beach access. **East Cape Explorers** (Calle Tiburon, tel. 624/242-6170, www.eastcapeexplorers.com) is the only dive shop located in San José del Cabo. Scuba diving excursions (US$95-160) run six days a week and explore nearby dive sites as well as Gordo Banks and Cabo Pulmo. Snorkeling tours (US$75) visit sites in Cabo San Lucas, the corridor, and Cabo Pulmo.

Playa California

SURFING

Surfers of all levels of experience can find waves at **Playa Costa Azul** (Mexico 1 Km. 28.5), one of the premier surfing beaches in the region. There are three breaks here. **Acapulquito (Old Man's)** is located in front of the Cabo Surf Hotel and has good waves for beginners and longboarders. **La Roca (The Rock)** is located just east of Acapulquito and is a right break. **Zippers,** just east of

Playa Costa Azul

the viewpoint before the bridge, is the most well-known break of Los Cabos, where the Los Cabos Open of Surf takes place every year.

Costa Azul Surf Shop (Mexico 1 Km. 28, tel. 624/142-2771, www. costa-azul.com.mx) offers board rentals (US$25), surf lessons (US$85), and surf excursion trips (US$180). **Mike Doyle Surf School** (Mexico 1 Km. 28, tel. 624/142-2627 or 624/142-2666, U.S. tel. 858/964-5117, www. mikedoylesurfschool.com) is conveniently located inside Cabo Surf Hotel. It offers board rentals (US$29-40), surf lessons (US$79-109), and clinics (US$215-290).

surfers at Playa Costa Azul

FISHING

San José del Cabo is a premier sportfishing destination, with regular catches including dorado, sailfish, wahoo, marlin, roosterfish, grouper, and yellowfin tuna. Gordo Banks is the area's most famous spot, well-known for the large sportfish regularly caught here. There are also productive inshore reefs northeast of Gordo Banks at Iman and La Fortuna Banks. In the past, most fishing charters in Los Cabos departed from Cabo San Lucas, but with the new Puerto Los Cabos Marina, charters now depart from San José del Cabo directly. **Catch Fish Cabo** (U.S. tel. 778/382-8688, www.catchfishcabo.com) has a fleet based out of the Puerto Los Cabos Marina with charters starting at US$250 a day, a variety of boats to choose from, and attentive guides. **Angeles Fleet** (tel. 624/197-0854, www.angelesfleetloscabos.jimdo.com) is also based out of Puerto Los Cabos Marina (with an office in downtown San José del Cabo) and offers personal service for an outstanding experience.

HIKING

While there is no hiking directly in San José del Cabo, trails in the East Cape and the Sierra de la Laguna can be reached within an hour's drive. **Cabo Outfitters** (Manuel Doblado and Blvd. Mijares, tel. 624/142-5222, www.cabo-outfitters.com) operates hiking tours from San José del Cabo to the Sierra de la Laguna and Cañon de la Zorra for US$120.

GOLF

There are two courses at **Puerto Los Cabos Golf Club** (Bulevar Mar de Cortez, tel. 624/173-9400, www. puertoloscabos.com, US$210): One designed by Jack Nicklaus and the other by Greg Norman. Both courses are currently only 9 holes but will eventually be 18 each.

Beginner and expert golfers will enjoy the 9-hole course at **Punta Sur Golf Course** (formerly Mayan Palace, Blvd. San José, tel. 624/172-5812, US$63 9 holes, US$98 18 holes), where the prices are more affordable than at other courses in the region.

SPAS

Located at the Tropicana Inn, **Seven Zenses** (Blvd. Mijares 30, tel. 624/130-7124, www.sevenzensescabospa.com.

mx) provides massage, facial, wrap, body polish, manicure, and pedicure services. It regularly offers spa packages at special discounted prices.

With a convenient location in the historic center, Zafiro Spa (Blvd. Mijares, tel. 624/142-0402, www.zafirospa.com) is known for its massages (US$40-60), but also offers facials and body wraps. Bring the whole family—massages and other services are available for kids as well.

If you're staying in the *zona hotelera* and want spa services at a more affordable rate than what's offered at your resort, try Reflex Wellness Corner (Paseo Malecón, tel. 624/105-2029, info@reflexwellness.com). It offers full-body massages and holistic facials as well as acupuncture and reflexology treatments.

ENTERTAINMENT AND EVENTS

NIGHTLIFE

San José del Cabo doesn't have the nightlife that Cabo San Lucas does. If you're looking for big nightclubs, you won't find them here. But you will find a few friendly bars and a more laid-back scene.

One of the newest hot spots for locals and tourists is La Osteria (Paseo de los Cabos Zona Hotelera, tel. 624/146-9696, 6pm-11pm Mon.-Wed., 6pm-3am Thurs.-Sat.). Live Latin, jazz, and Latin rock music is played almost every night. Patrons enjoy margaritas and Mexican wines in the open-air space. The full menu includes dishes like rib eye and *queso fundido.*

Beer lovers will enjoy Baja Brewing Co. (Morelos 1227, tel. 624/142-5294, www.bajabrewingcompany.com, noon-midnight Sun.-Wed., noon-2am Thurs.-Sat.), a craft brewery with a restaurant and outdoor patio.

Its signature Cabotella ale is joined by a wheat beer, blond ale, stout, red ale, and seasonal creations.

Cuervo's House (Blvd. Mijares 101A, tel. 624/142-5650, www.cuervoshouse.com, 10am-11pm Wed.-Mon.) is home to Cabo's only piano bar. The large space houses a Mexican restaurant during the day, with the piano bar starting around 9pm.

Located at Vidanta Hotel, OMNIA Dayclub (Blvd. San José, tel. 624/104-9743, www.omniaclubs.com/los-cabos) features four venues—OMNIA Dayclub, Herringbone, Casa Calavera, and SHOREbar—that provide entertainment from day to night with beachfront venues, restaurants, and bars.

FESTIVALS AND EVENTS

The Los Cabos Open of Surf (www.loscabosopenofsurf.com) is a professional surf and music event that takes place every June at the famous Zippers surf spot at Costa Azul. Both men's and women's competitions take place over six days. The event draws large crowds that gather to watch the surfing competitions and the live music performances.

Every November the Los Cabos International Film Festival (www.cabosfilmfestival.com) takes place over five days, screening films and bringing together filmmakers, actors, and film viewers from Mexico, Canada, and the United States.

SHOPPING

The handicraft market on Boulevard Mijares is home to about a dozen vendors who sell Mexican souvenirs like blankets, hammocks, pottery, and T-shirts. For higher-quality shopping, there are a number of shops around the plaza and art district.

Plenty of art galleries are in town to suit whatever your taste. **Silver Moon Gallery** (Blvd. Mijares 10, tel. 624/144-1269, 11am-8pm Mon.-Sat.) pioneered the notion of promoting Mexican folk art in the region. It sells pottery from Mata Ortiz, colorful Huichol beadwork, *alebrijes* from Oaxaca, and beautiful silver jewelry.

The chic space at **Santo Cabo** (Obregón, tel. 624/142-1665, www.santocabo.com, 9am-10pm Mon.-Sat.) is filled with handmade, locally sourced organic soaps and lotions. It also features organic produce and baked goods from Flora Farms, of Flora's Field Kitchen.

Curios Carmela (Blvd. Mijares, tel. 624/142-1617, 10am-8pm Mon.-Sat., 11am-5pm Sun.) has plenty of Mexican trinkets and souvenirs to take home to everyone on your shopping list. From T-shirts to traditional Mexican arts, it has a wide variety of offerings.

Young and trendy women looking for beachy straw bags and bold jewelry head to **Shima Shima** (José Maria Morelos, tel. 322/294-1812, www.shimashima.com.mx, 10am-7pm Mon.-Sat.). Many of its items are handmade and inspired by the Mexican beach culture around Los Cabos.

With a well-curated collection of colorful and well-designed handicrafts from all over Mexico, **Indita Mia** (Mexico 1, tel. 414/651-1213, www.inditamia.com) is a bright and cheerful shop carrying items that are 100 percent made in Mexico. It has a store in San José del Cabo located at the Selecto Chedraui, as well as a location at the airport in the international terminal for anyone looking for a last-minute gift to take home.

FOOD

Restaurants in touristy areas on Boulevard Mijares, near the plaza, or near the *zona hotelera* have higher prices. For more authentic food at more affordable prices, head a bit farther out from the center. The hip farm-to-table restaurants are located just outside town in the rural Las Animas Bajas area of San José.

CENTRO HISTÓRICO
Mexican

The charming and intimate **El Matador** (Paseo los Marinos, tel. 624/142-2741, www.elmatadorrestaurante.com, 5pm-10pm daily, US$20-33) is a family-owned operation with owner Pablo often present. Pablo began bullfighting at the age of 14 and did this professionally until moving to Los Cabos in 1988. There's plenty of bullfighting memorabilia in the restaurant, and the waitstaff dress as matadors. The service is impeccable, going above and beyond to attend to the needs of customers. The quality of the meats—veal, rack of lamb, filet—is unparalleled. There's an appealing outdoor patio and often live entertainment.

For modern Mexican from one of Baja's top chefs, head to ✪ **La Revolución Comedor de Baja California** (Álvaro Obregón 1732, tel. 624/688-6915, www.larevolucioncomedor.com, 1pm-midnight Tues.-Wed., 1pm-1am Thurs.-Sat., 1pm-11pm Sun., US$12-17). Executive Chef Benito Molina serves dishes like clam and octopus ceviche and fish tiradito alongside pork loin and tomahawk steak in a sleek and modern setting. The well-crafted food is accompanied by creative craft cocktails and a nice wine selection.

La Revolución Comedor de Baja California

For tacos and mezcal, local hipsters and chic travelers flock to ✪ **La Lupita** (Calle José Maria Morelos, tel. 624/688-3926, 2pm-midnight Tues., 2pm-2am Wed.-Sat., noon-midnight Sun., tacos US$2-4). The exposed brick, whitewashed walls, wood pallet furniture, and minimal decor create a Zen-like atmosphere. The wide variety of tacos includes rib eye, lamb, octopus, and nopal. There's an extensive mezcal menu as well as a decent selection of craft beers. Everything is reasonably priced for being in a tourist area, plus there's a lovely outdoor patio and bar.

Situated on the popular Boulevard Mijares, **Don Sanchez Restaurante** (Blvd. Mijares, tel. 624/142-2444, www.donsanchezrestaurant.com, 5:30pm-10:30pm daily, US$15-37) serves contemporary Mexican cuisine. This is fine dining complete with artful plating and higher pricing. The service is attentive, and the wine list is extensive. There are a variety of vegetarian options (like chile portobello) in addition to seafood dishes (lobster in white mole) and meats (lamb shank *mixiote*).

Also on Mijares and operated by the same owner as Don Sanchez is **Habanero's Gastro Grill and Tequila Bar** (Blvd. Mijares, tel. 624/142-2626, www.habanerosgastrogrill.com, 8am-10:30pm daily, US$13-25). Breakfast, lunch, and dinner can be enjoyed on the outdoor sidewalk seating or in the dining room. There's an impressive selection of tequila at the bar and an extensive menu featuring steaks, seafood, pastas, and traditional Mexican dishes.

Traditional Mexican restaurant **Jazmin's** (José Maria Morelos 133, tel. 624/142-1760, www.jazminsrestaurant.com, 8am-10:30pm daily, US$11-24) is in the art district downtown, a few blocks away from the plaza. This large restaurant is formed from a collection of different rooms and outdoor spaces with colorful walls, Mexican decor, and strung lights outdoors. It serves typical Mexican dishes.

Housed under a giant *palapa*, **El Herradero Mexican Grill and Bar** (Miguel Hidalgo, tel. 624/142-6350, www.elherraderoloscabos.com, 8am-10pm daily, US$11-16) serves traditional Mexican dishes for breakfast, lunch, and dinner. The casual and comfortable setting complements the flavorful food, live music, and friendly service.

Las Guacamayas (Paseo de los Marinos, tel. 624/109-5473, 11:30am-10:30pm daily, US$3-8) has authentic and affordable Mexican food. The large venue has a fun and lively atmosphere the whole family will enjoy. Another location is in Cabo San Lucas.

Seafood

An easy walk from downtown San José, **Mariscos El Toro Guero** (Calle

Ildefonso Green, tel. 624/130-7818, noon-6pm daily, US$8-10) is where locals and tourists alike go for fresh seafood, large portions, and affordable prices. Enjoy fresh ceviche and seafood cocktails as well as items like bacon-wrapped shrimp stuffed with cheese.

International

La Vaca Tinta (Manuel Doblado, tel. 624/142-1241, 5pm-11pm Tues.-Sat., 2pm-9pm Sun., US$8-15) has a great selection of Mexican wines on the menu. It grills steaks to perfection and also serves salads, soups, empanadas, and cheese appetizers.

For a meal set in a lovely garden courtyard, head to Casa Don Rodrigo (Blvd. Mijares 29, tel. 624/142-0418, www.casadonrodrigo.com, 11am-11pm Mon.-Sat., US$11-17). It serves seafood, meats, salads, and cheeses that come from the family's local ranch. The restaurant is located in an old house with a lovely courtyard that provides a beautiful and romantic setting.

Serving Argentinian barbecue, Barrio de Tango (Morelos, tel. 624/125-3023, 6pm-11pm Tues.-Sun., US$12-15) is a great place to go for steak. Dining is casual and outdoors here, and the place gets busy, so it's best to make a reservation.

If you want farm-to-table dining without wandering out of town, the sister restaurant to Huerta los Tamarindos, Tequila Restaurant (Manuel Doblado 1011, tel. 624/142-1155, 6pm-11pm daily, US$11-14) uses the same fresh ingredients in dishes served right in downtown San José. There's a lush garden dining patio, a walk-in humidor, and a nice wine list. Tequila shrimp, rack of lamb, lobster bomb (a giant lobster wonton), and beef tenderloin in guajillo sauce are some of the restaurant's specialties.

Street Food

For a more local experience, head to Las Cazuelas del Don (Malvarrose at Guijarro, tel. 624/130-7386, 1pm-9:30pm Mon.-Fri., US$4-6), where diners enjoy grilled steak, fresh fish, and local vegetables cooked in a traditional *cazuela* cooking pot. This family-run restaurant serves delicious and authentic food at affordable prices. On Saturdays you can find them at the San José Mercado Organico 9am-3pm.

You'll have to venture a bit off the tourist path to get to Taqueria Rossy (Mexico 1 Km. 33, tel. 624/142-6755, 8am-9pm daily, US$2-8). Don't be fooled by the basic setting—these are some of the best fish tacos in the area. It also serves a number of seafood dishes, from ceviche tostadas and marlin quesadillas to *pescado zarandeado,* a butterflied fish specialty.

Cafés

Located in the art district, Lolita Café (Manuel Doblado, tel. 624/130-7786, 9am-4pm Wed.-Sun., US$9-12) has plenty of options for healthy eats, like a signature egg sandwich with marinated vegetable slices, sun-dried tomato, almond pesto, and chickpea dressing. This is artisan food with a Mexican touch served in a hip and unpretentious setting (don't miss the garden patio in the back).

For a good cup of java, Coffee Lab (Benito Juárez 1717, tel. 624/105-2835, www.coffeelab.mx, 7am-7pm Mon.-Sat., US$3-6) is a sleek and stylish coffee shop located in downtown. In addition to great coffee, it serves breakfast, sandwiches, and paninis.

ZONA HOTELERA
Mexican

With a romantic courtyard setting, Lugareño Cocina de Mexico (Plaza Villa Valentina, tel. 624/142-6612, www.cocinadelugar.com, 9am-3pm and 5pm-10pm daily, US$9-16) serves Mexican dishes with fresh local ingredients. The menu features items like *aguachile* and *tlayudas*. It also has a seasonal tasting menu available. Reservations are kindly requested.

Seafood

Restaurant and bar El Fish & Grill (Paseo Malecón, tel. 624/142-1040, www.elfishandgrill.com, noon-11pm daily, US$11-18) is a casual spot for enjoying ceviche, grilled fish, and shrimp, as well as steak. The bar features a variety of cocktails as well as beer and wine. Enjoy sitting outdoors on the patio or inside in the dining room at this family-friendly restaurant.

International

If you're looking for Italian food close to the *zona hotelera,* La Forchetta (Plaza del Pescador, tel. 624/130-7723, www.laforchetta.mx, 5pm-11pm daily, US$13-16) provides a break for guests from the all-inclusive food at resorts across the street. Pizza, pasta, ravioli, and Italian staples like chicken parmesan are all on the menu. Make sure to save room for desserts like cannoli or tiramisu. There's also a decent wine list.

Serving breakfast, lunch, and dinner, La Galeria (Paseo Malecón, tel. 624/142-0978, www. lagaleriarestaurant.com.mx, 8:30am-midnight daily, US$17-23) offers a fusion of cuisines from Mexican to Asian and Mediterranean. Soups, salads, seafood, and a variety of appetizers are complemented by cocktails and beer. Indoor and outdoor seating is available in a relaxed atmosphere.

At the Cabo Surf Hotel, 7 Seas Seafood Grille (Mexico 1 Km. 28, tel. 624/142-2666, www.7seasrestaurant. com, 7am-11pm daily, US$16-35) serves an international menu with mains like shrimp ravioli, beef tenderloin au jus, mango red snapper, and various surf-and-turf combinations. This is refined beachside dining with ocean views and an upscale open-air *palapa* setting.

For casual beachside dining, Zippers Bar & Grill (Mexico 1 Km. 28.5, tel. 624/172-6162, 11am-11pm daily, US$15-18) has decent food (a mix of American and Mexican offerings) and live music on most days. It's a spot for tourists and expats, but the views are great, and there's a large bar area with televisions. If you're not into watching sports, the restaurant is situated near one of the best surf spots in Cabo, so enjoy a beer while watching the waves instead.

PUERTO LOS CABOS
Mexican

Located at La Marina Inn, George's Restaurant (Calle los Pescadores, tel. 624/142-4166, 8am-10pm daily, US$8-14) is cozy and serves seafood and traditional Mexican dishes. Garlic shrimp, lobster, and oysters Rockefeller are some menu favorites. The restaurant serves breakfast, lunch, and dinner at affordable prices. Don't miss the large and delicious margaritas.

International

Fashioned out of a shipping container, The Container Restaurant & Bar (Puerto Los Cabos Marina, tel. 624/105-6628, 8am-10:30pm Mon.-Sat., 8am-5pm Sun., US$12-20) features prime marina views. The open-air restaurant has a fun atmosphere and offers breakfast, lunch, and dinner, as well as a full bar. Salads, seafood, and Mexican food are all on the menu.

In a funky two-story *palapa* overlooking the marina in La Playita, El Marinero Borracho/The Drunken Sailor (Calle Cabrilla, tel. 624/105-6464, elmarineroborracho@gmail.com, noon-10pm Tues.-Sun., US$8-10) features Mexican-style seafood with an international twist. Try the Vietnamese-style seafood taco and a *michelada* while enjoying sunset over the marina.

LAS ANIMAS BAJAS

To get to Las Animas Bajas from downtown San José del Cabo, head east past Puerto Los Cabos, on the Camino Cabo Este road. Take a left at the cement plant onto the dirt road. From here, follow the signs for the restaurants.

Farm-to-Table

For a farm-to-table experience, head to ✪ Flora's Field Kitchen (Animas Bajas, tel. 624/355-4564, www.flora-farms.com, 9am-2:30pm and 6pm-9:30pm Tues.-Sat., 10am-2:30pm Sun., US$15-25), where handmade food is crafted with fresh ingredients from the land. You won't find much Mexican food on the menu, but all meats are raised on the property (cruelty-free), and all the produce is local. Popular with expats and American tourists, the beautiful restaurant is set in lush gardens. Flora's runs farm tours a few times daily; check with the restaurant directly for set times. A market, bar, pizzeria, ice cream cart, and curated gift shops are also on the

Flora's Field Kitchen restaurant

property. Reservations are highly recommended.

Also tucked away in the farmlands of Las Animas Bajas is ✪ **Huerta los Tamarindos** (Animas Bajas, tel. 624/105-6031, www.lostamarindos. mx, noon-10pm Wed.-Mon., US$11-18). The restaurant can be difficult to find, but it's worth the effort. You'll follow the signs along the dirt road before arriving at a large property where a 100-year-old brick building houses an open-air restaurant overlooking an organic farm. Overgrown vines hang down from the *palapa* roof, providing a romantic feel. With the serene outdoor patio seating looking out onto the farm and surrounding hillsides, it's easy to forget you're in Los Cabos. The food is fresh and meticulously prepared, from unique ceviches and other seafood to free-range chicken and pork shank with green mole to the house "mezcalita" tamarind and mezcal cocktail. After your meal, head up to the roof to check out the views. In addition to the restaurant, you can take cooking classes or get a tour of the organic farm.

Restaurant and cocktail bar **Acre** (Calle Camino Real, tel. 624/171-8226, www.acrebaja.com, noon-3pm and 5pm-10pm Mon.-Fri., 10am-3pm and 5pm-10pm Sat.-Sun., US$20-35) is situated on 10 hectares (25 acres) of farmland that was formerly a mango grove. Its menu features fresh ingredients artfully prepared into dishes like beet salad and charred octopus. A seven-course tasting menu is available with or without a wine pairing. Sleek architecture creates an enjoyable setting, and there are pathways leading around the verdant grounds. The extensive cocktail list includes many

Acre restaurant and cocktail bar

drinks crafted from syrups that are house distilled using products sourced from the farm.

Markets

The **San José Mercado Organico** (Huerta Maria, tel. 624/142-0948, www.sanjomo.com, 9am-3pm Sat.) is an organic farmers market that takes place on Saturdays northeast of the historic downtown on the road to Las Animas from Calle Centenario. In addition to organic produce, there are arts and crafts, books, and souvenirs for sale. There's also prepared food and local music.

ACCOMMODATIONS

CENTRO HISTÓRICO

A solid budget option right in town is **Hotel Colli** (Hidalgo, tel. 624/142-0725, www.hotelcolli.com, US$50), a Mexican hacienda-style hotel that was established in 1972. Hard beds disappoint many guests, but the rooms are clean and comfortable with air-conditioning, and the plaza, restaurants, galleries, and shops of San José are just steps away.

Close to the center of town, **Tropicana Inn** (Blvd. Mijares 30, tel. 612/175-0860, www.tropicanainn. com.mx, US$75-100) offers traditional Mexican atmosphere with 37 rooms centered around a large courtyard with a heated pool. Rooms are basic, but there's a nice pool area and friendly staff.

Set in the art district in San José, **El Encanto Inn and Suites** (Calle Morelos 133, tel. 624/142-0388, www.elencantoinn.com, US$118-145) is a hacienda-style boutique hotel with Old Mexico charm. Rooms feature Mission-style wooden furniture and crisp white bedding. There are two buildings here—the main inn and another one about a block away. The courtyard pool rooms in the main building, which are a bit more expensive, are worth the splurge to look over the lush courtyard with its lovely pool. This is a pet-friendly property.

Independent boutique hotel **Drift San José** (Miguel Hidalgo between Obregón and Comonfort, no tel., www.driftsanjose.com, US$79-99)

draws a youthful hip crowd. The sleek minimalistic rooms have stylish furniture and finishes. The property features a dipping pool, breakfast bar, food cart, and a mezcal bar.

For the most luxurious accommodations in town, try ✪ **Casa Natalia** (4 Blvd. Mijares, toll-free U.S. tel. 888/277-3814, www.casanatalia.com, US$175-230). This boutique property just off the plaza has chic decor in neutral colors with bright Mexican accents. The courtyard has a nice pool, and the attached **Mi Cocina** restaurant serves Mexican fare.

ZONA HOTELERA (BEACH HOTELS)

Situated on 5 hectares (12.4 acres) of oceanfront property, **Cabo Azul Resort** (Paseo Malecón, tel. 624/163-5100, toll-free U.S. tel. 855/385-0611, www.caboazulresort.com, US$630)

the patio at Casa Natalia

is not an all-inclusive resort, but that doesn't keep those who love the resort lifestyle from staying here. Guests enjoy a three-level infinity-edge pool, with swim-up bar, plus two serenity pools. There's a luxurious day spa, beauty salon, and fitness center. Downtown San José del Cabo is about a 15-minute walk away, but there are enough restaurants and amenities on the property that many guests don't leave. Almost the entire property was renovated after Hurricane Odile.

The all-inclusive family resort Hyatt Ziva (Paseo Malecón 5, tel. 624/163-7730, www.hyatt.com, US$500) is welcoming to guests of all ages. This massive resort has seven restaurants on property, five swimming pools (including an adults-only pool and a children's pool complete with multiple slides), Cirque du Soleil-style live entertainment, and a plethora of activities to choose from. A full children's center, a variety of sports activities, and a full spa round out the selections.

The luxury Vidanta Los Cabos (Blvd. San José, toll-free U.S. tel. 800/292-9446, www.vidanta.com, US$650) originally opened as The Grand Mayan Hotel. The property features 154 rooms, eight pools, a golf course, an exclusive spa, and 10 restaurants and bars, including the OMNIA Dayclub. While the property is large and attracts many couples and families, some may find the loud music coming from OMNIA during the day to be disruptive.

Design aficionados will want to stay at the slick Viceroy (Paseo Malecón, tel. 624/104-9999, www. viceroyhotelsandresorts.com, US$425 standard, US$725 all-inclusive), which opened in 2018 and was formerly Mar Adentro. The resort's modern concept is the brainchild of architect Miguel Ángel Aragonés. Distinct water features cover the outdoor area, only to be interrupted by a unique woven "nest" that houses a restaurant. All-white interiors maintain the contemporary feel throughout the property. The 192 rooms have private balconies, some with Jacuzzis, all overlooking the pools and white sand beach. Rooms can be booked standard or all-inclusive.

The family-run Casa Costa Azul Hotel (Mexico 1 Km. 28.5, tel. 624/172-6632, www. hotelcasacostazulcabo.com, US$222-247) is a small boutique hotel with a prime location right on the beach. The 14 rooms are clean with comfortable beds, wooden Mission-style furniture, and Mexican accents. A continental breakfast is included in your stay. It's worth the extra money for an oceanview room. There's no elevator so guests on the upper floors will need to take the stairs.

The small Marisol Boutique Hotel (Paseo San José 161, tel. 624/132-9089, www.marisolboutiquehotel.com, US$50) has eight rooms. You won't find a swimming pool here, but the property is two blocks away from the beach, and guests are provided beach towels, umbrellas, and beach chairs. No children under 15 years old are allowed.

Surfers coming to the region stay at Cabo Surf Hotel (Mexico 1 Km. 28, tel. 624/142-2666, www.cabosurf. com, US$280-325), where boutique accommodations are situated right on Acapulquito (Old Man's), one of the best surfing beaches in Los Cabos. There are 36 rooms decorated in a

DAY TRIPS FROM LOS CABOS

Get out of town for a day trip. If you don't have a car or just don't feel like driving yourself, there are many tour operators who will take you to many of these locations:

Cabo Pulmo: Over on the East Cape is a 20,000-year-old coral reef that makes up the Cabo Pulmo national marine park. Divers and snorkelers flock to see the marinelife that inhabits one of only three living coral reefs in North America (page 81).

Cañon de la Zorra: Up in the nearby Sierra de la Laguna, a 10-minute hike will get you to a beautiful waterfall. The surrounding pools and rocks provide an unforgettable day of swimming and relaxing in nature (page 104).

El Triunfo: The small old mining town of El Triunfo is having a resurgence. With its historic old colonial buildings and new cafés, shops, and restaurants opening up, it's becoming a popular day trip for travelers to Baja Sur (page 108).

Todos Santos: The colonial town of Todos Santos on the West Cape is a popular spot for visitors who want to get away from the mega-resort crowds for a day (page 149).

laid-back California style with beautiful views of the ocean.

PUERTO LOS CABOS

For budget accommodations, ✪ El Delfin Blanco (Calle Delfines, tel. 624/142-1212, www.eldelfinblanco. net, US$57) has six separate casitas, all with air-conditioning and a mini-refrigerator. There's a courtyard with a fountain and plenty of seating, as well as an outdoor kitchen. You'll get personal attention here, unlike an experience at one of the larger hotels and resorts in the area. Don't miss the Swedish pancakes for breakfast.

Creative types looking for a more laid-back vibe will undoubtedly find themselves at ✪ Hotel El Ganzo (Blvd. Tiburón, tel. 624/104-9000, www.elganzo.com, US$300), a 69-room hotel in a tranquil area near the marina at Puerto Los Cabos. The hotel is understated but hip, with sleek, undeniable style. Artists in residence leave their mark on the hotel, whether through murals and other artwork, or by using the underground recording studios. Guests enjoy a rooftop infinity pool, a spa, and Ganzo Downstairs—the signature restaurant

Hotel El Ganzo

on the property—as well as the hotel's own weekly farmers market.

Boutique hotel La Marina Inn (Calle los Pescadores, tel. 624/142-4166, www.lamarinainn.com, US$125-250) was originally built in 1953 but has been refurbished. It has a nice pool area, 23 rooms, and three suites. The remodel has brought modern updates to the classic Mexican architecture and charm. All rooms feature televisions, air-conditioning, and Wi-Fi.

The adults-only Secrets Puerto Los Cabos Golf & Spa Resort (Av. Paseo de los Pescadores, tel. 624/144-2600, www.secretsresorts.com, US$1,345) is an "unlimited-luxury" (all-inclusive) romance resort with 500 suites. The property is pristine with excellent service. There are plenty of activities to choose from as well as dining options and live entertainment day and night.

Scheduled to open in 2019, the Zadún Ritz-Carlton Reserve Hotel (www.ritzcarlton.com) will be coming to the Puerto Los Cabos area. The "Reserve" label for Ritz-Carlton is its more elite sub-brand that brings luxury to one-of-a-kind boutique hotel experiences. There will be 115 suites and villas with panoramic views of the Sea of Cortez, as well as an exclusive spa.

LAS ANIMAS BAJAS

If you've always dreamed of sleeping in a tree house, enjoy a stay at Acre (tel. 624/129-9607, www.acrebaja. com, US$295). The 12 tree house units are stylishly rustic and outfitted with plush furniture, Mexican artisan decor, and a curated mini-bar. Breakfast and morning yoga are included in your stay. This adults-only property features a pool and is also home to a popular outdoor restaurant and mezcal bar. Note that the tree houses are not handicap-accessible.

INFORMATION AND SERVICES

TOURIST ASSISTANCE

The Los Cabos Tourism office (tel. 624/146-9628, www.loscabos.gob.mx) is in Plaza San José. It has brochures and information about the area.

THE U.S. CONSULATE

The United States has a consular agency (Tiendas de Palmilla, Mexico 1 Km. 27.5 Local B221, tel. 664/748-0129) just outside San José del Cabo.

It can provide emergency services for U.S. citizens as well as routine services such as notarial services, reports of birth abroad, and applications for U.S. passports. This location is unable to provide visa-related information or services.

MEDICAL SERVICES

The new state-of-the-art hospital, H+ Los Cabos (Mexico 1 Km. 24.5, tel. 624/104-9300, www.hmas.mx/loscabos) is a large modern facility with a 24/7 ambulance, doctors who can provide specialty care, and the latest modern technology. The Walk in MediClinic (Mexico 1 Km. 28, tel. 624/130-7011) has an emergency room, ambulance, and pharmacy. Call 911 for emergencies.

TRANSPORTATION

GETTING THERE

Air

The commercial airport for the region, Los Cabos International Airport (SJD, tel. 624/146-5111, www. sjdloscabosairport.com), is located in San José del Cabo, 13 kilometers (8.1 miles) north of the center of town. Direct flights are available from the United States, Canada, and other areas of Mexico.

From Los Cabos International Airport

Ruta del Desierto (tel. 624/128-3760) is a bus service that will take you to San José for US$5. You can collect the bus from Terminal 1 at the airport, and it will drop you at the bus station in San José del Cabo, 1.5 kilometers (0.9 mile) from Plaza Teniente José Antonio Mijares. It's a quick and cheap solution for airport transportation.

A taxi to downtown San José or the *zona hotelera* from the airport costs around US$30. Many large hotels and resorts have their own airport shuttle service that will be cheaper than a cab; check with your accommodations.

There are many rental car companies in Los Cabos, most of which are familiar names to U.S. travelers. Even if you do not rent a car at the Los Cabos airport (though note this is the cheapest option), there are rental car offices around San José del Cabo (many along the *zona hotelera*). Remember that you are legally required to purchase the Mexican auto insurance when renting a car. **Cactus Rent a Car** (tel. 624/146-1839, toll-free U.S. tel. 866/225-9220, www.cactuscar. com) is a local company that will quote you a full price (insurance included) so there are no unwelcome surprises at pickup. Another car rental company that will quote you for the full price is **BBB Rent a Car** (tel. 624/172-2436, www.bbbrentacar.com), although its prices tend to be expensive. Gas stations and car services are plentiful throughout the area.

Car
If you're going by car, there's the Autopista San José del Cabo-Cabo San Lucas toll road connecting San José del Cabo to the airport. The trip to downtown San José takes 25 minutes, and the toll is US$2. To the *zona hotelera,* the drive is 20 minutes, and the toll is US$2, which must be paid in cash (both dollars and pesos are accepted).

From Todos Santos and the West Cape, take Mexico 19 south to catch either Mexico 1 or the toll road in Cabo San Lucas. Continue east another 30 kilometers (19 miles) to San José del Cabo. The route is 100 kilometers (62 miles) and takes just over an hour.

From La Paz the 185-kilometer (115-mile) journey takes just over two hours, traveling south on Mexico 19 and then east on Mexico 1.

Bus
The main bus station in San José del Cabo is on Calle González. **Aguila** (toll-free Mex. tel. 800/026-8931, www. autobusesaguila.com) and **Autobuses de la Baja California** (ABC, tel. 664/104-7400, www.abc.com.mx) have services to and from La Paz and Todos Santos. From La Paz, the bus ride to San José del Cabo takes three hours and costs US$22, with buses running about every hour. From Todos Santos, the two-hour bus ride costs US$9, with buses departing every hour.

The bus station is located 1.5 kilometers (0.9 mile) from the *centro histórico* and 2 kilometers (1.2 miles) from the *zona hotelera*. A 25-minute walk or a cab ride (US$5) will get you to either location.

GETTING AROUND
The downtown San José area is pleasant and easy to explore by foot. If you're planning on staying mostly at a resort or in the downtown area, you can get away with not renting a car. The *zona hotelera* is located 1.5 kilometers (0.9 mile) from the *centro histórico,* a 20-minute walk or US$5 cab ride.

Car
The Autopista San José del Cabo-Cabo San Lucas toll road connects San José del Cabo with the airport, the corridor, and Cabo San Lucas. Depending on where you are getting on and off the road, the fee will be US$2-4.

From Cabo San Lucas, San José del Cabo is 30 kilometers (19 miles) along Mexico 1, and the drive takes 45 minutes. On the faster toll road, the drive takes 30 minutes, and the toll is US$4.

Parking is generally easy to find around San José and all of Los Cabos, and there are plenty of gas stations. Having a car will give you the freedom to explore on your own schedule without having to rely on bus services or taxis.

Bus

Aguila (toll-free Mex. tel. 800/026-8931, www.autobusesaguila.com) and Autobuses de la Baja California (ABC, tel. 664/104-7400, www.abc.com.mx) have services to and from Cabo San Lucas. The bus ride takes 30 minutes and costs US$3; buses run every half hour.

Ruta del Desierto (tel. 624/128-3760) is a bus service that will pick you up in the San José bus station and go to Cabo San Lucas or the corridor for US$2. It takes about an hour to get from San José to Cabo San Lucas, with frequent stops along the route.

Taxi

Taxis are available around the downtown area and the *zona hotelera*. A taxi will cost around US$40 to go to Cabo San Lucas. Make sure to negotiate your cab fare in advance. It costs about US$5 to get from the *zona hotelera* to the *centro histórico*.

Ridesharing service Uber (www.uber.com) is now available in Los Cabos. Uber is not currently available for rides to or from the Los Cabos International Airport.

THE EAST CAPE AND THE SIERRA DE LA LAGUNA

East of San José del Cabo, the

resorts and crowds of Los Cabos fade away and you're left with the pure natural beauty of Baja California Sur.

The East Cape is home to deserted white sand beaches, coral reefs teeming with sealife, charming colonial towns, and the lush Sierra de la Laguna.

It's a more relaxing and intimate alternative to the glamour and crowds of Los Cabos, but still within close proximity of the airport. The few small towns here are nestled into the foothills of

HIGHLIGHTS

○ **DIVING AND SNORKELING IN CABO PULMO:** The coral reef and national park are home to abundant marinelife and offer some of the best diving on the peninsula (pages 82 and 83).

○ **KITEBOARDING IN LOS BARRILES:** The El Norte winds and warm waters attract kiteboarders from all over the world, especially in winter months (page 90).

○ **SPORTFISHING:** The summer months bring anglers to the East Cape to catch marlin, dorado, yellowtail, roosterfish, and sierra (page 92).

○ **CAÑON DE LA ZORRA:** This beautiful and remote canyon is home to a large waterfall and natural pools that make for an exciting day trip (page 104).

○ **SANTA RITA HOT SPRINGS:** This is the best spot for soaking in the area (page 105).

○ **EL TRIUNFO:** This old colonial mining town is worth a day trip to explore the mine ruins, museums, cafés, and restaurants (page 108).

the mountains or dotted along the Sea of Cortez, attracting close-knit expat communities. There are no nightclubs or mega-resorts here—in fact, quite the opposite. Most of the region is off the grid and quiets down not long after sunset. This is an area prime for families and those who love to get outdoors, whether your idea of being outdoors is relaxing on a pristine beach or hiking to waterfalls in the sierra. Anglers, kiteboarders, surfers, hikers, divers, and snorkelers will all find plenty to fill their days with here.

Los Barriles is the largest town on the East Cape, and many visitors end up staying here, along with the surrounding communities like Buena

Beautiful beaches stretch all along the East Cape.

Vista and Punta Pescadero. Cabo Pulmo's coral reef to the south is one of the premier diving and snorkeling destinations in Baja. Inland toward the Sierra de la Laguna are a number of quaint towns that act as gateways to the mountains that shelter scenic hikes, hot springs, waterfalls, and natural pools.

PLANNING YOUR TIME

Although the East Cape is a relatively small area, there's plenty to do here for outdoor enthusiasts. When, where, and how long to go are all largely dependent on the activities you're interested in.

A week gives you enough time to relax, explore the area, and fit in a range of activities. Despite the heat, summer is usually when anglers come to Los Barriles, Buena Vista, or Punta Pescadero for offshore sportfishing. Summer is also the season for divers and snorkelers who arrive in Cabo Pulmo to enjoy its coral reef abounding with marinelife. In the wintertime, kiteboarders head to Los Barriles to take advantage of the El Norte winds. If you're planning a multiday trek into the Sierra de la Laguna, allow at least 3-4 days.

Many travelers staying in Los Cabos take day trips to the East Cape for activities such as snorkeling or diving in Cabo Pulmo, trekking to the Cañon de la Zorra waterfall just outside Santiago, or exploring the towns of Los Barriles and El Triunfo.

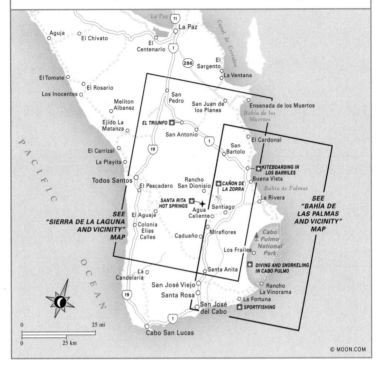

Parque Nacional Cabo Pulmo and Vicinity

Parque Nacional Cabo Pulmo is one of the most popular destinations for scuba diving and snorkeling on the peninsula. With the living coral reef and an abundance of sealife, it's no wonder that the area is a highly protected national park. Divers and snorkelers flock to see the colorful tropical fish, moray eels, octopus, lobsters, and sea lions. This region has been fighting back large development for years and so far remains occupied mostly by small family-run hotels and dive shops.

The area that surrounds Cabo Pulmo is mostly centered on the nearby beaches and the East Cape coastal road, Camino Cabo Este. The road departs from Mexico 1 at kilometer 93 and heads east to the coast. It then follows the coast along the East Cape and reconnects with Mexico 1 at San José del Cabo. The road is paved for a few kilometers along the northern part until La Ribera, and for a few kilometers out of San José del Cabo along the southern part. There have been plans for over a decade to pave the entire road, but for now, most stretches remain dirt.

There is no bus service to the area.

Cabo Pulmo Visitor Center

CABO PULMO

One of only three coral reefs in North America, the Cabo Pulmo reef is 5,000 years old and the only living coral reef in the Sea of Cortez. The marine reserve was established in 1995 to protect the reef, and in 2005, UNESCO recognized it as a World Heritage Site. There are eight separate fingers of the reef, four close to shore and the other four out in the bay. The reef begins just a few meters off the shore, which makes Cabo Pulmo an extremely appealing dive and snorkel spot. Commercial and sportfishing are banned within the park.

The waters here are teeming with marinelife, and divers and snorkelers have the ability to see sea turtles, dolphins, parrot fish, angelfish, damselfish, mobula rays, sharks, and whales. Large schools of tropical fish provide impressive sights for those who explore this part of the Sea of Cortez.

The little town of Cabo Pulmo is completely off the grid. The rustic, dusty town is inhabited by a small group of Mexicans and expats who

a tour boat departing from the beach access in Cabo Pulmo

operate the dive shops, accommodations, and restaurants in town. There are not many services here (no ATMS or gas stations) and just a handful of small lodging options and restaurants. Travelers who visit are usually divers or those looking for a remote and peaceful escape.

SIGHTS

There's a new Cabo Pulmo Visitor Center (tel. 612/121-2800, 8am-6pm daily) on the main street in town. There are three modern wood buildings that contain informational and interpretive exhibits showcasing the local wildlife and reef system. Captions for exhibits are in both English and Spanish.

BEACHES

Los Arbolitos

Five kilometers (3.1 miles) south of town, Los Arbolitos is the best beach in the area for snorkeling. There aren't many services out here, so if you don't have your own snorkel and mask, you'll need to rent one in town before coming out to Los Arbolitos. There are primitive bathroom and shower facilities. You'll need to pay US$2 to park your car and for access to the facilities.

Los Arbolitos

Playa La Sirenita

Also known as Dinosaur Egg Beach or Los Chopitos, this beach is difficult to access. Playa La Sirenita can only be reached by kayak, boat, or from a walking path from Los Arbolitos. The attractive narrow beach has white sand speckled by rocks. Hidden at the base of a cliff, the beach has protected waters that provide an excellent area for snorkeling around the rocks just offshore.

Los Frailes

When the winds kick up in the afternoons, divers and snorkelers head to Bahía de Los Frailes. Nine kilometers (5.6 miles) south of Bahía Cabo Pulmo, this sheltered bay provides a calm location for diving. The long beach has a few *palapas* for shade, but otherwise very few services. Snorkeling and diving take place at the northern part of the beach where the rocky point is. Camping is allowed, and this is a popular spot for dry camping and RVers.

SPORTS AND RECREATION

✪ Snorkeling

Because the coral reef begins just a few meters from the shoreline, it's possible to snorkel directly from shore at Cabo Pulmo without having to take a boat out to reach the good spots. Los Arbolitos, about 5 kilometers (3.1 miles) south of town, is the prime spot for snorkeling off the beach. If it's too windy at Arbolitos, head down to the more protected Los Frailes, where the snorkeling is good along the point on the north end of the beach. It's important to note that while snorkeling or free diving in reef areas, you are required to wear a life jacket and must maintain a distance of 2.5 meters (8.2 feet) or more from the reef.

If you want to go on an organized

snorkeling trip, any of the tour operators that run dive trips can accommodate snorkeling trips as well. There are stands and information for tours in town where the beach access is (next to La Palapa restaurant). The tour operators can take you out on boats to certain beaches and spots that you can't access on your own.

Snorkeling trips with Eco Adventures (tel. 624/157-4072, www.cabopulmoecoadventures.com, US$45-60) last 2.5 hours and include snorkeling equipment, water and soft drinks, snacks, the national park entrance fee, and a guide. For those with younger kids, the company offers a special device with a Plexiglas viewer that allows them to see underwater without using snorkeling gear.

✪ Diving

There's good scuba diving year-round in Cabo Pulmo, but the best seasons are summer and fall when the visibility is best (30 m/98 ft or more) and water temperatures are warm. Divers can find themselves surrounded by large schools of fish like snappers, bigeye jacks, and porkfish. Moray eels, sea turtles, octopus, sharks, and manta rays are also common sights. Guided drift diving is how most tours operate, with divers drifting along with the current and the captain following with the boat. Night dives and private tours are available through most tour providers by request. Scuba divers are not allowed to wear gloves while diving, and must maintain a distance of 2.5 meters (8.2 feet) or more from the reef.

In the center of town on the main street, Cabo Pulmo Beach Resort (tel. 624/141-0726, www.cabopulmo.com) is a PADI-certified dive center that offers well-maintained gear and professional and experienced guides who can handle beginning to

Los Frailes is a good beach for snorkeling on windy afternoons.

BEST RESTAURANTS IN THE EAST CAPE AND THE SIERRA DE LA LAGUNA

✪ **CAMPESTRE TRINY:** For an excellent meal, delicious margaritas, and outdoor seating, this spot is a safe bet (page 92).

✪ **LAZY DAZE BEACH BAR:** This casual beach bar is a great place for hanging out and watching the kiteboarders in Los Barriles (page 94).

✪ **LA CASITA:** Specializing in sushi and other international dishes like pastas and steak, this is some of the most upscale dining in Los Barriles (page 94).

✪ **ROADRUNNER CAFÉ & BAKERY:** Visitors come here for the best breakfast in town (page 94).

✪ **BAR EL MINERO:** Offering a chic indoor space as well as a large outdoor area, this El Triunfo bar and eatery is home to a weekly Sunday paella fest (page 110).

advanced divers. It operates a hotel as well, and offers complete packages including accommodations, food, and diving.

With a stand near the beach access in town, Cabo Pulmo Sport Center (tel. 624/157-9795, www.cabopulmosportcenter.com) offers dive tours that start at US$95 for one dive. It also handles snorkeling tours, equipment rental, sportfishing, kayaking, and whale-watching. In case you want to video your underwater adventure, it also rents GoPros.

Cabo Pulmo Divers (tel. 612/157-3381, www.cabopulmodivers.com) and Cabo Pulmo Watersports (tel. 624/228-5676, www.cabopulmowatersports.com) are two more options for dive operators.

FOOD

Because of the remote location, restaurant prices in Cabo Pulmo can be unexpectedly high since everything needs to be brought in. During the summer, restaurants will likely have a weekly schedule where they are closed more days than in other times of the year, but there is always at least one restaurant in town that will be open on any given day.

In the center of the action next to the beach access in town, La Palapa (tel. 624/130-0195, noon-9pm, US$5-12) is a great place to grab a cold beer and some food after returning from a day of snorkeling or diving. The ocean views and casual atmosphere make it a popular spot for hanging out and enjoying some shrimp or tacos with a margarita.

Just off of the main street on the north side of town, El Caballero (tel. 624/211-6317, 7am-10pm Fri.-Wed., US$6-12) is open for breakfast, lunch, and dinner serving homemade Mexican food. This is one of the best spots in town for breakfast and a good cup of coffee. There's also a small store selling an assortment of groceries and snacks.

With a popular Saturday night buffet, Tito's Bar and Restaurant (tel. 624/175-8884, US$8-11) is also known for serving great margaritas. It's open for breakfast, lunch, and dinner, serving traditional Mexican fare along with cold beer and a selection of mixed drinks. Tito's is located on the north end of the main street in town and accepts cash only.

Located on the 2nd story of the turquoise Cabo Pulmo Dive Center, Coral Reef Restaurant (tel. 624/141-0726, US$14-17) is open for lunch and dinner. It has a good happy hour, and there are flat-screen satellite TVs for watching sports. Patrons enjoy nice ocean views, but many people feel that the prices are a bit expensive for what you get. This is one of the few restaurants in town that accepts credit cards.

ACCOMMODATIONS

Rustic charm is the standard in Cabo Pulmo, so visitors shouldn't expect to find fancy resorts or large hotels. Accommodations here are small, with only a few rooms available at each property. The entire town is off-grid, relying on solar (and generators as backups), so air-conditioning is not available at most places. If visiting in summer, take this into consideration. Many accommodations offer kitchenettes or access to kitchens, but be sure to buy groceries before getting to Cabo Pulmo, where there are no large markets.

Exhibiting the peaceful and unpretentious character that Cabo Pulmo is known for, ✪ Baja Bungalows (www.bajabungalows.com, US$85-95) is a welcoming and comfortable place to stay. It has a convenient location just west of the main street in town, beaches for snorkeling, and local restaurants. It also offers snorkel and beach gear for guest use. Kent and Veronica are wonderful hosts, providing guests with helpful information, personal attention, and great recommendations. A two-night minimum stay is required.

In the center of town on the main street, Cabo Pulmo Beach Resort (tel. 624/141-0726, www.cabopulmo. com, US$60-145) has a pool on the property and villas with full kitchens. There's also a dive shop where diving and snorkeling tours can be arranged as well as surfing and mountain biking excursions. It has a wide variety of accommodations to fit various budgets and also offers a few deluxe bungalows that have air-conditioning.

Guests stay in solar-powered *palapa*-roof bungalows at Cremin's Casas (www.creminscasas.com, US$79-89). The beach and town are both a short walk away from the property, which is situated slightly inland from the center of town. Guests enjoy the views, tranquility, and personal attention from host Cremin.

With three suites, El Encanto de Cabo Pulmo (www.encantopulmo. com, US$105-125) is located near the center of town on the main street and has a convenient location close to dive shops, beaches, and restaurants. Air-conditioning, which can be difficult to find at other places in town, is available here for an extra charge. The colorful and eclectic decor includes folk art that has been collected over the years.

INFORMATION AND SERVICES

Because it's off the grid and caters to a very small population, services are minimal in Cabo Pulmo. There are no banks or ATMs here, and very few places accept credit cards, so it's important to get cash in Los Barriles or La Ribera. The nearest gas station is in La Ribera. Groceries, a health center, and other services can be found in Los Barriles.

BEST ACCOMMODATIONS IN THE EAST CAPE AND THE SIERRA DE LA LAGUNA

✪ **BAJA BUNGALOWS:** You'll feel right at home at this peaceful and unpretentious spot in Cabo Pulmo (page 85).

✪ **VILLA DEL FARO:** This gorgeous and secluded property is the place to go when you want to take a beach vacation to get away from it all (page 87).

✪ **CAPTAIN NEMO'S LANDING:** You can spend the night in a tepee or casita, as well as take kiteboarding lessons (page 95).

✪ **RANCHO LEONERO:** The rugged beauty of the East Cape shines through at Rancho Leonero, where guests spend their days fishing or relaxing in hammocks poolside (page 96).

✪ **HOTEL BUENA VISTA BEACH RESORT:** The whole family will enjoy a stay on these lush grounds, with a beautiful beach providing a backdrop for a range of activities (page 97).

GETTING THERE
It's possible to use either La Paz's Manuel Marquez de Leon International Airport (LAP) or Los Cabos International Airport (SJD) to get to the East Cape. The Los Cabos airport is the more popular choice because there are more flights. Travelers arriving at either airport can rent a car to drive to the East Cape, which takes 1-1.5 hours, depending on where you're going.

If you're driving from Los Cabos, head north on Mexico 1, branching off on the road to La Ribera to arrive at Cabo Pulmo. The last few miles into Cabo Pulmo are unpaved, but graded. It's about 100 kilometers (62 miles) and takes about 1.75 hours to drive from San José del Cabo. Those with a four-wheel-drive vehicle can take the unpaved Camino Cabo Este road along the coast, which is about 70 kilometers (43 miles) and 2 hours from San José del Cabo.

Because this is such a renowned area for diving, there are a number of tour operators in the Los Cabos area who bring divers to Cabo Pulmo by boat from Los Cabos for the day.

BOCA DE LA VINORAMA

In between Cabo Pulmo and San José del Cabo is a beautiful and remote stretch of coast, home to a number of great surf breaks, gorgeous empty beaches, and a few services along the way. Those who have 4-wheel drive and a sense of adventure can drive the coastal Camino Cabo Este that goes from San José del Cabo through Cabo Pulmo and up to La Ribera where it meets up with Mexico 1. It's best to check with locals about the condition of the road before deciding to take this route, as the southern part between San José del Cabo and Boca de la Vinorama can be in rough condition. There's a large community of expensive beachfront homes here, and a project to pave the roads lasted from San José del Cabo to a few kilometers east. Once the pavement ends, the washboard dirt roads begin. Easier access to this stretch of coast can be had via an inland route that goes through the tiny village of Palo Escopeta.

The inland route meets the coastal road right near **VidaSoul Hotel** (1000 Camino Cabo Este, tel. 624/154-6966, U.S. tel. 626/840-0485, www.vidasoul.com, US$129). The impeccably modern and sleek hotel grew out of what started as a small *palapa* serving beer and tacos to surfers who came to the nearby Punta Perfecta break. There are now 16 rooms in the eco-lodge (it runs on solar) with floor-to-ceiling windows, ocean views, polished concrete construction, and features like rain showerheads, iPod docks, and 400-thread-count sheets. Food and beer is still served on the property at the **Crossroads Bar and Restaurant.** There's a pool on-site and air-conditioning in the rooms. The prime beach location and remote site make this a wonderful spot to relax and escape.

Travelers looking for a secluded stay in paradise will find it at ✪ **Villa del Faro** (Camino Cabo Este Km. 65, no tel., www.villadelfaro.net, US$190-340). The 5 hectares (12.4 acres) of lush grounds look out onto stunning private beaches. Tucked into the exquisite oasis are a main house and a number of casitas with architecture reminiscent of a mix between a Mexican hacienda and an Italian villa. An afternoon lounging around the pool will make you feel as though you're vacationing at a private mansion along the Italian Riviera. This off-the-grid eco-lodge is a truly magnificent retreat where guests can walk or swim on the secluded beach, hike into the nearby arroyo, or watch the gray and humpback whales go by. There are eight options for accommodations, ranging from the large Casa Alberca pool house to the rustic stone cottage right on the beach. The property was

the pool at Villa del Faro in Boca de la Vinorama

originally built as a family's retreat, and the operation is still family-run today. There's a restaurant on-site, and a full breakfast is included with your stay. Table d'hôte dinners are available upon request.

LA RIBERA

Located just north of Cabo Pulmo, La Ribera is the last town on the Camino Cabo Este with municipal water and power (and paved roads), before heading out to the coast. There are some services like gas stations, OXXO convenience stores, an ATM, and small markets. The small town is home to local fishers, ranchers, and farmers.

A few large developments are taking shape along the coast. Many locals and preservationists are fighting to halt large developments, and the area is caught in a perpetual struggle between developers wanting to make it an extension of Los Cabos and those who want to preserve the natural beauty and peace of the region. Costa Palmas (www.costapalmas.com) is a 400-hectare (988-acre) beachfront development that will be home to 3.2 kilometers (2 miles) of swimmable beach, a 250-slip marina, an 18-hole golf course, 7 hectares (17.3 acres) of orchards and farms, and its own beach and yacht club. Costa Palmas will also be home to the Four Seasons Resort Los Cabos and Aman's Amanvari Resort and Residences, both opening in 2020.

The waters off La Ribera are home to the same sportfishing species that the East Cape is famous for, such as marlin, wahoo, roosterfish, dorado, and sailfish. But because La Ribera isn't a town that caters to tourists, most anglers choose to stay in and get fishing charters out of Los Barriles and Buena Vista.

Just east of La Ribera is Punta Colorada, at the southern point of Bahía de las Palmas. The Punta Colorada resort is currently closed.

FOOD AND ACCOMMODATIONS

You can expect personal attention and a welcoming atmosphere at Efren's Restaurant and Bar (Calle Brisa del Mar at Calle Casa Ejidal, tel. 624/100-4264, 10am-10pm daily, US$8-12). Seafood, steaks, hamburgers, and Mexican dishes can all be enjoyed on the large outdoor patio upstairs with views of town and the Sea of Cortez.

There isn't much in terms of accommodations in La Ribera, but Cabañas Vista La Ribera (Carrera a Cabo Pulmo Km. 13.5, tel. 624/172-7021, www.vistalaribera.com, US$140) is the nicest option. It has four casitas, all nicely decorated with modern features and offering mini-refrigerators, microwaves, and air-conditioning. You aren't right on the sea here, but there's a nice outdoor space with a pool, lounge chairs, and fire pit. All-inclusive dining packages are available for guests through the on-site restaurant (7am-10pm daily, US$8-15) that serves Mexican plates and fresh seafood. The restaurant is also open to the public.

Los Barriles and Vicinity

Los Barriles is the largest town on the East Cape and a popular destination for kiteboarders and windsurfers as well as anglers. The dusty streets lined with taco shops, small produce stands, and *tortillerías* are now filled in winter months with retiree snowbirds on ATVs and kiteboarders in search of El Norte winds.

While there's a strip mall and a growing number of expat mansions, at its heart, Los Barriles is still a small, laid-back town, especially when compared to Los Cabos. But because there are a number of options for accommodations, restaurants, and activities, Los Barriles can be a great place to stay as a home base for exploring the rest of the East Cape.

Los Barriles and the surrounding communities are situated on the Bahía de las Palmas, a large bay that is 32 kilometers (20 miles) long. The area was discovered by anglers in the 1960s and was a popular spot for fly-in fishing resorts during that time. Anglers are still drawn to the area, especially in the summer months when offshore sportfishing is at its prime.

The coastal areas north and south of Los Barriles are small communities but are constantly growing because of new housing developments. South of Los Barriles, Buena Vista has expat homes and beachfront hotels where fishing and relaxation are the focus. North of Los Barriles, Punta Pescadero also has a few hotels that

Kiteboarders flock to Los Barriles.

Bahía de las Palmas and Vicinity

lure anglers, but the area is generally less developed, in part because of dirt roads that can be rough driving.

LOS BARRILES

The town of Los Barriles has grown from a sleepy fishing village into a friendly and vibrant town over the past number of years due to an influx of American and Canadian expats. While large beachfront homes and a small strip mall have had their influence, you can still get an authentic Baja vibe here at the small markets and taco stands. It's been a popular destination for anglers since the 1960s, and in more recent decades has grown into

a world-class destination for windsurfers and kiteboarders. While the town has large grocery stores and a number of services, it's still devoid of nightlife or luxury resorts. Retirees come here to relax and enjoy the slow-paced life, while families are drawn to the region for the water sports and friendly feel.

SPORTS AND RECREATION
✪ Kiteboarding and Windsurfing
Over the past number of years, Los Barriles has established itself as a world-class spot for kiteboarding and windsurfing. The sandy bottoms and shore break make this is good spot for beginners, while the large swells that

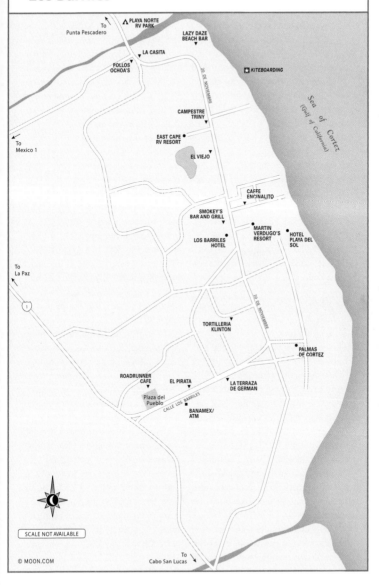

Los Barriles

To Punta Pescadero

△ PLAYA NORTE RV PARK

LAZY DAZE BEACH BAR

LA CASITA

POLLOS OCHOA'S

★ KITEBOARDING

Sea of Cortez
(Gulf of California)

20 DE NOVIEMBRE

CAMPESTRE TRINY

EAST CAPE RV RESORT

To Mexico 1

EL VIEJO

CAFFE ENCINALITO

SMOKEY'S BAR AND GRILL

MARTIN VERDUGO'S RESORT

HOTEL PLAYA DEL SOL

LOS BARRILES HOTEL

To La Paz

1

20 DE NOVIEMBRE

TORTILLERIA KLINTON

PALMAS DE CORTEZ

ROADRUNNER CAFE

EL PIRATA

LA TERRAZA DE GERMAN

Plaza del Pueblo

CALLE LOS BARRILES

BANAMEX/ATM

SCALE NOT AVAILABLE

© MOON.COM

To Cabo San Lucas

pick up in the afternoons bring excellent waves for more experienced riders. November-April the El Norte winds arrive, with consistent wind speeds between 18 and 25 knots. Playa Norte is considered the best kiteboarding beach in the region. The IKO-affiliated ExotiKite Kiteboarding School (U.S. tel. 541/380-0948, www.exotikite.com) has been in operation since 1998. It has an experienced staff and all the equipment and knowledge you need to learn kiteboarding. In addition to classes, the school has a restaurant, SUP center, and store, and can help with accommodations. Another option is Kiteboarding Baja (tel. 624/166-0986, www.kiteboardingbajaschool. com), offering private or group lessons for all levels of kiteboarders. It's IKO-certified and also has a location in La Ventana.

TOP EXPERIENCE

✪ Sportfishing

The Sea of Cortez waters on the East Cape are home to an abundance of fish, making this some of the best angling in Baja. In shallow waters, the catch can include cabrillas, jack crevalle, roosterfish, pompano, triggerfish, snappers, sierra, ladyfish, and barred pargo. Marlin, wahoo, sailfish, dorado, and tuna can be hooked in deeper waters. (Many sportfishing operations in the area encourage catch and release to help conserve natural resources.)

The waters get deep just offshore here, so it's common to catch roosterfish and jack crevalle from the shore. Punta Pescadero, Punta Colorada, and Punta Arena are three good places for this.

If you want to check out the deeper waters, many of the hotels in Los

Barriles and Buena Vista have their own fishing fleets or can arrange for a charter for you. Expect to pay US$700-1,200 a day, which will cover the boat, captain, crew, lunch with non-alcoholic drinks, and a daily fishing license. Bait and fishing gear rental will cost about US$40 extra. Boats usually leave by 7am and return around 3pm, and don't travel farther than 50 miles out for the day.

Independent sportfishing companies include Baja's Awesome Sportfishing (tel. 624/141-0231, www.bajasawesomesportfishing. com), headquartered at East Cape RV Resort. It operates two cruisers and can provide all tackle. Rates start at US$675 per day for up to four anglers. Baja on the Fly (U.S. tel. 760/522-3720, www.bajafly.com) is operated by well-known Baja fisherman and writer Gary Graham and his wife, Yvonne. They arrange complete East Cape fishing packages for single anglers or groups, taking care of hotel accommodations as well as guided beach, *panga,* or cruiser trips on private or hotel cruisers. Other activities like diving, kayaking, and whale-watching can be arranged for family members who don't fish.

The Dorado Shootout (www.doradoshootout.com) is the largest fishing tournament in Baja Sur and takes place for one day in July each year in Los Barriles. The Bisbee's East Cape Off Shore (www.bisbees. com) is based out of Buena Vista and takes place over four days in late July/early August.

FOOD

Mexican

Serving typical Mexican dishes and combo plates, ✪ Campestre Triny (20 de Noviembre, tel. 624/124-8067, noon-10pm daily, US$11-16) has a friendly staff and makes great margaritas. It offers both indoor and outdoor seating. The fresh grilled fish is usually a good bet for an excellent meal. Staff will also prepare your own catch.

Campestre Triny

Seafood

Specializing in seafood, La Terraza de German (Valentin Ruz, tel. 624/129-6334, 5:30pm-midnight Thurs.-Tues., US$8-12) also has meat, chicken, and taco dishes on the menu, which varies depending on what fresh seafood is available. There's a lovely 2nd-floor outdoor terrace, and all the food is cooked on a charcoal grill at one end of the patio.

If you want beach dining where you can have your toes in the sand, head to El Gecko Beach Club (Playa Norte, tel. 624/142-8212, US$13-17). Local expats cruise up on their ATVs for 2-for-1 happy hour and stay for the savory seafood and Mexican dishes. This is a great spot to enjoy Sea of Cortez views, and to do some kiteboarding and windsurfing spectating.

Taco Stands and Street Food

Great for a casual breakfast or lunch, El Viejo (20 de Noviembre, no tel., 8am-3pm Mon.-Sat., breakfast US$3-5, tacos US$1-2) has a central location

downtown with comfortable outdoor seating under the *palapa*. For breakfast, there's a large selection of egg dishes like huevos rancheros or omelets, in addition to pancakes and *chilaquiles*. The taco selection includes clam, scallop, shrimp, fish, chicken, or beef.

Specializing in seafood, El Pirata (Valentin Ruiz Gonzalez, no tel., noon-8pm daily, US$8-15) is the perfect casual spot if you're craving a quick bite of ceviche, *aguachile*, fish tacos, or grilled shrimp. Ask the chef what she recommends if you're looking for the fresh catch or a unique dish.

Stop by Tortilleria Klinton (Av. de la Juventud, tel. 624/144-4499, 6am-10am Mon.-Sat., 6am-9am Sun., US$1/dozen tortillas) to watch the women making tortillas, and buy some to take with you.

A favorite for locals is Pollos Ochoa's (Los Barriles-Santa Teresa, no tel., 8am-8pm daily), where grilled chicken is the specialty. Served with fresh tortillas, salsa, and french fries, this is a deliciously filling and affordable meal.

International

Don't let the sports bar atmosphere, expat crowd, or the throng of ATVs parked in the lot steer you away from Smokey's Grill and Cantina (20 de Noviembre, no tel., 11am-10pm daily, US$7-12). This restaurant serves large portions of great food made from fresh ingredients. The extensive menu features pastas, sandwiches, build-your-own burgers, and the option to have the chefs prepare your fresh-caught fish. Don't miss the tasty jalapeño poppers to start. With a half dozen flat-screen TVs, occasional live music, and a fun casual atmosphere, the place is usually packed with locals

Smokey's Grill and Cantina

and tourists who cruise up on their four-wheelers or stumble upon the place during their explorations along the main drag.

Right on the beach and popular with locals and expats is ✪ Lazy Daze Beach Bar (no tel., 10am-8pm daily), serving cold beers, great margaritas and Bloody Marys, and pub fare. This casual spot is an inviting place to come spend the afternoon in the sand playing volleyball and corn hole or watching the kiteboarders. The owner, Rexe, is the mother of motocross superstar Carey Hart (married to the singer Pink) and creates an enjoyable and welcoming environment with music, good food, and fun crowds.

You'll need a reservation if you want to eat at ✪ La Casita (Santa Teresa, tel. 624/124-8259, noon-10pm Tues.-Sun., US$8-16), opened by the same owners as the beloved La Casita restaurant in Todos Santos. It specializes in sushi but also offers a variety of dishes like fresh salads, mango shrimp, New York strip, and pastas.

Cafés

For house-roasted, fair trade coffee, head to **Caffé Encinalito** (17 Costa Brava, tel. 624/213-8986, 8am-3pm daily). Here, customers will find hand-pulled espresso (the beans come from Nayarit, Mexico) served in a sweet outdoor setting with chairs, pillows, and hammocks for lounging. There's free wireless Internet, and it also serves small bites like homemade granola and baked goods.

For some of the best breakfast in town, go to ✪ **Roadrunner Café & Bakery** (Plaza del Pueblo 5, tel. 624/124-8038, www.roadrunnercafe. com.mx, 7am-4:30pm Mon.-Fri., 7am-2pm Sat.-Sun.). It serves hearty egg dishes and fresh pastries from its bakery, along with great coffee for breakfast anytime. Fresh salads and sandwiches are available for lunch. There's a classic diner setting inside or a large shady patio outside.

Caffé Encinalito

Known for its gooey cinnamon sticky buns, **Caleb's Café** (20 de Noviembre, tel. 624/141-0330, 7:30am-3pm Tues.-Sat., US$4-7) serves breakfast until closing and also has a lunch menu. Located on the main drag in town, it's a good spot for people-watching.

ACCOMMODATIONS
Hotels

If you've always wanted to spend the night in a tepee, ✪ **Captain Nemo's Landing** (North Beach, tel. 624/124-8078, toll-free U.S. tel. 800/657-1664, www.captainnemoslanding.com, casita US$48, tepee US$35, camping US$25) will afford you that opportunity. It also offers regular casitas as well as camping. In addition to accommodations, it provides a wide range of activities like kiteboarding lessons, fishing, kayaking, horseback riding, and ATV rentals.

Located centrally in town with 20 rooms, **Los Barriles Hotel** (20 de Noviembre, tel. 624/141-0024, www.losbarrileshotel.com, US$85) offers spacious, basic, neat accommodations that all look over the pool. You won't get beachfront here, but the beach is within walking distance and there's a nice pool area with a *palapa* bar. The hotel offers secure parking and has a helpful staff and management team.

Just steps from the beach, **Agave Hotel y Cantina** (formerly Casa Miramar Hotel, tel. 624/168-3547, www.agavehotelandcantina.com, US$115, three-night minimum), located in a large house outside the town, operates more like a vacation rental with property managers who do not stay on-site. There are nine rooms available, and guests can choose from standard rooms, suites, or a separate beachfront casita. There's a pool on the property, and staff can help arrange a number of activities for guests such as ATV or horseback riding.

The Van Wormer Resorts operate multiple properties in Los Barriles. **Hotel Playa del Sol** (20 de Noviembre, tel. 624/141-0044, www.vanwormerresorts.com, US$140 meals included) has a great location on the beach just off the main drag in town. Room rates include three meals a day, and there's a bar on the property as well. The 26 rooms are a bit dated and there are no televisions in the rooms, but there's a nice pool area and beachfront views. Kiteboarding and windsurfing equipment is available for rent, as are bicycles. The hotel has its own sportfishing fleet with cruisers, super *pangas,* and English-speaking captains.

The larger Van Wormer property just south of Hotel Playa del Sol is **Palmas de Cortez** (tel. 624/141-0044, www.vanwormerresorts.com, US$150). The hotel offers 50 rooms, an infinity-edge pool, swim-up bar, and hot tub. An optional meal plan can be purchased for US$37 per day to include breakfast, lunch, and dinner. There are a number of activities to choose from such as golf, spa services, ATV rentals, and excursions. While it provides some of the nicest accommodations for the area, the property is older and disappoints many who are looking for true resort lodgings like those found in Los Cabos.

Popular with anglers, **Martin Verdugo's Beach Resort** (20 de Noviembre, tel. 624/141-0054, www.verdugosbeachresort.com, US$85-95) is located right on the beach in Los Barriles. The rooms are small and basic but have air-conditioning, and some have fridges and kitchenettes. There's also an RV park and campground (US$17 for dry camping, US$25 for RV hookups). It has a fleet of super *pangas* and 28-foot super cruisers for fishing.

Camping and RV Parks

In addition to Martin Verdugo's Beach Resort, there are a few other options for RV parks and campgrounds.

If you have a big rig, you'll want to head to East Cape RV Resort (20 de Noviembre, tel. 624/141-0231, www.eastcaperv.com, US$35, discounts for longer stays), where there's lots of room and 30-amp power. The property is nice with palm trees and vegetation throughout. Wi-Fi is available around the property, and there's a swimming pool and laundry facilities. The location is great for walking to restaurants, markets, and the beach. The owners have two sportfishing boats and can also help arrange daytrip excursions.

Playa Norte RV Park (20 de Noviembre, U.S. tel. 425/252-5952, www.playanortervpark.com, US$27-45) sits on 5 hectares (12.4 acres) of beachfront property just north of Los Barriles. It offers full services like municipal water, power (30 amps), septic, laundry, free wireless Internet, and the waterfront Gecko Restaurant. The park features 60 rental sites, 20 of which are waterfront. There's also a designated caravan area. Large pull-through sites will accommodate rigs up to 21 meters (69 feet) long and 10 meters (33 feet) wide. Sites for tent camping are also available. Kids and pets are welcome, and there's even an on-site veterinarian clinic. The Windsurfer's Club is located waterfront for quick beach access.

SERVICES

For medical and dental services, the East Cape Health Center (Plaza Libertad 1, tel. 624/124-8203, www.eastcapemedical.com, 9am-5pm Mon.-Fri., 8am-2pm Sat.) is your local clinic. It has a 24/7 emergency phone line.

GETTING THERE

Los Barriles is about 80 kilometers (50 miles) and a 1.25-hour drive from San José del Cabo, heading north on Mexico 1. It takes just under 2 hours to drive the 105 kilometers (65 miles) from La Paz, heading south on Mexico 1.

Autobuses de la Baja California (ABC, tel. 664/104-7400, www.abc.com.mx) and Aguila (toll-free Mex. tel. 800/026-8931, www.autobusesaguila.com) have services to Los Barriles, with the same routes and prices. Buses to Los Barriles run every 2-3 hours from San José del Cabo (US$8, 1.5 hours), Cabo San Lucas (US$10, 2 hours), and La Paz (US$10, 1.5 hours).

BUENA VISTA

Just south of Los Barriles is the quieter and smaller community of Buena Vista. There's no town center here as the community is a collection of a few hotels and beachfront houses. Because of the remote location, hotels in Buena Vista offer meal plans for guests. The peaceful area attracts anglers, families, and expats who come to fish and relax.

Outstanding sportfishing and true relaxation await you at ✪ Rancho Leonero (Mexico 1 Km. 103.5, tel. 624/141-0216, toll-free U.S. tel. 800/646-2252, www.rancholeonero.com, US$223-296). This intimate and rustic property is dappled with palm trees, large lawns, and *palapa*-roofed structures that will make you feel like you're spending time in a natural paradise. There are 34 rooms, a pool area, and a restaurant and bar. It has a large fishing fleet ranging from super *pangas*

Rancho Leonero in Buena Vista

to large cruisers. The whole family will enjoy activities ranging from fishing, snorkeling, diving, and stand-up paddleboarding to just relaxing in a poolside hammock. There's also a small gym on the property. Breakfast, lunch, and dinner are all included in your room stay.

The family-run ✪ Hotel Buena Vista Beach Resort (Mexico 1 Km. 105, toll-free U.S. tel. 800/752-3555, www.hotelbuenavista.com, US$145-185) offers 40 Mediterranean-style bungalows tucked into lush grounds and set on a beautiful beach. This is a great spot to bring the family to enjoy sportfishing, snorkeling and diving, or relaxing in a beach cabana. The property sits on an underground river of natural hot springs that run into the Sea of Cortez, creating the soothing tropical paradise. Guests of all ages will enjoy the pool that has a *palapa* swim-up bar, large Jacuzzi, and water volleyball. You can book your room with just breakfast included or with all meals included.

Built in 1952, the historic Rancho Buena Vista (Mexico 1 Km. 106, tel. 624/141-0177, US$100) is the oldest fishing resort along the East Cape. Situated on a beautiful point, the property was once the premier destination for anglers back in its heyday. Today, the hotel is still in operation but currently a shadow of its former self. Just a portion of the rooms are being used, but the pool is kept in great condition and the bar is open (the restaurant is closed). Rooms are basic but clean with Saltillo tiles and hammocks hanging outside. Today the resort attracts mostly Mexican families.

Aguila (toll-free Mex. tel. 800/026-8931, www.autobusesaguila.com) offers bus service to Buena Vista from San José del Cabo (US$7, 1.5 hours) every 3 hours. Every 2-3 hours, buses run to Buena Vista from Cabo San Lucas (US$9, 2 hours) and La Paz (US$10, 2 hours). Buses run between Buena Vista and Los Barriles (US$1, 5 minutes) every 3 hours.

the beach in Buena Vista

PUNTA PESCADERO

Fifteen kilometers (9.3 miles) north of Los Barriles is the small town of Punta Pescadero, with private homes and a few options for accommodations. The area attracts anglers and is a good snorkeling spot as well. The dirt road out to Pescadero can be rough at times, so be sure to ask locally about recent conditions. The hotels in town can help with making arrangements for fishing charters leaving directly out of Punta Pescadero.

The boutique **Hotel los Pescaderos** (Colonia Buenos Aires, tel. 624/121-8786, www.fisheastcape. com, US$107) is a charming spot for anglers and families. Fishing charters here start at US$385 for a full day and are less expensive than you'll find at the bigger hotels in Los Barriles. There's a pool, restaurant, and bar on the property. The beach is a 5- to 10-minute walk away. Continental breakfast is included with your stay.

The remote **Punta Pescadero Paradise Hotel & Villas** (Camino de Los Barriles al Cardonal Km. 14, tel. 612/175-0860, www.punta pescaderoparadise.com, US$150) has 24 villa-suites with beautiful views of the Sea of Cortez. There's a nice pool, bar, and restaurant. If you stay more than three nights, you have the option of including all meals with your room price. The hotel can arrange for transportation to and from Los Cabos airport for US$300.

EL CARDONAL

North of Punta Pescadero, El Cardonal is located on the south end of Bahía de los Muertos, 23 kilometers (14.3 miles) north of Los Barriles. El Cardonal is a small, sleepy fishing village on the Sea of Cortez, with not much to offer travelers who are not there for fishing. For accommodations, **Las Terrazas del Cortés** (tel. 612/180-3225, www.lasterrazasdelcortes.com. mx, US$70-100) has five modern and well-appointed suites for rent as well as a new pool. Staff can help arrange for activities like horseback riding, kayaking, and ATV riding. Restaurant **Cielito Lindo** on the property serves traditional Mexican dishes.

Sierra de la Laguna and Vicinity

Inland from the beaches of the East Cape, travelers will find a very different terrain within the steep mountains and lush green hillsides of the Sierra de la Laguna. The rich mountains are home to waterfalls, hot springs, and plenty of hiking areas. Offering some of the least-explored terrain on the peninsula, the Sierra de la Laguna is a UNESCO-designated biosphere reserve and home to a variety of different ecosystems. There are a few little towns scattered along the foothills that provide some services and access to the mountains.

MIRAFLORES

In the foothills of the Sierra de la Laguna sits the small agricultural town of Miraflores. The town has a source of natural springwater and is extremely lush with mangoes, avocados, and pitayas growing everywhere. There's one paved road in this quaint village; the rest of the roads are all dirt.

Los Agaves restaurant in Miraflores

The Sierra de la Laguna provides a backdrop for the colonial buildings, a town plaza, a cultural center, and a number of small markets. This is not a town that's centered on tourism—there are no hotels here and very few tourist services. It is, however, a lovely glimpse into local life in Baja Sur. The entrance to Miraflores is at kilometer 71 on Mexico 1. There's a gas station on the highway. The wide paved road will lead you west from the highway into town.

The welcoming restaurant **Los Agaves** (tel. 624/161-2234, 9am-5pm daily, US$6-12) is definitely worth a stop if you're passing through Miraflores. The open-air *palapa* serves Mexican dishes like fajitas, enchiladas, and tacos. If the lobster tacos are on special, they are definitely worth a try. Don't miss the piña colada made with locally grown pitaya. Cosme, the friendly owner, is a wealth of knowledge about the area and can direct you to a guide if you want to venture into the Sierra de la Laguna.

Near the entrance of town is the small **Talabartería** (open daily), a tannery and leatherworks shop. Visitors can go inside to see them at work with the leather. The shop has a small selection of leatherworks for sale like belts, bags, bracelets, and wallets.

Behind town is a paved road that heads west to the *ejido* (communal land) of **Boca de la Sierra.** There, travelers can park their car, pay US$3 per group, and walk in five minutes to natural pools set in a palm oasis.

Just south of Miraflores in Caduaño is the large and impressive **Parque Acuático Wet Fun** (Mexico 1 Km. 66, tel. 624/188-0518, www.wildwetfun.com, 10am-6pm Tues.-Sun. late spring-early fall, US$11 adults, US$8 kids ages 3-10). Kids of all ages will enjoy splashing around

Sierra de la Laguna and Vicinity

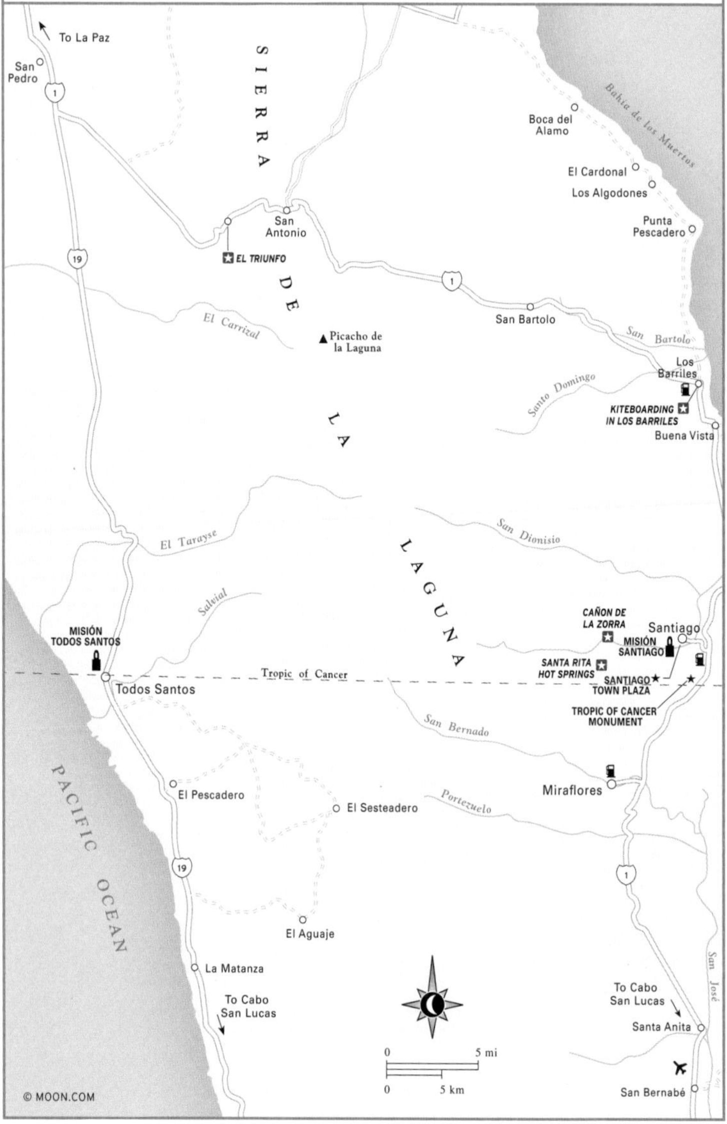

S I E R R A

To La Paz

San Pedro

Boca del Alamo

Bahía de los Muertos

El Cardonal
Los Algodones

Punta Pescadero

San Antonio

✚ EL TRIUNFO

D E

El Carrizal

▲ Picacho de la Laguna

San Bartolo

San Bartolo

Santo Domingo

Los Barriles

KITEBOARDING ✚
IN LOS BARRILES

Buena Vista

L A

El Tarayse

San Dionisio

Salsial

L A G U N A

CAÑON DE LA ZORRA
✚

Santiago

MISIÓN SANTIAGO

MISIÓN TODOS SANTOS

SANTA RITA
HOT SPRINGS
✚

SANTIAGO ★
TOWN PLAZA

★

Tropic of Cancer

Todos Santos

San Bernado

San Bernardo

TROPIC OF CANCER MONUMENT

P A C I F I C   O C E A N

El Pescadero

El Sesteadero

Portezuelo

Miraflores

El Aguaje

La Matanza

To Cabo San Lucas

To Cabo San Lucas

Santa Anita

San José

0   5 mi
0   5 km

San Bernabé

© MOON.COM

100

Santiago to Miraflores

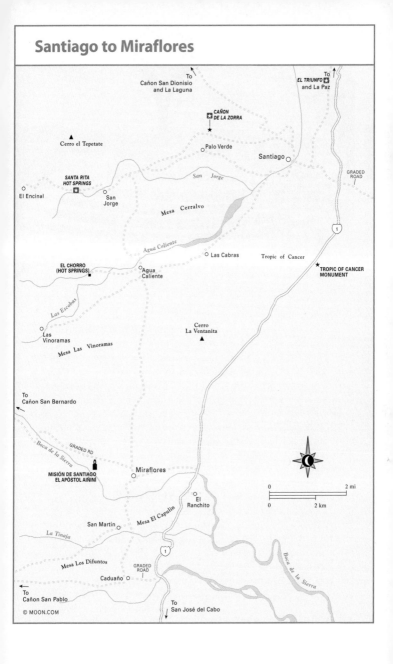

To Cañon San Dionisio and La Laguna

To El Triunfo and La Paz

CAÑON DE LA ZORRA

Cerro el Tepetate

Palo Verde

Santiago

GRADED ROAD

SANTA RITA HOT SPRINGS

San Jorge

El Encinal

San Jorge

Mesa Cerralvo

Agua Caliente

Las Cabras

Tropic of Cancer

TROPIC OF CANCER MONUMENT

EL CHORRO (HOT SPRINGS)

Agua Caliente

Las Escobas

Cerro La Ventanita

Las Vinoramas

Mesa Las Vinoramas

To Cañon San Bernardo

Boca de la Sierra

GRADED RD

MISIÓN DE SANTIAGO EL APÓSTOL AIÑINÍ

Miraflores

El Ranchito

0   2 mi
0   2 km

San Martín

Mesa El Capulín

La Tinaja

Mesa Los Difuntos

GRADED ROAD

Caduaño

To Cañon San Pablo

To San José del Cabo

Boca de la Sierra

© MOON.COM

the Tropic of Cancer, also called the Northern Tropic

on huge waterslides, pirate ships, and swimming pools. The grounds are well maintained, and the pools are very clean. There are plenty of shaded areas with tables and chairs for relaxing. No food or beverages are allowed in the park, but there's a grill and snack bar inside with inexpensive prices.

Miraflores is located about 45 minutes and 45 kilometers (28 miles) north of San José del Cabo on Mexico 1. **Aguila** (toll-free Mex. tel. 800/026-8931, www.autobusesaguila.com) offers bus service to Miraflores from Los Cabos and La Paz multiple times a day. Buses from San José del Cabo to Miraflores (US$4, 1 hour) run every two hours. Buses to Miraflores from Cabo San Lucas (US$6, 1.5 hours) and La Paz (US$13, 2.5 hours) run every three hours.

TROPIC OF CANCER

At kilometer 81.5 on Mexico 1, between Miraflores and Santiago where drivers pass over the Tropic of Cancer (currently latitude 23.26°N), is a nice newer facility (built in 2013) that's worth a quick stop. There are a few sculptures and monuments, a small open-air chapel, and some shops that sell artisan crafts from nearby villages. The Tropic of Cancer, also called the Northern Tropic, is the most northerly line of latitude where the sun appears directly overhead at its culmination. This event only occurs once a year, on the Northern Solstice, which happens between June 20 and June 22 each year.

SANTIAGO

The largest town along the eastern foothills is Santiago. The town was originally founded as a mission settlement and today subsists on agriculture. The small town plaza is surrounded by colonial architecture, and a modern church resides on the old mission spot. The water coming from the sierras supplies a large natural lake in town, shaded by palm trees. This is a great starting point for hiking into the Sierra de la Laguna and also is home to nearby hot springs and waterfalls that make for interesting and easy day trips.

The town is off the highway and easy to miss if you aren't looking for the turnoff from Mexico 1 at kilometer 84. You'll head west on a paved road for 2 kilometers (1.2 miles) to come into town.

SIGHTS

Santiago Town Plaza

Palm trees and benches line the sleepy but charming town plaza of Santiago. This picturesque spot is surrounded by beautiful examples of colonial architecture, a post office, a gas station, and a few little markets. It serves as a gathering spot for locals and the venue for events and festivals.

Misión Santiago Apóstol Aiñiní

In 1721, Padre Ignacio Mario Nápoli set out on an expedition to find a location for a mission between La Paz and Cabo San Lucas. He founded the mission Santiago de los Coras in a location he named "Santa Ana" (a few miles south of the town of San Antonio). The project was soon abandoned after the uncompleted church collapsed in a storm, killing many of the people inside. Padre Nápoli eventually rebuilt the mission in 1724 in a new location in the land of the Pericú natives, who called the area Aiñiní. The mission was attacked in the giant Pericú Revolt of 1734 and was ruined. The father in residence, Padre Lorenzo Carranco, was killed. Survivors of the attack rebuilt the mission in 1736 (a few miles south of the 1724 site), but this was eventually abandoned in 1795. A modern church that was built in 1958 still stands on the mission site on the south hill in town. It is often referred to by the mission's original name, **Misión de Santiago de los Coras.**

Parque Ecológico

Formerly the Santiago Zoo, the **Parque Ecológico** (Camino a Matancitas, no tel.) opened in early 2018. Primarily open for school groups, the park features well-manicured exhibits with birds and farm animals and hosts educational workshops. Entry is free.

FOOD AND ACCOMMODATIONS

One of the only spots for accommodations in town is the historic **Palomar Restaurant and Bar** (Calzada Maestros Misioneros de 1930, tel. 624/130-2394, palomarsergio66@hotmail.com, restaurant 10am-6:30pm Mon.-Sat., 10am-3:30pm Sun., rooms US$38). The current owner, Sergio, is the son of the founder who started the operation in 1966. Palomar has hosted a wealth of Hollywood elite ranging from Barbra Streisand, Harrison Ford, and Susan Sarandon. Santiago used to be home to the best white-winged dove hunting in Baja, a sport that attracted notable figures like Dwight D. Eisenhower, Bing Crosby, and John Wayne, who would arrive via the nearby private airstrip (now closed). Sergio proudly shows off a photo of his mother, Virginia, with Bing Crosby to anyone who asks.

Palomar Restaurant and Bar in Santiago

Fruit trees are all around the property—ponderosa lemon, mandarin, almond, avocado, mango, banana, and coconut. Fruit falls everywhere, giving a lush, overgrown Garden of Eden feel to this peaceful and secluded space. There are five rooms that are very basic but have air-conditioning, and there is wireless Internet on the property. The restaurant and bar open starting at 10am every day. There's also an area for camping.

Another option for accommodations is Hospedaje San Andres (24 de Febrero and Francisco J. Mujica, tel. 624/130-2047, US$55), which offers basic single or double rooms with air-conditioning, televisions, wireless Internet, and a secure parking lot.

On the road out to Cañon de la Zorra, Taqueria la Cascada (Francisco J. Mujica, no tel., 8am-4pm Mon.-Fri., 8am-6pm Sat.-Sun.) serves staples like tacos and carne asada. Right next door is Tortilleria El Palmar, where you can stop by in the mornings to pick up a dozen fresh handmade tortillas.

Camping and cabin accommodations are available north and west of Santiago at ranches that are within the Sierra de la Laguna biosphere reserve, such as Rancho Ecológico Sol de Mayo (tel. 624/130-2055, US$45-75), where access is granted to Cañon de la Zorra; Rancho la Acacia (tel. 612/136-4688, US$75 for two-bedroom cabin), where Cañon San Dionísio is located; and Rancho Santa Rita (no tel., US$50), where the hot springs are located.

✪ CAÑON DE LA ZORRA

Just outside Santiago is the striking Cañon de la Zorra. The centerpiece of the canyon is an impressive 10-meter (33-foot) waterfall that cascades into natural pools below. It's a great spot for swimming and sunbathing on the rocks. Go in the morning to get the most light as the sun disappears behind the mountains putting the water into shade by early afternoon.

Because the canyon is within the biosphere reserve of the Sierra de la Laguna, a minimal entrance fee must be paid to visit. Access to Cañon de la Zorra is only gained through Rancho Ecológico Sol de Mayo (tel. 624/130-2055, US$6), where you will purchase your entry bracelet and be directed to the trail to the waterfall. Ranch owner Prisciliano de la Peña Ruiz is the fifth generation of his family to have lived on the ranch, and if you speak Spanish, he's a wealth of information about the region. Guests can camp at the ranch for US$7. There are also eight *cabañas* for rent (US$47-78) that can hold 2-6 people.

To get to the canyon and waterfall from the ranch is a steep 10-minute hike. There are now steps that have been carved out of the rocks (visitors used to have to use a rope to scale the large rocks to get down to the pools), but even with the steps, it's a moderate hike, and travelers should watch their step.

To get to Sol de Mayo and Cañon de la Zorra, enter the town of Santiago and turn right on Francisco J. Mujica (before you get up to the plaza). Follow the road to an intersection, where you'll follow signs for "Sol de Mayo" to make a soft left to go up a small hill. Here the pavement ends, but the dirt road is in good condition. Continue to follow signs for "Cañon de la Zorra" and "Sol de Mayo" for another 10 kilometers (6.2 miles) until arriving at Rancho Sol de Mayo.

✪ SANTA RITA HOT SPRINGS

There are three hot springs areas to visit—Agua Caliente, El Chorro, and Santa Rita. The best is the Santa Rita Hot Springs (8am-7pm daily, US$3), set in a lush palm-filled canyon. These natural hot springs have shallow sandy-bottom pools that are nestled in between large boulders and palm trees. It's a beautiful and serene spot to relax for a few hours. The pools are hot, but there's a cold river below where you can cool off if needed. The nearby camping facility has bathrooms and a barbecue area. It's US$6 to camp overnight or US$50 for a cabin. Food and alcohol are not allowed in the hot springs. Santa Rita can be reached either from Cañon de la Zorra or by taking the road in Santiago next to the zoo. You'll head to the *ejido* of San Jorge and then follow signs to Santa Rita. Keep following the power lines overhead. The road is rough, and you'll need a four-wheel-drive vehicle with high clearance to make the trek.

GETTING THERE

Santiago is about an hour's drive and 60 kilometers (37 miles) north of San José del Cabo on Mexico 1. Aguila (toll-free Mex. tel. 800/026-8931, www.autobusesaguila.com) offers bus service to Santiago from Los Cabos and La Paz multiple times a day. Buses to Santiago from San José del Cabo (US$5, 1 hour) run every 2 hours. Buses from Cabo San Lucas (US$8, 2 hours) run every 2-3 hours. Buses from La Paz (US$12, 2 hours) run every 3 hours.

SIERRA DE LA LAGUNA

The Sierra de la Laguna is one of the most beautiful and least-explored areas of the peninsula. UNESCO

the road through the Sierra de la Laguna to Cañon de la Zorra

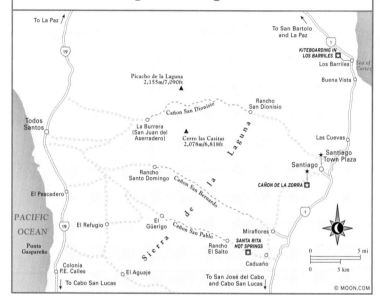

Sierra de la Laguna Hiking Trails

designated the 11,600 hectares (28,664 acres) of this mountain range a biosphere reserve in 1994. There are more than 900 plant species in the sierra, ranging from cacti to palms. Over 20 percent of them are endemic to the peninsula. As a microclimate, the Sierra de la Laguna receives far more rainfall than any other part of the peninsula, providing a drastic change in scenery from the desert below. The highest peak in the range, Picacho de la Laguna (elev. 2,161 m/7,090 ft), is also the highest peak in all of Baja California Sur. The Sierra de la Laguna can be approached either from the East Cape or the West Cape, depending on the final destination. All sierra access from the East Cape is self-guided, while most tours and guided hikes depart from the West Cape.

The mountains experience heavy rains July-October. November-early spring is the most popular time for hiking. Temperatures can drop below freezing at night during the winter.

There are three access points into the sierra from the eastern side: Cañon San Dionísio from Santiago, Cañon San Bernardo from Miraflores, and Cañon San Pablo from Caduaño. Most hikes use an assortment of trails, canyons, and cow paths that wind through the sierra.

The Cañon San Dionísio trail begins at Rancho San Dionísio, in the mouth of the canyon, 23 kilometers (14.3 miles) from Santiago. Inquire in town about how to get out to the ranch. Cañon San Bernardo is the easiest cross-sierra hike, beginning in Boca de la Sierra on the east side of the range and ending at Santo Domingo on the west side. There are permanent water pools that provide drinking water throughout the 22.5-kilometer (14-mile) hike that takes three days to complete.

The most popular overnight hike is to **Picacho de la Laguna,** though the lake in the name is now a meadow instead of a pool. This hike is best approached from the western side of the sierras, from La Burrera ranch near Todos Santos. This is the only trail in the Sierra de la Laguna that is shown on topo maps. Allow three days for the full round-trip hike.

Trails in the Sierra de la Laguna can be difficult to find and follow. If you aren't an expert or a local who knows your way around, it's better to go with a guide. **Baja Sierra Adventures** (tel. 624/166-8706, www.bajasierradventures.com) leads guided treks through the sierra with a range of day trips and overnight trips.

El Triunfo and Vicinity

As the Mexico 1 highway winds along the northern foothills of the Sierra de la Laguna between La Paz and Los Barriles, a few small towns pop up along the way. Silver and gold were found nearby in the mid-19th century, which led to the establishment of mining towns in the region. El Triunfo, one of these former mining towns, had been mostly abandoned after the mines were closed nearly 100 years ago. But today, the former ghost town is becoming a must-stop for travelers with its interesting history, chic cafés, and beautiful colonial architecture that's now getting a second life. This entire area is fed by natural springs in the Sierra de la Laguna, providing a lush backdrop for the towns and the picturesque drive. Accommodations are scarce in this area, but the small settlements and scenic vistas make for a lovely day trip from both Los Barriles and La Paz.

SAN BARTOLO

As travelers wind along Mexico 1 north of Los Barriles, they'll find themselves in a lush, semitropical setting with an abundance of mango

and avocado trees, palm-filled canyons, and roadside fruit stands populating the highway. The small village of San Bartolo (Mexico 1 Km. 128) is nestled in this fertile region, which is fed by a natural springs from the Sierra de la Laguna. There's a tiny plaza in town, and along the highway there are a number of markets, small eateries, and *dulcerías* selling homemade candy. Down in the canyon of San Bartolo are small cement pools that capture the natural springwater and are a popular spot for locals to take a dip in the heat of summer. To get to the pools and springs from town, take Ramon Cota off Mexico 1.

The springs in San Bartolo can also be reached from Los Barriles by taking an ATV or four-wheeler along the Arroyo San Bartolo, a dry riverbed that runs from Los Barriles to San Bartolo. It's a sandy gravel route frequented by ATV tours and adventurous tourists.

SAN ANTONIO

This small town doesn't have too much to offer tourists, but it is a hub for local ranchers and farmers. There's a town plaza and a few markets. There's even a gas station on the south side of town off the highway. Just north of town is a turnoff from Mexico 1 for La Ventana and Bahía de los Muertos at kilometer 155.5. The road is 22 kilometers (13.7 miles) long and meets up with Mexico 286 at San Juan de los Planes.

Just off the highway in San Antonio, travelers will find Pizza Gourmet (tel. 612/177-5806, noon-7pm Fri.-Sun., US$6-9), offering pizzas and salads made from fresh ingredients. The friendly atmosphere features an agreeable garden setting. It also has homemade breads and jams (they're sold at the Los Barriles Community Market on Saturday as well). It currently only accepts cash.

Between San Antonio and San Bartolo is Rancho LaVenta (Mexico 1 Km. 144.5, tel. 612/156-8947, www.rancholaventawines.com, US$75-100), a 350-acre historic ranch that has been in existence since the late 1700s. The ranch offers guests a range of activities, from enjoying the spring-fed granite pool and sauna to horseback riding or bird-watching. Owners Liz and Bob Pudwill grow grapes and make wine on the property, and wine-tasting is available by appointment. In addition to red wines, they make a unique mango wine as well as mead from local honey.

✪ EL TRIUNFO

For decades, it felt like time had forgotten the old mining town of El Triunfo (Mexico 1 Km. 163). What was once the largest and richest town in Baja Sur during its glory days became a virtual ghost town after the mine closed in 1926. The dusty streets were lined with abandoned and derelict colonial buildings in a hauntingly sad reminder of the town's glorious past. The sleepy

settlement was mostly empty except for some local families who had lived here for generations.

But in recent years, a restored interest has brought new life to El Triunfo. There are some new restaurants, shops, and galleries, and plenty of history to explore. Saturday afternoons the town is packed with day-trippers who come to walk around the old mine ruins, eat at the local cafés, and enjoy the historical charms. There are no options for accommodations, but it's an easy (45-minute) drive from La Paz or Los Barriles, making it an interesting and fun day trip.

the town of El Triunfo

SIGHTS
The Old Mine and Mirador

A trip to El Triunfo isn't complete without a walk through the town's historic mining ruins. Access to the area can be found on Calle Libertad (just head toward the tall smokestack). Here, visitors will find old mining equipment, brick ruins, and old smokestacks. The largest smokestack, "La Romana," is 35 meters (115 feet) tall and rumored to have been designed by Gustave Eiffel (of Eiffel Tower fame). Follow the path lined by the white rocks to head up to the *mirador.* At this lookout you'll get a beautiful view of the town and the surrounding mountains. Halfway up the path is a side jaunt to the walled-in Panteon Ingles, a cemetery with 13 white aboveground mausoleums of English citizens who once worked in the mines.

Museo Ruta de Plata

Opened in November 2018, the Museo Ruta de Plata (Calle Ayuntamiento, tel. 612/229-5587, www.museorutadeplata.com, 10am-5pm Wed.-Mon., US$6) is a historical mining museum. The museum features a short video and interactive exhibits explaining the rich history of the region from 1750 to 1930. There's a small wine cellar serving wine and beer on the weekends. The museum is on the same property as Bar El Minero and shares a courtyard with the restaurant.

Museo de la Música

Housed in a white and amber colonial building on the east side of Mexico 1 is the music museum, the Museo de la Música (no tel., 8am-2pm daily, US$1.50).

During the prosperous years of El Triunfo, the town was a cultural center for music and dance. Pianos and other instruments were shipped from Europe and other parts of the world. Pianist Francisca Mendoza would entertain wealthy patrons with concerts during El Triunfo's heyday. The Museo

Museo de la Música

de la Música was opened in 2003 to honor that heritage. The late curator of the museum, Nicolás Carrillo, who was known regionally as the "Liberace of Baja," passed away a few years ago, and the museum has declined recently.

Santuario de los Cactus

Outside the town, just a few kilometers north on the highway, is the turnoff for the Santuario de los Cactus (Mexico 1 Km. 167, no tel., 9am-5pm daily, US$4). This 50-hectare (124-acre) cactus sanctuary is an ecological reserve home to cacti and plants found only in this part of the world. There are a few informational signs along the path that point out some of the unique flora and fauna found in the area. Those interested in learning more in-depth information should take along a copy of Jon P. Rebman's *Baja California Plant Field Guide*.

ENTERTAINMENT AND EVENTS

Every spring the El Triunfo Festival Artesanal is a daylong event with *ballet folklórico* dancing and entertainment, and booths with arts and regional products. The small town comes alive with bright colors, lively music, and festive crowds.

FOOD

When it comes to dining options in El Triunfo, it's quality over quantity. There are currently only two places to eat and drink in town (aside from little roadside markets), but they're both excellent options.

Open for breakfast and lunch, Caffé El Triunfo (Ayuntamiento, tel. 612/157-1625, 9am-5pm daily, US$7-10) is the only full restaurant in town. The restaurant has a wood-burning oven where staff bake fresh breads

Bar El Minero

and make pizzas that are a favorite of all who pass through. There's a café in the front (the restaurant is in the back), so if you stop by in the morning, buy a few loaves of bread or some of its famous cinnamon rolls. There are various areas and outdoor patios for eating, drinking, and relaxing. The owner, Marcus Spahr, previously ran Caffé Todos Santos for 16 years. If you're visiting on a weekend when there are lots of tourists in town, be patient as service can get bogged down when the place gets busy.

The new, refreshingly chic ✪ **Bar El Minero** (Calle Progreso, tel. 612/194-2093, www.barelminero. com, 11am-6:30pm Thurs.-Mon., closed July-Sept., US$6-8) resides in a building that is over 120 years old and once housed the laboratory for the mines. Today the space is beautiful and inviting with upcycled bottle light fixtures, locally crafted wooden tables, and a long bar. The expansive outdoor space has plenty of seating, fire pits, and views of the old smokestacks. El Minero serves craft beer on tap, as well as house-made artisanal sausages, salads, and local cheeses. Chef Felipe studied the culinary arts in San Diego and Tijuana, and his sophisticated understanding of flavor profiles shines through in everything he makes. On Sunday there's a large paella fest that draws locals and visitors for a fun afternoon. Don't visit without dressing up to take your photo with the bronze sculpture of Sofia and Juan Matute in the courtyard.

GETTING THERE

El Triunfo is a 1.75-hour drive from Cabo San Lucas, traveling north on Mexico 19 and then southeast on Mexico 1, or about a 2-hour drive from San José del Cabo on Mexico 1. El Triunfo is also a popular day trip from La Paz, since it takes just 45 minutes traveling south on Mexico 1.

Aguila (toll-free Mex. tel. 800/026-8931, www.autobusesaguila.com) offers bus service to El Triunfo from La Paz, Los Cabos, and Los Barriles. Buses depart every two hours from Cabo San Lucas (US$15, 3 hours) and La Paz (US$4, 45 minutes). From San José del Cabo (US$12, 2.5 hours) and Los Barriles (US$5, 1 hour), buses depart every three hours.

LA PAZ

As the capital of Baja California

Sur, La Paz has culture, history, beaches, and islands, and is one of the best places in Baja for water sports and fishing.

Even with so much to offer, La Paz still retains a friendly small-town feel. Downtown La Paz is centered on the beautiful *malecón* that wraps around the bay and makes for a popular spot for locals and tourists to enjoy the views and get a pulse on the city. Many locals refer to La Paz as a "real Mexican town," a comment comparing it to the more commercialized Los Cabos region.

HIGHLIGHTS

⭐ **MALECÓN ÁLVARO OBREGÓN:** The heart of La Paz is this walkway with shops, restaurants, and bars on one side and beautiful white sand beaches on the other (page 114).

⭐ **PLAYA EL TECOLOTE:** Locals and tourists come to Playa El Tecolote's turquoise waters and white sands to swim, relax, and eat and drink beachside (page 119).

⭐ **ISLA ESPÍRITU SANTO:** The large island off the coast of La Paz is home to a colony of sea lions, whales, and other marinelife (page 121).

⭐ **DIVING AND SNORKELING:** Dive shipwrecks and snorkel with sea lions along the beaches and islands of La Paz (pages 124 and 125).

⭐ **SPORTFISHING:** May-November, anglers enjoy catching wahoo, dorado, tuna, marlin, and roosterfish (page 126).

⭐ **KITEBOARDING AND WINDSURFING:** In the winter months, La Ventana draws crowds of kiteboarders and windsurfers following the El Norte winds (page 141).

A number of restaurants, hotels, and shops line the *malecón,* and the museums and cultural sites are just a few blocks off the boardwalk. And while the city itself has a lot to offer, the main draw for most tourists coming to La Paz are the beaches and nearby islands. Travelers can take boat tours out to Isla Espíritu Santo where they can snorkel with sea lions, swim with whale sharks, or enjoy sandy beaches on deserted islands. There are also a number of famous beaches accessible by car from downtown La Paz—Playa El Tecolote and Playa Balandra being the most beautiful and popular, with white sand and clear turquoise waters. Nearby Bahía de la Ventana is a mecca for kiteboarders and windsurfers who come from all over the world for the warm waters and thermal winds.

La Paz is also a famous destination for scuba divers and snorkelers who visit to experience the marinelife

La Paz and Vicinity

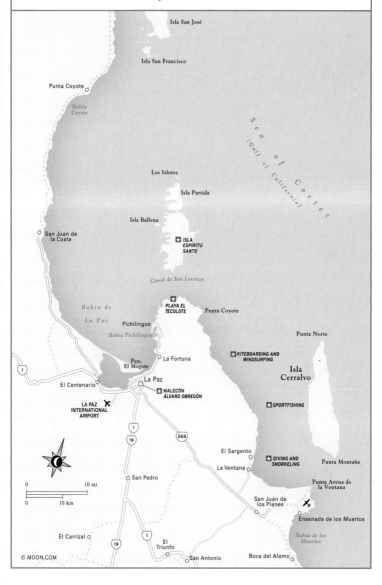

Isla San José

Isla San Francisco

Punta Coyote

Bahía Coyote

Sea of Cortez
(Gulf of California)

Los Islotes

Isla Partida

Isla Ballena

San Juan de la Costa

🔲 *ISLA ESPÍRITU SANTO*

Canal de San Lorenzo

Bahía de La Paz

🔲 **PLAYA EL TECOLOTE**

Punta Coyote

Pichilingue

Bahía Pichilingue

Punta Norte

Pen. El Mogote

🔲 La Fortuna

🔲 **KITEBOARDING AND WINDSURFING**

Isla Cerralvo

El Centenario

La Paz

🔲 **MALECÓN ÁLVARO OBREGÓN**

✈ **LA PAZ INTERNATIONAL AIRPORT**

(1)

(19)

(266)

🔲 **SPORTFISHING**

El Sargento

La Ventana

🔲 **DIVING AND SNORKELING**

Punta Montaña

0   10 mi

0   10 km

San Pedro

Punta Arena de la Ventana

San Juán de los Planes

✈

Ensenada de los Muertos

© MOON.COM

El Carrizal

(19)

(1)

El Triunfo

San Antonio

Boca del Alamo

Bahía de los Muertos

of the Sea of Cortez around La Paz's islands and nearby reefs. Jacques Cousteau once called the Sea of Cortez "the aquarium of the world," and nowhere is that more apparent than around La Paz. Manta rays, whales, sea lions, tropical fish, dolphins, and whale sharks delight those who come in search of marinelife. Anglers also flock to the area for the roosterfish, marlin, wahoo, dorado, and tuna.

For first-time travelers to La Paz, the orientation can be slightly confusing. Because of the city's location on the bay and the Pichilingue Peninsula, the water is actually to the west of the city, even though La Paz in on the east side of the peninsula. This is the only place on the Sea of Cortez where you'll get beautiful sunsets over the water.

Summers can be extremely hot and humid here, but the rest of the year, the climate is pleasant. February is the liveliest time for La Paz with the large, multiple-day Carnaval celebration that takes place along the *malecón*.

PLANNING YOUR TIME

Since La Paz is only a two-hour drive from Los Cabos, some travelers split their trip, spending a few days in Los Cabos and a few days in La Paz.

Because La Paz has lots to offer, you'll ideally want to allow 3-4 days to explore the city and beaches, and to take a boat trip out to the islands. With a week or more, you'll have plenty of time to get to know La Paz and to take day trips to surrounding places like La Ventana.

Sights

✪ MALECÓN ÁLVARO OBREGÓN

The heart of La Paz is the large 4.8-kilometer-long (3-mile) *malecón* along Álvaro Obregón street with shops, restaurants, and bars on one side and the beautiful white sand beaches and shallow turquoise bay of the Sea of Cortez on the other. Day or night, this is a great place to stroll, do some people-watching, and get a feel for the pulse of the city. The views at sunset are stunning. Palm trees line the wide sidewalk and *palapas* dot the beach. Ornate ironwork benches painted white provide lovely places to sit while enjoying a *paleta* on a warm day. A white two-story gazebo is the focus of Plaza Malecón, which is considered the heart of the *malecón*, and the boardwalk is dotted with copper statues denoting whales, pearls, dolphins, and other representations of La Paz life. The nearby 16 de Septiembre is one of the main streets in La Paz and is a good stroll to check out shops, cafés, and restaurants.

PLAZA DE LA CONSTITUCIÓN

A few blocks inland from the *malecón,* the central plaza of La Paz is a square block bounded by Avenida Independencia and 5 de Mayo and Revolución de 1910 and Madero. While the center of activity for La Paz

La Paz

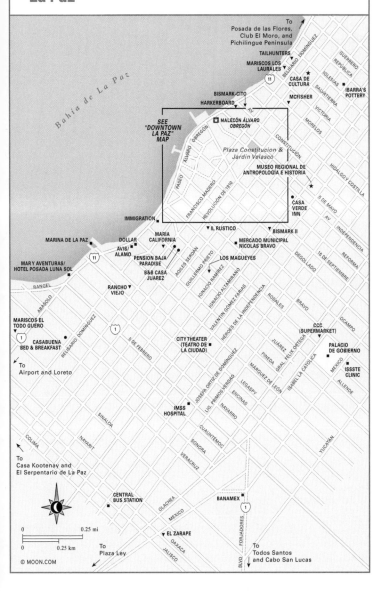

To
Posada de las Flores,
Club El Moro, and
Pichilingue Peninsula

TAILHUNTERS

MARISCOS LOS LAURALES

Bahía de La Paz

BISMARK-CITO

HARKERBOARD

CASA DE CULTURA

MCFISHER

IBARRA'S POTTERY

MALECÓN ÁLVARO OBREGÓN

SEE "DOWNTOWN LA PAZ" MAP

Plaza Constitucion & Jardin Velasco

MUSEO REGIONAL DE ANTROPOLOGÍA E HISTORIA

CASA VERDE INN

IMMIGRATION

IL RUSTICO

BISMARK II

MARINA DE LA PAZ

DOLLAR

MARIA CALIFORNIA

MERCADO MUNICIPAL NICOLAS BRAVO

AVIS/ ALAMO

LOS MAGUEYES

MAR Y AVENTURAS/ HOTEL POSADA LUNA SOL

PENSION BAJA PARADISE

B&B CASA JUAREZ

RANCHO VIEJO

MARISCOS EL TODO GUERO

CCC (SUPERMARKET)

CASABUENA BED & BREAKFAST

CITY THEATER (TEATRO DE LA CIUDAD)

PALACIO DE GOBIERNO

To Airport and Loreto

ISSSTE CLINIC

IMSS HOSPITAL

To Casa Kootenay and El Serpentario de La Paz

CENTRAL BUS STATION

BANAMEX

0   0.25 mi
0   0.25 km

To Plaza Ley

EL ZARAPE

To Todos Santos and Cabo San Lucas

© MOON.COM

115

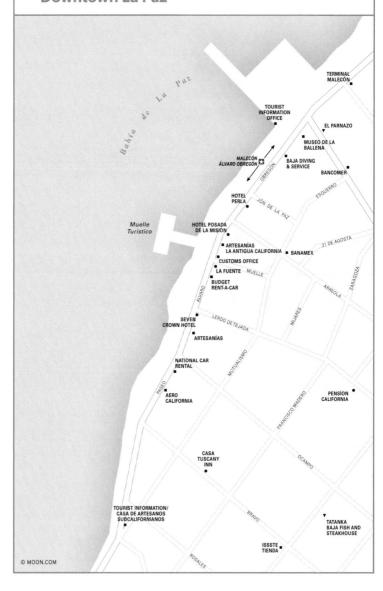

Downtown La Paz

Bahia de La Paz

Muelle Turistico

TERMINAL MALECÓN

EL PARNAZO

TOURIST INFORMATION OFFICE

MUSEO DE LA BALLENA

MALECÓN ÁLVARO OBREGÓN

BAJA DIVING & SERVICE

BANCOMER

OBREGÓN

ESQUERRO

HOTEL PERLA

CALLÓN DE LA PAZ

HOTEL POSADA DE LA MISIÓN

21 DE AGOSTA

ARTESANÍAS LA ANTIGUA CALIFORNIA

BANAMEX

CUSTOMS OFFICE

ZARAGOZA

LA FUENTE

MUELLE

ARREOLA

BUDGET RENT-A-CAR

MIJARES

SEVEN CROWN HOTEL

LERDO DE TEJADA

ALVARO

ARTESANÍAS

NATIONAL CAR RENTAL

MUTUALISMO

PENSIÓN CALIFORNIA

PASEO

AERO CALIFORNIA

FRANCISCO MADERO

CASA TUSCANY INN

OCAMPO

TOURIST INFORMATION/ CASA DE ARTESANOS SUDCALIFORNIANOS

BRAVO

TATANKA BAJA FISH AND STEAKHOUSE

ISSSTE TIENDA

ROSALES

© MOON.COM

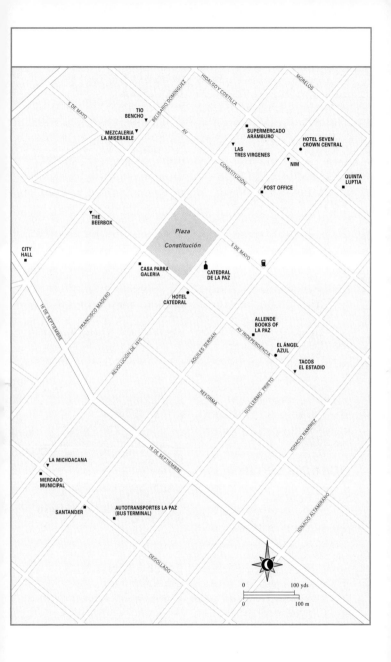

is the *malecón* and not the Plaza de la Constitución, the plaza is still a pleasant and quiet place to sit and relax on a day of walking around the city. Locals and tourists alike enjoy the benches, a gazebo, and a fountain with a replica of the mushroom rock found at Playa Balandra. On one side of the plaza is the Catedral de La Paz.

MISIÓN NUESTRA SEÑORA DEL PILAR DE LA PAZ AIRAPÍ

Jesuit Padres Jaime Bravo and Juan de Ugarte established the original mission in La Paz in 1720. Its success was short-lived as La Paz was a region fraught with conflict between the several indigenous tribes as well as the Spaniards. The mission was ruined in the Pericú Revolt of 1734 and finally closed and moved to Todos Santos in 1748. The possible first mission site is marked by a plaque on the wall of the pink and white Biblioteca de los Misioneros on Ignacio Zaragoza (Zaragoza 31). The Catedral de La Paz that stands on Plaza de la Constitución is a modern church with no relation to the original mission.

MUSEO REGIONAL DE ANTROPOLOGÍA E HISTORIA

The Museo Regional de Antropología e Historia (Ignacio Manuel Altamirano, tel. 612/122-0162, 9am-6pm daily, US$3, an extra US$4 to take photos) is set in the heart of town and is an interesting place to learn about the La Paz region and the Baja peninsula. The museum features exhibits about the history of the area, displays of Baja California cave paintings and pictographs, historical photographs, fossils dating back 60 million years, and a botanical garden. Displays and signs throughout the museum are only in Spanish.

MUSEO DE LA BALLENA

Remodeled in 2018, the Museo de la Ballena (Obregón and 16 de Septiembre, tel. 612/129-6987, www.museodelaballena.org, 9am-6pm Tues.-Sat., 10am-6pm Sun., US$9 adults, US$4 children) is a fun stop for families and those interested in both whales and other marinelife such as dolphins, sharks, and sea turtles. There's a complete skeleton of a gray whale as well as exhibits with history, artifacts, videos, and art related to whales. Kids will enjoy an interactive element where visitors can touch baleen and whale bones. Most of the exhibits are in Spanish, but knowledgeable guides who speak English are available to walk you through the museum for free.

Museo de la Ballena

EL SERPENTARIO DE LA PAZ

El Serpentario de La Paz (Brecha California, tel. 612/122-5611, www.elserpentariodelapaz.org.mx, 10am-4pm Tues.-Sun., US$2.50 adults, US$1.50 children) has reptile exhibits and lectures for guests. The serpentarium focuses on education about conservation and rehabilitation in the region. Lizards, snakes, turtles, reptiles, and fish are all on display for visitors to see. Kids will love the hands-on aspect of getting to hold creatures such as lizards or tarantulas. The aviary provides an opportunity to feed birds and rabbits.

Beaches

The best beaches in La Paz are north of the city, away from the city center and any hotels or large developments. Services at and around the beaches are somewhat limited, but travelers will find stretches of white sand and clear turquoise waters for enjoying a day of snorkeling, kayaking, swimming, and relaxing.

PLAYA PICHILINGUE

East of the ferry terminal, Playa Pichilingue is a white sand beach on a calm bay. The shallow and protected waters are good for kayaking or snorkeling. When you've worked up an appetite, there's a *palapa* restaurant right on the beach, La Luna Bruja (Km. 18, tel. 612/122-2598, 11am-8pm daily, US$6-15), specializing in *pescado zarandeado* (a full fish butterflied and grilled). Its fresh ceviches and *aguachiles* are also worth trying.

PLAYA BALANDRA

Known for its famous mushroom-shaped rock, Playa Balandra is arguably the most beautiful beach in the area. There are a few *palapas* on the beach for shade but no restaurants or services (there are porta-potties that are sometimes open). You can buy some snacks and rent kayaks for US$12 an hour. Because the beach is situated on a bay, kayakers will enjoy paddling around the protected waters to see the famous mushroom rock, as

well as exploring nearby mangroves. Go early in the day to snag one of the *palapa* umbrellas and to enjoy the beach in peace before the crowds come in the afternoon. Swimming is also better in the morning, as the tide lowers in the afternoon and the water in the entire bay becomes awkwardly shallow—about knee-deep. Beware of stingrays here and be sure to shuffle your feet in the sand when entering the water.

Playa Balandra

✪ PLAYA EL TECOLOTE

Just 1.5 kilometers (0.9 mile) north of Playa Balandra, Playa El Tecolote has the same white sands and clear waters, but a few more services, including restaurants. Tecolote attracts visitors who come to play and swim in the sea and eat and drink barefoot in the sand. This is a popular beach for families because of the sandy bottom and gentle slope into the water, providing

Beaches and Islands Near La Paz

Isla Partida

Isla Ballena

ISLA ESPÍRITU SANTO

Sea of Cortez (Gulf of California)

Bahía San Gabriel

Canal de San Lorenzo

PLAYA EL TECOLOTE

Puerto Balandra
Playa Balandra

PALAPA AZUL

Playa Pichilingue

BAJA DIVING & SERVICE

Pichilingue

BAJA FERRIES TO MAINLAND

Bahía Pichilingue

0   2 mi

0   2 km

Playa El Tesoro

Bahía de La Paz

Playa El Coromuel

Playa Palmira

MARINA COSTA BAJA/ COSTABAJA RESORT

Peninsula El Mogote

Playa El Comitán

Canal de La Paz

CLUB EL MORO

La Paz

Ensenada de La Paz

Playa Las Hamacas

El Centenario

LA PAZ INTERNATIONAL AIRPORT

To Cabo San Lucas

© MOON.COM

(tel. 612/165-1428, 8am-9pm daily, US$8-12), patrons can enjoy chocolate clams, ceviche, and buckets of beers while sitting on the beach enjoying views of the Sea of Cortez and nearby Isla Espíritu Santo. Palapa Azul can also help with arrangements for a fishing charter or to get out to the islands for the day for a cheaper rate than leaving from La Paz. Next door, El Tecolote (tel. 612/127-9494, 8am-9pm daily, US$8-14) offers similar food and drink options.

workers repairing *palapa* roofs at Playa El Tecolote

PLAYA COYOTE

Beyond Playa El Tecolote, the road continues around the east side of the Pichilingue Peninsula to Playa Coyote. The beaches on this side of the peninsula turn rocky with gray sand. The kayaking and snorkeling can be good here because of the clear and calm waters, but many tourists prefer white sand beaches like Balandra or El Tecolote.

shallow spots for wading and playing. There's plenty of parking for those arriving by private vehicle. Mornings and weekdays are your best chance for peaceful beach time, as the winds pick up in the afternoons and weekends can get crowded. At Palapa Azul

The Islands

No trip to La Paz is complete without a visit to the islands. Teeming with marinelife, they make for an excellent boating day trip for those who want to snorkel, dive, or just enjoy the island bays with white sand beaches. Visitors can arrange for an organized day trip from La Paz, or there are *pangas* that leave from Playa El Tecolote and take travelers for US$55 per person. Tours generally pick up clients in the morning, and fees include snorkel or dive equipment, the national park entrance fee, drinks for the day, and lunch.

Boats headed to Isla Espíritu Santo leave from La Paz.

✪ ISLA ESPÍRITU SANTO

The large island 25 kilometers (15,5 miles) off the coast of La Paz is Isla Espíritu Santo, a designated UNESCO World Heritage Site. It's considered by many to be the most beautiful island in the Sea of Cortez and boasts dozens of bays with white sand beaches and waters full of marinelife.

Most travelers experience Isla Espíritu Santo on a boat day trip from La Paz. These boat trips focus on diving and snorkeling in the waters around the island because of the rich marinelife that lives around the rock and coral reefs. Visitors will have a chance to see and swim with sea lions, orca, dolphins, manta rays, sea turtles, and blue or humpback whales.

The island isn't inhabited, but tent camping is permitted. Todos Santos Eco Adventures (tel. 612/145-0189, www.tosea.net) has a new seasonal glamping spot, Camp Cecil (open Nov.-Apr.), that offers the only fixed accommodations on the island. This is the only way to spend any substantial amount of time exploring the island since the boat trips stop only briefly to allow some swimming and snorkeling. Camping gives visitors the unique experience of exploring the island and waters by day and enjoying stargazing at night. There are 10 designated hiking paths on the island that are great for getting out in the terrain and encountering mammals, reptiles, birds, and amphibians. Because the islands are protected, camping requires getting a US$4 permit in advance from the SEMARNAT office (Ocampo 1045, tel. 612/123-9300, www.gob.mx/semarnat). Fun Baja (www.funbaja.com) can arrange for multiday camping trips on the island.

ISLA PARTIDA

Connected to Isla Espíritu Santo by a narrow sandbar, Isla Partida is a much smaller island, but still has beautiful bays, beaches, dive sites, hiking, and camping opportunities.

Isla Espíritu Santo, Isla Partida, and Los Islotes

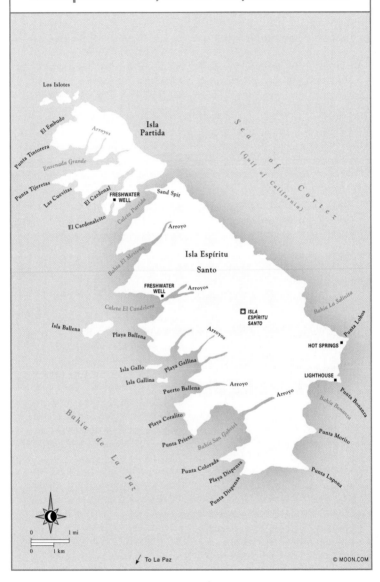

Los Islotes

El Embudo

Punta Tintorera

Isla Partida

Arroyos

Ensenada Grande

Sea of Cortez
(Gulf of California)

Punta Tijeretas

Las Cuevitas

El Cardonal

FRESHWATER WELL

Sand Spit

El Cardonalcito

Caleta Partida

Arroyo

Isla Espíritu Santo

Bahía El Mezteño

FRESHWATER WELL

Arroyos

Caleta El Candelero

ISLA ESPÍRITU SANTO

Bahía La Salinita

Isla Ballena

Playa Ballena

Arroyos

Punta Lobos

HOT SPRINGS

Isla Gallo

Playa Gallina

Isla Gallina

LIGHTHOUSE

Puerto Ballena

Arroyo

Punta Bonanza

Arroyo

Bahía Bonanza

Playa Coralito

Bahía de La Paz

Punta Morito

Punta Prieta

Bahía San Gabriel

Punta Colorada

Punta Lupona

Playa Dispensa

Punta Dispensa

0   1 mi
0   1 km

To La Paz

© MOON.COM

122

There are small fishing camps at either end of the island, but otherwise the island in uninhabited. You'll need to bring in your own drinking water and provisions. Just like Isla Espíritu Santo, camping here requires getting a permit in advance from SEMARNAT for US$4 (Ocampo 1045, tel. 612/123-9300, www.gob.mx/semarnat).

LOS ISLOTES

At the northern tip of Isla Partida and Espíritu Santo are smaller Los Islotes, where a large colony of hundreds of sea lions resides. Friendly interaction with the sea lions is highly likely, and these islets are a popular stop on the island day trips for snorkelers and divers who want to get in the water with the sea lions.

Sports and Recreation

With water and land sports aplenty, the options for outdoor activities in La Paz are seemingly endless. Water sports include fishing, kayaking, diving, snorkeling, and stand-up paddleboarding. When you tire of the water, land activities like horseback riding, cycling, yoga, and hiking are all easily accessible.

ORGANIZED TOURS

The best way to fully take advantage of what La Paz has to offer is to go with an organized tour company. Island excursions, fishing charters, whale shark encounters, dive and kayak trips, and whale-watching tours are all available. Most hotels can make arrangements for tours, or you can go directly to the tour operators, calling or booking online.

Fun Baja (Carretera a Pichilingue Km. 7.5, tel. 612/106-7148, www.funbaja.com, US$75-150) is highly recommended for snorkeling and scuba diving trips. All the guides speak English, Spanish, and Japanese. It also has whale shark adventures, whale-watching trips, and day trips to Los Cabos, Todos Santos, and El Triunfo.

Baja Outdoor Activities (BOA) (tel. 612/125-5636, www.kayactivities.com, US$600-1,300) has extensive options for multiday kayaking trips, fly-fishing, stand-up paddleboarding excursions, whale-watching, and other custom trips.

Mar Y Aventuras, Sea & Adventures (tel. 612/122-7039, www.kayakbaja.com, US$95-145) offers trips for island-hopping, kayak excursions, and whale shark adventures. Day trips and multiday trips are available. It also rents kayaks and gear to experienced kayakers.

Espiritu & Baja Tours (Obregón 2130-D, tel. 612/122-4427, www.espiritubaja.com.mx, US$75-150 per person) has the usual snorkeling, whale-watching, kayaking, fishing, and whale shark excursions. It can also provide airport shuttle services for US$30 one-way.

Baja Expeditions (Sonora 585, tel. 612/125-3828, www.bajaex.com, US$68-150) offers sailing trips as well as diving, snorkeling, kayaking, and whale-watching trips. Single- and multiple-day trips are available.

Baja Adventure Co. (tel. 612/106-7242, www.bajaadventureco.com, US$80-250) provides tailor-made adventure trips. Its custom excursions allow for travelers to choose the activities that they want to include on their adventure, from spearfishing to island outings.

KAYAKING

The islands of La Paz offer some of the best kayaking on the peninsula, with stunning bays featuring clear waters, white sand beaches, and plenty of wildlife. Birds, manta rays, whale sharks, sea lions, dolphins, and whales are all common sights while kayaking. Most kayakers join organized tours for overnight, multiday trips to explore the islands, as there's too much to see in just a single day trip. Some kayak tour operators will rent kayaks to experienced kayakers who prefer to explore on their own. Those who want to venture out for the day solo can find beaches and mangroves along the mainland of the peninsula.

Baja Outdoor Activities (BOA) (tel. 612/125-5636, www.kayactivities. com, US$55 for half-day trip, US$600-1,200 for multiday trips) has extensive options for single and multiday kayaking trips. It offers up to 12-day excursions exploring many of the islands around La Paz as well as the rest of the peninsula by kayak.

Mar Y Aventuras, Sea & Adventures (tel. 612/122-7039, www. kayakbaja.com, US$130 for day trip, US$1,100-1,600 for multiday trips) offers trips for island-hopping, kayak excursions, and whale shark adventures. Day trips and multiday trips are available. It also rents kayaks and gear to experienced kayakers.

✪ DIVING

La Paz is a popular scuba diving destination with abundant marinelife, islands, seamounts, reefs, and shipwrecks to explore. Diving is good

kayaking at Isla Espíritu Santo

year-round, but conditions are best July-October when visibility can reach 30 meters (98 feet) and water temperatures can rise to 29 degrees Celsius (84°F). Dive sites range from beginner to experienced, and the various outfitters can also accommodate all levels of divers. Popular sites include the sea lion colony at Los Islotes and other island inlets around Isla Espíritu Santo and out at Isla Cerralvo. Shipwrecks include the *Salvatierra,* a ferry that sank in 1976, and the Las Gaviotas wrecks—two wooden boats that were scuttled to create underwater reefs. Advanced divers can head to El Bajo, an underwater seamount where divers go to see manta rays and a chance to catch sight of schools of the hammerhead sharks that used to be prevalent here. After a 15-year hiatus, the giant manta rays returned in 2018 in strong numbers to La Reina dive site, a small rock outcrop north of Isla Cerralvo. These large rays can grow up to 6 meters (20 feet) and weigh up to 2,950 kilograms (6,500 pounds). Most dive sites in the area are a 45- to 60-minute boat ride from La Paz, and waters can be choppy, so remember to take seasickness medicine.

With a fleet of guides that all speak English, Spanish, and Japanese, **Fun Baja** (Carretera a Pichilingue Km. 7.5, tel. 612/106-7148, www.funbaja.com, US$135) is great for snorkeling and scuba diving trips. It can also handle diving certification with PADI and SSI courses.

Running a professional top-notch operation, **Dive in La Paz** (tel. 612/167-8914, www.diveinlapaz.com, US$125-145) has gear that's in great condition and captains and guides who are knowledgeable and helpful. Many divers take multiday trips that combine diving along with snorkeling

with sea lions or swimming with whale sharks.

Based at Club Cantamar, **Baja Diving & Service** (tel. 612/122-7010, www.clubcantamar.com, US$135-190) has been running dive trips since 1983. It has the largest and most comfortable fleet in La Paz and offers a variety of dive courses as well as excursions including live-aboard trips. It is based at Pichilingue beach but also has an office in town on the *malecón.*

The **Cortez Club Dive Center** (tel. 612/121-6120, www.cortezclub. com, US$165-199) is a reputable company that has been running dive trips since 1995. It can assist with all levels of PADI courses, from those just learning to dive to those looking to become certified as scuba instructors.

✪ SNORKELING

Most of the kayak and dive outfitters in La Paz handle organized snorkeling excursions as well. The most popular snorkeling trip in the region takes visitors out to Isla Espíritu Santo where the highlight is snorkeling with the sea lions at Los Islotes. The tour outfitters will provide snorkeling gear, the park entrance fee, lunch, and beverages. In recent years, since the whale sharks have been more prevalent around La Paz, snorkeling with the whale sharks has become a popular organized tour as well. Those who prefer to snorkel on their own can drive to the beaches along the Pichilingue Peninsula, where you can snorkel from the beach. You should bring your own snorkel equipment or rent it in town before heading out to the beaches.

WHALE-WATCHING

Diverse whales can be spotted around La Paz, including humpback, pilot, fin, orca, and blue whales. Most

GRAY WHALE EXCURSION TO BAHÍA MAGDALENA

Looking for a whale-watching experience that's more up close and personal? Take an excursion from La Paz to Bahía Magdalena to see (and touch!) gray whales.

While gray whale sightings are rare on the Sea of Cortez, they are frequent on the Pacific side of the Baja peninsula, where gray whales migrate to three lagoons, January-April. **Bahía Magdalena** is the southernmost lagoon of the three and the easiest and closest option for visitors to Baja California Sur. Travelers head out onto the lagoons in small *panga* fishing boats and the whales engage in friendly behavior, coming right up to the boats so that people can pet and hug the whales.

It takes three hours to drive from La Paz across the peninsula to Bahía Magdalena, so tour companies in La Paz offer both multiday trips as well as long one-day trips (about 12 hours). **Baja Outdoor Activities (BOA)** (tel. 612/125-5636, www.kayactivities.com) has a number of options and can also accommodate private groups. **Fun Baja** (Carretera a Pichilingue Km. 7.5, tel. 612/106-7148, www.funbaja.com) offers both one- and two-day trips from La Paz. Tour prices range US$250-395.

whale sightings occur during day trips out to the islands. **Baja Outdoor Activities (BOA)** (tel. 612/125-5636, www.kayactivities.com) offers multiday whale-watching trips on the Sea of Cortez—as well as excursions up to Bahía Magdalena on the Pacific Coast to see gray whales.

TOP EXPERIENCE

✪ SPORTFISHING

The best fishing around La Paz takes place May-November. Anglers will enjoy catching wahoo, dorado, tuna, marlin, and world-record roosterfish. The best and most-consistent fishing is on the other side of the Pichilingue Peninsula near La Ventana and Isla Jacques Cousteau. Most anglers opt to take a one-hour van ride and launch at Punta Arena de la Ventana, rather than going by *panga* from La Paz over to the area.

Because the waters are so calm in the channel of Isla Cerralvo, flyfishing and kayak fishing are common in addition to traditional fishing. Catch from inshore fishing includes snapper, grouper, sea bass, and mackerel. Many anglers are after the world-record *pez gallo* (roosterfish) in this region.

There are many professional fishing charters in La Paz, with options ranging from *pangas* to big cruisers. Serious fishers should ask around town for recommendations based on their specific wants and needs. One of the most popular choices is **Tailhunter International** (Obregón 755, U.S. tel. 626/638-3383, www.tailhunter.com) on the *malecón*. It has a variety of packages for fly-fishing, spearfishing, and sportfishing. **Baja Pirates Fishing Fleet** (U.S. tel. 866/454-5386, www.bajapiratesoflapaz.com, US$950 for up to 4 people) employs knowledgeable and helpful captains. It offers a range of packages from one-day excursions to all-inclusive multiday packages with accommodations and airport transportation included.

BOATING

La Paz is a popular spot for boaters exploring the Sea of Cortez, as it has the largest bay along the coast. The city has an impressive selection of marinas, boatyards, boating services, and supplies. **Marina de La Paz** (tel. 612/122-1646, www.marinadelapaz.

com), on the west side of the *malecón,* has a launch ramp, fuel dock, convenience store, laundry facilities, yacht maintenance, and dive center.

Next to the Costa Baja resort, Marina Costa Baja (tel. 612/121-6225, www.marinacostabaja.com) has 250 slips that can accommodate vessels up to 67 meters (220 feet). Amenities include wireless Internet, TV, phone, dry storage, showers, parking, and shuttle service to La Paz. Marina Cortez (tel. 612/123-4101, www.marinacortez.com) is an ecofriendly option with 50 slips up to 37 meters (120 feet) in length. Amenities here include on-boat massage services, grocery delivery, and assistance with immigration and customs paperwork, car rental arrangements, and special tours.

A new project, Marina Santa Cruz, is a 90-acre facility being planned at Km. 16 on the La Paz-Pichilingue highway.

GOLF

There are a few options for golfing in La Paz with rates that are much more affordable than those found in Los Cabos. The peninsula visible across the bay from town, called El Mogote (the antler) has an 18-hole golf course and a putting green at El Mogote Golf Club of La Paz (formerly Paraiso del Mar, Peninsula El Mogote, tel. 612/189-6332, www.mogotegolflapaz.com, US$60 includes golf cart and club rental). Costa Baja (Carretera a Pichilingue Km. 7.5, tel. 612/175-0122, www.costabajagolf.com, US$110, US$85 for tee time after noon, US$65 for nine holes) also has an 18-hole course. Both will provide players with ocean views.

Entertainment and Events

NIGHTLIFE

Compared to other towns in Baja, La Paz has a fairly lively nightlife scene. You won't find the huge clubs and touristy spots that you will in Cabo—the scene here is more laid-back with mostly young locals. Most bars don't open until around 7pm and usually close around 2am.

For a sophisticated and tranquil evening, Mezcaleria La Miserable (Belisario Dominguez 274, tel. 612/129-7037, 7pm-2am Mon.-Sat.) has a large selection of artisanal mezcal served in a refined and stylish atmosphere. It has mezcals for sipping, mezcal-crafted cocktails, as well as beers on the menu.

Craft beer aficionados will want to head to The BeerBox (Independencia 201, tel. 612/129-7299, 6pm-midnight Mon.-Wed., 6pm-2am Thurs.-Sat.), where there's a large selection of rotating craft beers from Mexico and other parts of the world. The friendly and bilingual staff will help you find the perfect cerveza to enjoy in this intimate space.

For a more refined evening, head to La Morante Art Bar (Revolución de 1910 635, tel. 612/129-6635, 6pm-2am Tues.-Sat.), where you can enjoy live music over a glass of wine. The intimate bar has seating available in the open courtyard or the balcony. There are events most nights related to music, drama, or art, and therefore usually a small cover fee is charged.

The young kids of La Paz congregate at **El Parnazo** (16 de Septiembre 15, no tel.), a fun and rowdy bar with liter draft beers for US$2. **Clandestino** (Madero 1440, tel. 612/157-3322, 7pm-3am daily) is another bar popular with the locals, who go for the cheap beer and live music.

For those looking for a quieter evening, there are a number of movie theaters in town. **Cinépolis** (Blvd. Forjadores 4215, www.cinepolis.com) has numerous theaters, and **Cinemex** (Avenida Constituyentes 1975 No. 4120, www.cinemex.com) has a location in town as well. Movies cost US$3, and there are showings in English.

FESTIVALS AND EVENTS
CARNAVAL
La Paz is home to the largest **Carnaval celebration** (www.culturabcs.gob.

mx) on the Baja peninsula. The six-day festival takes place every February on the *malecón* with parades featuring floats, costumes, and music. There are also fair rides and other family-friendly activities. There's a new theme each year, and all the floats and costumes are based around it. This is La Paz's busiest time of year, so if you plan on traveling here in February, advance hotel reservations are required.

SCORE INTERNATIONAL OFF-ROAD RACES
The famous **Baja 1000** (www.score-international.com) off-road race held annually in November always starts in Ensenada, and every other year it ends in La Paz. It currently comes to La Paz in even years.

Shopping

ARTESANÍA
At the family-run weaving studio **Artesanias Cuauhtemoc** (Mariano Abasalo 3315, tel. 612/141-3018, 10am-5:30pm Mon.-Sat.), visitors can watch the weavers making bedcovers, blankets, and rugs on giant looms. All the products are 100 percent cotton and produced on-site on one of the many looms in the studio. There's a small gift shop where they carry their own items as well as handicrafts from mainland Mexico. Bring pesos if you plan on making any purchases, as you'll need to pay in cash.

All the pottery is made on-site at **Ibarra's Pottery** (Guillermo Prieto 625, tel. 612/122-0404, 9am-3pm

Mon.-Fri., 9am-2pm Sat.), where you can watch the artists molding their creations as they explain the process. The colorful products are also available to purchase at reasonable prices.

Casa Parra Galeria (Madero, tel. 612/124-2528, www.casaparra. com.mx, 11am-8pm Mon.-Sat.) stocks a large selection of Mexican folk art, furniture, home decor items, and jewelry. For all things Talavera, head to **Quinta Lupita** (Constitución 422, tel. 612/123-0599, www.quintalupitalavera.com). The shop has serving ware, tiles, sinks, murals, shingles, and more, all in the colorful traditional Mexican pottery style.

BOOKSTORES

For a well-curated selection of books in English, locals and visitors can go to Allende Books (Independencia 518, tel. 612/125-9114, www.allendebooks.com, 10am-6pm Mon.-Sat.). Owners Bruce and Kathleen Bennett take great care in supplying quality titles across a wide variety of genres. There's a solid selection of language books, Baja books, field guides, fishing charts, fiction, coffee-table books, and children's books. Pick up something to learn about the region or take home a beautiful illustrated book as a memento of your trip.

Food

Because La Paz is a major city, the culinary scene has a variety of quality Mexican, seafood, and international options. Nicer restaurants and those in the tourist zone will be more expensive than the local taco stands and *mariscos* spots outside the tourist area. Street tacos and the prevalent evening hot dog carts are great for a cheap snack on the go.

MEXICAN

Famous for its traditional Mexican food, ✪ El Zarape (México 3450, tel. 612/122-2520, www.elzarapelapaz.com, 7:30am-11pm Tues.-Sun., US$10-15) has a large Mexican buffet for US$10, or you can order dishes off the menu like *molcajetes,* chiles rellenos, or taco platters. On Sunday it has dancers for entertainment, and there's often live music throughout the week.

For traditional hearty Mexican dishes and large margaritas, travelers enjoy Los Magueyes (Allende 512, tel. 612/128-7846, 8am-10pm Tues.-Sat., 9am-6pm Sun., US$6-9). The charming Mexican decor creates a welcoming ambience, and the staff is friendly. Don't forget to order flan for dessert.

For an old-fashioned Mexican restaurant with a romantic setting, ✪ Tres Virgenes (Madero 1130, tel. 612/123-2226, 11am-11pm daily, US$15-25) is a favorite for locals and tourists. The outdoor courtyard has a serene garden setting and a fire where chefs cook the steaks. Dishes like filet mignon, pork shank, and tuna tostadas grace a menu rounded out by a nice selection of wines, many from Mexico. Reservations are suggested.

Another option for upscale dining is ✪ Tatanka Baja Fish and Steakhouse (Revolución between Bravo and Ocampo, tel. 612/187-2042, 6pm-11:30pm Mon. and Wed.-Thurs., 2pm-11:30pm Fri.-Sat., 2pm-9pm Sun., US$15-20). Opened in 2017, this restaurant is quickly becoming a favorite of foodies who appreciate delicious food and beautiful presentation. Chef Carlos Valdez artfully prepares dishes ranging from delicate seafood *tiraditos* to hearty Sonoran steaks. It also carries a nice selection of Mexican wines.

With multiple locations, Rancho Viejo (tel. 612/128-4647, open 24 hours, US$4-10) has an extensive menu of authentic Mexican dishes. The casual atmosphere, flavorful food, affordable prices, and the fact that it's open 24 hours make it a popular choice for locals and travelers alike. The large original venue is on

✪ **EL ZARAPE:** Visitors love the delicious, traditional Mexican food and large buffet (page 129).

✪ **TRES VIRGENES:** A lovely patio setting and gourmet dishes create a perfect combination for a night out on the town (page 129).

✪ **TATANKA BAJA FISH AND STEAKHOUSE:** Delicate seafood dishes and hearty steaks are artfully served at this upscale restaurant (page 129).

✪ **TACOS EL ESTADIO:** Head to the most popular place in town for fish and shrimp tacos (page 131).

✪ **EL RINCON DE LA BAHÍA:** On the beach in La Ventana, this restaurant and bar was one of the first in the area (page 142).

Marquez de Leon, and there's a smaller location on the *malecón*.

For breakfast, head to Maria California (Benito Juárez 105, tel. 612/140-0342, www.mariacalifornia. com, 7:30am-2pm daily, US$5-9) for great coffee and a large selection of savory traditional Mexican dishes like poblanos in cream sauce, *chilaquiles,* and *huitlacoche* omelets. The brightly colored Mexican decor, friendly staff, and occasional live music add to the welcoming atmosphere.

Popular with U.S. and Canadian tourists, Tailhunter (Obregón 755, tel. 626/638-3383, www.tailhunter. com, 8am-midnight Sun.-Thurs., 8am-1am Fri.-Sat., US$7-11) on the *malecón* has three floors of ocean views. This sports bar serves up traditional Mexican dishes as well as burgers and some Hawaiian dishes. It can also arrange for fishing charters and trips.

SEAFOOD

When it's a nice day, head to Bismark-cito (Obregón at Hidalgo, tel. 612/138-9900, www.restaurante sbismark.com, 8am-11pm daily, US$10-19) for *malecón* and ocean views in the open-air *palapa.*

Specializing in seafood, it serves fish, shrimp, and lobster almost any way you could imagine. The original location, Bismark (Degollado and Altamirano, tel. 612/122-4854, www. restaurantesbismark.com), has been a landmark in town since 1968.

For fresh seafood in a casual atmosphere, locals go to McFisher (Morelos, tel. 612/12-4140, 8:30am-6pm Tues.-Sat., 8:30am-5pm Sun., US$5-10). There's a large menu with lots of options for seafood cocktails, tacos, fish fillets, and shrimp.

Chocolate clams, octopus, tuna sashimi, and ceviche are just some of the seafood dishes you'll get at Mariscos El Toro Guero (Mariana Abasalo, tel. 612/122-7892, 10am-7pm daily, US$4-8). This casual spot is popular with the locals and a welcome treat for tourists looking for affordable and fresh food.

Located right on the *malecón,* Mariscos Los Laureles (Obregón, tel. 612/128-8532, www.mariscos loslaureles.com, 11am-9pm daily, US$6-9) has a nice front patio that's perfect for people-watching. The casual spot is often packed with locals. Chocolate clams and *pescado zarandeado* are among the most popular choices on the menu.

TACO STANDS AND STREET FOOD

The most popular place in town for fish and shrimp tacos is ✪ Tacos el Estadio (corner of Independencia and Guillermo Prieto, tel. 612/157-2472, US$1.50-2). This rustic taco stand has been serving up tacos since 1979. Be prepared to wait, as this is a popular spot with the locals and lines can form in the afternoon around lunchtime. You'll need to pay with the cashier first and then get in line to get your tacos and dress them with all the usual toppings and sauces. As with most fish taco places, it opens in the morning and closes early afternoon when the food runs out.

For ceviche and seafood cocktails, Mariscos El Molinito (Carretera a Pichilingue Km. 2, tel. 612/128-4747, www.mariscoselmolinito.com.mx, 10am-8pm daily, US$6-10) serves up fresh seafood in a casual atmosphere. The menu is extensive and the prices are cheap, which makes it a popular spot with locals.

MARKETS

The large public market in town, Mercado Municipal Nicolás Bravo (corner of Nicolás Bravo and Guillermo Prieto), is open seven days a week and offers fresh produce, meat, seafood, and dry goods. There are also stands with prepared foods where locals love to enjoy a cheap breakfast or lunch.

INTERNATIONAL

Il Rustico (Revolución 1930, tel. 612/157-7073, www.ilrusticolapazbcs.com, 6pm-11pm Mon. and Wed.-Sat., 2pm-9pm Sun., US$7-10) is the top choice for Italian in La Paz with

fish tacos from Tacos el Estadio

wood-fired pizzas, pastas, and substantial salads. The lovely outdoor patio has lush trees and hanging lanterns.

For Japanese food in La Paz, Jiro Sushi (Obregón 210, tel. 612/146-3617, www.jirosushi.com, 1pm-11pm daily, US$7-9) has fresh and tasty rolls, sashimi, and seafood plates. It has a location on the *malecón* and a second operation in Plaza Náutica.

International foods come together at Nim (Revolución 1110, tel. 612/122-0908, www.nimrestaurante.com, 1pm-10:30pm Mon.-Sat., US$8-14), where you can enjoy mole chicken or lamb meatballs in tzatziki for dinner and baklava for dessert. There's indoor seating as well as an outdoor patio.

Savor your burgers, pizzas, and salads, alongside craft beer on tap, on the great rooftop patio at Harkerboard (Obregón 299, tel. 612/122-7661, 3pm-midnight Mon.-Tues., 11am-midnight Wed.-Sun., US$5-10). It also rents out paddleboards, so this is a great place to stop in after a day of SUP for a margarita, a bite of food, and a view of the sunset over the bay.

Locals and tourists in need of a break from Mexican food and seafood head to Bandido's (Navarro and Topete, tel. 612/128-8338, 5pm-midnight daily, US$5-8), where the cooks barbecue food on a car converted to a grill (where the engine was). Hamburgers, ribs, and chicken burgers are served up in a fun atmosphere with good service.

CAFÉS AND ICE CREAM

For a dose of coffee and baked goods, Doce Cuarenta (Madero 1240, tel. 612/178-0067, www.docecuarenta.com, 7am-10pm Mon.-Sat., 8am-9pm Sun.) is a great place to pop in for a quick cup of coffee to-go or to hang out on the patio and take advantage of the free wireless access. Sandwiches and salads are made from fresh ingredients and come in large portions. The GotBaja? store is located within Doce Cuarenta, where you can pick up free Baja city maps or check out the selection of cheeky T-shirts, mugs, pillows, and other merchandise.

A bit outside the tourist area, Café la Choya (Colima 1650, tel. 612/128-7118, www.cafelachoya.com.mx, 7:30am-2pm and 4pm-8pm Mon.-Fri., 7am-2pm Sat.) is another option for a good cup of coffee. In addition to brewing coffee, it also sells coffee beans from all over Mexico.

You can't visit La Paz without getting a *paleta* at the famous La Fuente (Álvaro Obregón, 9am-11pm daily). This La Paz institution is where locals and tourists head on a hot day for a Mexican-style popsicle to help cool down. Grab your *paleta* and head for a stroll along the *malecón*.

✪ **EL ÁNGEL AZUL HACIENDA:** Stay in an old renovated hacienda, conveniently located in town near all the restaurants, shops, and the *malecón* (page 133).

✪ **HOTEL CATEDRAL:** This modern 72-room hotel has a prime in-town location for an affordable price (page 134).

✪ **COSTA BAJA:** This resort has well-appointed rooms, an infinity-edge pool, restaurants, and spa services on the property (page 135).

✪ **CAMP CECIL:** This luxury glamping experience offers a unique opportunity to stay on Isla Espíritu Santo (page 136).

✪ **VENTANA BAY RESORT:** This resort in El Sargento offers private bungalows and a restaurant and bar, as well as a certified kiteboarding school (page 143).

Accommodations

UNDER US$50

Popular with backpackers, divers, and budget travelers, **Pensión Baja Paradise** (Madero 2166, tel. 612/128-6097, baja_paradise@yahoo.com.mx, US$28) has clean rooms and comfortable beds. The property provides a cute and funky decor just two blocks away from the *malecón*. There's a communal outdoor kitchen area, air-conditioning, TV with basic channels, good wireless Internet, hot showers, and a coin laundry.

Since 1965 **Pensión California** (Degollado 209, tel. 612/122-2896 pensioncalifornia@prodigy.net.mx, US$20) has been a popular spot for motorcyclists and other backpackers. The bold gold and blue building has plenty of character and offers basic and clean accommodations with a friendly staff.

With a great location on the *malecón* in the center of town, **Hotel Posada de la Mision** (Alvaro Obregón 220, tel. 612/128-7767, www.posadadelamision.com, US$37) offers modest and clean accommodations at an affordable price. Rooms have air-conditioning and flat-screen TVs. The junior and master suites (US$60-75) are almost like full apartments with equipped kitchens, living rooms, and separate bedrooms. Master suites have private balconies looking out onto the *malecón* and water. Be aware that there are no elevators here.

US$50-150

With a prime in-town location just up from the plaza, ✪ **El Ángel Azul Hacienda** (Independencia 518, tel. 612/125-5130, www.elangelazul.com, US$80-110) affords guests the chance to stay in a remodeled historical hacienda. Swiss-born owner Esther Ammann came to La Paz in 1998 and spent years remodeling the historic building that was originally the courthouse for Baja California into

El Ángel Azul Hacienda

the hacienda it is today. There are nine regular rooms as well as a suite, all built around a lush and eclectic courtyard. Coffee is ready each morning in the communal kitchen, and there's an honor bar for guests to enjoy. Towels and coolers are available for guests to use at the beach. Discounted rates for extended stays are offered.

Above the offices for Mar y Aventuras is Posada LunaSol (Topete 564, tel. 612/122-7039, www.posadalunasol.com, US$55-85), a hotel with 20 rooms that have air-conditioning, pillow-top beds, and in-room safes. Suites with kitchens are available. Guests can enjoy the fountain pool, continental breakfast at the café, and bay views from hammocks up on the rooftop terrace. The hotel is owned by the same people as Mar Y Aventuras (tel. 612/122-7039, www.kayakbaja.com), so it can easily book kayaking or whale-watching adventures for guests.

✪ Hotel Catedral (Independencia 411, tel. 612/690-1000, www.hotelcatedral.mx, US$75-95) offers modern accommodations in the heart of town for an affordable price. The 72-room hotel is built around a central courtyard and features a rooftop pool with views of town and the Sea of Cortez. A delicious traditional Mexican breakfast is included with your stay. Rooms feature flat-screen TVs, marble bathrooms with rain showerheads, coffeemakers, and in-room safes. Secure underground parking is available for cars.

Popular with anglers because of its location overlooking Marina Palmira, Hotel Marina (Carretera a Pichilingue Km 2.5, tel. 612/121-6254, www.hotelmarina.com.mx, US$54) has 89 basic but clean rooms. There's a nice pool area as well as the Dinghy Dock restaurant and Liparoli bar on-site. The hotel can be noisy, so light sleepers should bring earplugs. Anglers who like a more intimate and personal experience stay at Leo's Baja Oasis (Ignacio Allende, tel. 250/448-6405, www.leosbaja.com, US$100), where staff can arrange for fishing charters and also freeze and package the fish for you. There's a main house and three additional bungalows that are all open to lodgers. All units have full kitchens, king-size beds, air-conditioning, and wireless Internet. Common areas include a pool, hot tub, barbecue area, and laundry facilities.

Hotel Catedral

An institution in town, **Hotel Perla** (Obregón 1570, tel. 612/122-0478, www.hotelperlabaja.com, US$60) has been around since 1940 and offers 110 rooms. The central location on the *malecón* means it is within walking distance to everything in town. It's been updated in recent years and offers basic but clean and modern accommodations. The pool area is small but pleasant, and the wireless signal is strong.

Hotel Seven Crown Centro (Revolución 1090, tel. 612/129-4562, www.sevencrownhotels.com, US$80) also has a central location and offers 54 clean and quiet rooms around a nice courtyard pool. There's a bar and café in the lobby. A second location a few blocks away on the *malecón* has rooms starting at US$68, but it doesn't have a pool and the rooms aren't as nice.

La Posada Hotel and Beach Club (Nueva Reforma 115, tel. 612/146-3269, www.laposadahotel.mx, US$137) is a boutique hotel just south of the *malecón* offering spacious and modern accommodations with unobstructed views of the Sea of Cortez. With great service, it also offers a range of amenities with a restaurant, gym, and spa on the property. Staff can also arrange for you to take a day trip out to Isla Espíritu Santo, whale-watching, or other water activities.

Just north of town, **La Concha Beach Hotel and Condominiums** (Carretera a Pichilingue Km. 5, tel. 612/175-0860, www.laconcha.com, US$95) has a beach location that's still within walking distance to town. It's an older property and the rooms are dated, but the grounds are nice with lawns, palm trees, and a relaxing pool area all within steps to the beach. There's a restaurant and bar on-site as well as an attached dive and snorkel shop that can help you arrange any water activities. Condos, with up to three bedrooms, are in a building next to the hotel and can also be booked for overnight stays.

On the far north end of the *malecón,* **Club El Moro** (Carretera a Pichilingue Km. 2, tel. 612/122-4084, www.clubelmoro.com.mx, US$70-115) has distinct Moorish architecture that sets it apart from other hotels in the area. The rooms could use an update, but are ample and well equipped. The suites have kitchenettes. There are multiple options for sleeping arrangements, with rooms that can accommodate up to five people. There's a well-maintained courtyard with gardens, palm trees, a pool and Jacuzzi, and *palapas.* An on-site café serves breakfast and lunch.

US$150-250

The iconic ✪ **Costa Baja** (Carretera a Pichilingue Km. 7.5, tel. 612/123-6000, toll-free U.S. tel. 877/392-5525, www.costabajaresort.com, US$250) was purchased in October 2018 and will be undergoing a US$5 million renovation and renamed **Puerta Cortés.** Located a few kilometers north of town on the beach, this luxury resort offers all the amenities. It has a golf course, beaches, and tennis courts. There's a beautiful infinity edge pool that looks out onto the Sea of Cortez. There are two restaurants on the property, including the very popular **Azul Marino** (www.azulmarinorestaurante.com). The neighboring beach club facility has a second pool and a fitness center that hotel guests may use. A free shuttle takes guests between the resort and town, or a local taxi will cost you about US$8. The hotel often has special packages and deals if you book directly.

Posada de las Flores La Paz (Alvaro Obregón 440, tel. 612/125-5871, www.posadadelasflores.com, US$160) provides guests elegant but modern amenities with Mexican charm and details like traditional mission-style furniture, art, and pottery. Breakfast is included and served daily. Other services cover daily afternoon tea service, a welcome cocktail, and help arranging excursions. There's a pool in the central courtyard, and rooms on the 2nd floor have ocean views. The property was remodeled in 2016.

For a truly unique experience, join Todos Santos Eco Adventures at its glamping experience on Isla Espíritu Santo, ✪ **Camp Cecil** (tel. 612/145-0189, www.tosea.net, open Nov.-Apr., US$750). Located on La Paz's most cherished and uninhabited island, accommodations consist of eight luxury tents with real beds and furniture like bedside tables and chairs. Guests spend their time hiking, exploring rock art, swimming with the sea lions, stand-up paddleboarding, or just relaxing. There's an on-site chef who makes all the meals, as well as bilingual guides who are all interpretive naturalists. This is one of the few opportunities to stay on one of Baja's most iconic islands.

BED-AND-BREAKFASTS

A charming B&B with a prime location, **Casa Tuscany Inn** (Nicolas Bravo 10, tel. 612/128-8103, US$108-143) houses guests a block off the *malecón* in the central district. There are four rooms with Mexican decor, all centered around a lush courtyard. Owner Carol Dyer is a welcoming host, helping guests with recommendations and suggestions around town.

B&B Casa Juarez (Benito Juárez 443, tel. 612/132-2959, www.casajuarez.mx, US$68-90) is a pet-friendly property with a nice central location, walking distance to restaurants, shops, and the *malecón*. The rooms are bright, clean, and nicely appointed with air-conditioning and wireless access. The quiet central courtyard has a small swimming pool. There are three rooms as well as two apartments that have kitchens and living rooms. Breakfast is included.

For value bed-and-breakfast accommodations, **Casabuena Bed & Breakfast** (Belisario Domingues 3065, tel. 612/122-5538, www.casabuena.net, US$57) is a comfortable spot that's popular with language students, families, and budget travelers. You won't find fancy accommodations here, but there are 13 comfortable rooms and a simple pool and grilling area. The property is dog- and kid-friendly, and many rooms have multiple beds and kitchens, great for families.

Situated in a restored historic colonial house, **Casa Verde Inn** (Independencia 563, tel. 612/165-5162, www.casaverdeinn.com.mx, US$90-100) has three beautiful and comfortable rooms. The decor is a nice nod to Mexican charm, but rooms still have modern amenities. There's a small courtyard pool for cooling off when temperatures are warm. It also has two guesthouses in other areas of central La Paz that are equally as well-appointed and available to rent (US$90-100/night, three-night minimum stay).

Anca Mi Nana (Guillermo Prieto 1050A, tel. 612/123-2499, www.

ancaminana.wix.com/ancaminana, US$75) offers three rooms that are beautifully decorated. Beach umbrellas, towels, coolers, and bicycles are provided for guest use. Natalia is a wonderful host who can recommend activities and restaurants in town and arrange day tours. A continental breakfast is served each morning.

Located right on the water, Casa Kootenay (Brecha California 1035, tel. 612/122-0006, www.casakootenay. com, US$88) boasts a great rooftop deck with lounge chairs and daybeds for enjoying the incredible views of the bay.

Information and Services

TOURIST ASSISTANCE

BCS State Tourism (Obregón at Allende, 8am-8pm Mon.-Fri.) has an information booth on the *malecón* with maps and brochures.

Inside the La Paz Cultural Center is the La Paz Hotel Association (16 de Septiembre, tel. 612/122-4624, www. golapaz.com, 9am-7pm Mon.-Fri.) where visitors can also pick up brochures and information.

One of the best, and free, resources for tourists is the La Paz map from Got Baja? (Madero 1240, tel. 612/125-5991, www.gotbaja.mx). Copies can be picked up at its location on Calle Madero or at hotels and restaurants all over town. *The Baja Citizen* recently became a glossy magazine (it was once a newspaper). This free English publication comes out every month with good information for both local expats and tourists.

MEDICAL EMERGENCIES

There are two hospitals in La Paz, Hospital Fidepaz (De Los Delfines 110, tel. 612/124-0402, www. hospitalfidepaz.com), on the highway, and Hospital Juan María de Salvatierra (Av. Paseo de los Deportistas 5115, tel. 612/175-0500, www.hgejms.gob.mx).

LANGUAGE COURSES

Baja doesn't have many Spanish language courses anymore, and La Paz is a city that used to have many but is now home to just one. El Nopal (Legaspy 1885, tel. 612/177-4098, www.elnopalspanish.com) has a wide variety of options for courses such as full immersion programs, a 10-month program, family packages, online classes, and a class for locals. It can also include cultural activities like Mexican cooking classes, market visits, and outdoor sports.

TAKING THE FERRY TO MAINLAND MEXICO

The ferry travels between La Paz and mainland Mexico.

La Paz is one of only two locations in Baja (the other being Santa Rosalía) where travelers can take the ferry from the peninsula over to the mainland. **Baja Ferries** (tel. 612/123-6397, toll-free tel. 800/337-7437, www.bajaferries.com) operates car and passenger ferry routes between La Paz and Mazatlán or Topolobampo, Mexico. It's a long journey (18 hours to Mazatlán and 7 hours to Topolobampo) but still more time- and cost-effective than driving up the peninsula and back down the mainland.

Transportation

GETTING THERE

AIR

La Paz has its own international airport, **Manuel Marquez de Leon International Airport (LAP)** (tel. 612/124-6307), 12 kilometers (7.5 miles) south of La Paz. There are currently no direct flights from the United States, but Calafia, Aeromexico, and Volaris have direct flights from Tijuana and other cities in Baja. Some visitors fly into the **Los Cabos International Airport (SJD)** because there are more options and direct flights from the United States. Travelers who choose this option can rent a car in Cabo and drive the two hours up to La Paz.

CAR

La Paz is about a two-hour drive and 160 kilometers (99 miles) north of Cabo San Lucas on highway Mexico 19 along the West Cape. It's also possible to drive to La Paz via the East Cape on Mexico 1, but this route takes almost an hour longer due to some windy mountain roads.

BAJA FERRIES

The car and passenger ferry arrives at La Paz from Topolobampo and Mazatlán in mainland Mexico. Ferries arrive from both locations multiple times a week. A full schedule and prices can be found by contacting **Baja Ferries** (tel. 612/123-6397,

Ferries only depart for particular cities on certain days, so make sure to check the schedule on the Baja Ferries website ahead of time. Purchase your ticket a few days in advance from either the ferry terminal office in Pichilingue or any one of the town's **Baja Ferries offices** (Ignacio Allende 1025, tel. 612/123-6600, 8am-5pm Mon.-Fri., 8am-2pm Sat.).

When purchasing your ticket, you will need to have your passport with you. If you are also taking a vehicle on board, you should bring the vehicle to be measured and will also need to show your temporary importation permit for it. If you do not already have your temporary car import permit (which is not required for driving in Baja California, but is for mainland Mexico), you can purchase this at the ferry terminal in Pichilingue. This should be taken care of a few days in advance of ferry travel. Vehicle permits are US$48 (plus a refundable deposit that can be up to US$400, depending on the value of your vehicle) and are valid for six months. You can also start the temporary vehicle import in advance by going online to **Banjercito** (www.gob.mx/banjercito).

If you are taking your vehicle on board the ferry, it will be measured to see how much it will cost. The ticket for the driver of the vehicle is included in the price of the ticket for the vehicle. Any other passengers will need to pay a separate ticket fee (US$70). These tickets will get you the standard passenger fare. This means you will get a seat on the ferry (very similar to a plane seat) in a room where movies are shown. Meals served in the cafeteria are included in the ticket price. There's a deck on the ferry for passengers to enjoy the fresh sea air.

Private cabins cost an additional US$50 and sleep up to four people on bunk beds. There's a bathroom, complete with a shower with hot water and great water pressure. Cabins come with windows and without windows. Specify your preference when booking. If not all of the cabins are booked ahead of time, Baja Ferries will also sell cabins to passengers once on board the ferry, although the price will be more expensive.

Be aware that there is also a separate port fee (US$10) that you will need to pay in cash when you arrive to board the ferry.

toll-free tel. 800/337-7437, www.bajaferries.com).

GETTING AROUND

CAR

For non-road-trippers who haven't arrived in La Paz in their own car, there are various rental agencies that have locations in the airport and also in downtown La Paz. Most visitors who fly into La Paz's **Manuel Marquez de Leon International Airport (LAP)** (tel. 612/124-6307) or **Los Cabos International Airport (SJD)** rent a car when arriving at the airport to drive around for their time in La Paz. This gives visitors the flexibility to explore the city and surrounding region. There are plenty of gas stations as well as mechanics and services around La Paz.

TAXI

Taxis are easily found in central La Paz. Fares are around US$5 to get around the center of town, US$8 to get to the closer resorts and beaches just north of town, US$15 to the airport, and US$20 to the ferry terminal or farther beaches like Playa Balandra and El Tecolote. Negotiate the price with the driver before getting in the taxi. The rideshare service **Uber** (www.uber.com) is also available. It's a safe way to get around the city and to the surrounding beaches and is generally a few dollars cheaper than taking a taxi.

BUS

For adventurous travelers, the *peseros* (*colectivos*) cluster downtown on Revolución de 1910, Aquiles Serdán, Santos Degollado, and Melchor Ocampo. Fares are less than US$1 (no transfers). The system is slightly convoluted, so you'll need to ask the driver which *pesero* to take to get to where you're going. There are routes, but the stops are usually not marked. The *peseros* operate between 6am and 10:30pm.

Vicinity of La Paz

Bahía de la Ventana

LIGHTHOUSE

El Sargento

La Ventana
SEE "LA VENTANA AND EL SARGENTO" MAP

Punta Arena de la Ventana
LIGHTHOUSE

266

San Juán de los Planes

Bahía de los Muertos

0   2 mi
0   2 km

To El Triunfo

© MOON.COM

BAHÍA DE LA VENTANA

Forty minutes southeast of La Paz, Bahía de la Ventana shelters the fishing villages of El Sargento and La Ventana. The area has become a premier destination for kitesurfing and windboarding during the months of November to April when the El Norte winds are blowing. Other people come to the area for fishing, stand-up paddleboarding, practicing yoga, and relaxing.

ISLA JACQUES COUSTEAU/CERRALVO

In 2009, the Mexican government officially changed the name of the 29-kilometer-long (18-mile) island off the coast of La Ventana from Isla Cerralvo to Isla Jacques Cousteau. The change was to honor the French oceanographer who led many expeditions in the area and famously referred to the Sea of Cortez as "the world's aquarium."

The change was met with much resistance from citizens in the area, and most people will still refer to the island as Cerralvo. The island is one of the largest in the Sea of Cortez and a popular spot for fishing as well as diving. Palapas Ventana (www.

the coast in La Ventana

palapasventana.com) runs multiday trips out to the island for diving.

SPORTS AND RECREATION
✪ Kiteboarding and Windsurfing
Windsurfers first discovered La Ventana in the 1990s, but in recent years, kiteboarding has become a popular activity as well. Nearly every establishment in town can assist with kiteboarding lessons and rentals including most accommodations, such as Playa Central and Palapas Ventana.

There are plenty of schools certified by the International Kiteboarding Organization (IKO). Elevation Kiteboarding School (tel. 612/177-9847, www.elevationkiteboarding.com) has customized kiteboarding lessons for all levels, and it provides all the gear (you'll need to provide your own wetsuit).

Family-run Baja Kite and Surf (tel. 612/155-5775, www.bajakiteandsurf.com) focuses mainly on kiteboarding lessons for different levels and backgrounds starting at US$150 for two hours of instruction. 4Elements Kiteboarding (tel. 612/136-9956, www.4elementskiteboarding.com) is great for those who are just learning to kiteboard because of its hands-on and patient instructors who are sticklers for safety.

The La Ventana Classic (www.laventanaclassic.com) takes place in January and runs multiple days for kiteboard and windsurf races, SUP races, and parties.

Fishing
Most of the best fishing in this region is around Bahía de la Ventana, Isla Jacques Cousteau, Punta Arena de la Ventana, and Bahía de los Muertos. Many fishing charters from La Paz will come over to this region to launch at Punta Arena de la Ventana. This is a

La Ventana is home to world-class kiteboarding and windsurfing.

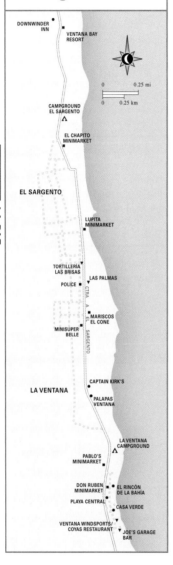

La Ventana and El Sargento

DOWNWINDER INN

VENTANA BAY RESORT

0   0.25 mi
0   0.25 km

CAMPGROUND EL SARGENTO

EL CHAPITO MINIMARKET

EL SARGENTO

LUPITA MINIMARKET

TORTILLERÍA LAS BRISAS

POLICE

LAS PALMAS

MARISCOS EL CONE

MINISUPER BELLE

CAPTAIN KIRK'S

LA VENTANA

PALAPAS VENTANA

LA VENTANA CAMPGROUND

PABLO'S MINIMARKET

DON RUBEN MINIMARKET

EL RINCÓN DE LA BAHÍA

PLAYA CENTRAL

CASA VERDE

VENTANA WINDSPORTS/ COYAS RESTAURANT

JOE'S GARAGE BAR

CTRA. EL SARGENTO A LA VENTANA

prime area for big-game fishing, with plenty of marlin, swordfish, dorado, sailfish, yellowfin tuna, and large roosterfish.

FOOD AND ACCOMMODATIONS

One of the original restaurants in the area, ✪ El Rincon de la Bahía (tel. 612/140-1082, 3pm-9pm Tues.-Fri., 1pm-9pm Sat.-Sun.) is on the beach in La Ventana. Try the specialty, *pescado relleno con camerón* (fish stuffed with shrimp). It also has a full bar.

For authentic Mexican food and seafood dishes, locals head to Mariscos El Cone (tel. 612/114-0121, 8am-9:30pm daily, US$5-10). The casual eatery is situated under a large open-air *palapa*. The menu is extensive, but the grilled shrimp dishes are a favorite.

Even more than a restaurant/coffee shop/bar, Playa Central (tel. 612/114-0267, www.playacentralkiteboarding. com, 8am-midnight daily) has become a gathering place for the kiteboarding community. It regularly features live music as well as events like salsa lessons and open mic nights. November-March, it hosts the La Ventana farmers market (9am-noon Thurs.). It also runs a concierge service to help travelers plan their entire trip to the area, from airport shuttle service to accommodations and kite lessons.

Baja Joe's (tel. 612/114-0001, www. bajajoe.com, US$95) has individual cabins for rent that are air-conditioned and surrounding a common courtyard. The bar on the property, Joe's Garage Bar (tel. 612/114-0001, www. bajajoe.com, 4pm-10pm Mon.-Sat.) has specialty drinks like margaritas and fresh mint mojitos, in addition to 10 beers on tap.

Palapas Ventana (tel. 612/114-0198, www.palapasventana.com, US$68-88 pp) has two casita styles to choose from, regular (for up to two people) and specialty (up to four). The regular casitas do not have private bathrooms. All casitas have *palapa* roofs and overlook the ocean. Staff can arrange boat trips, fishing charters, snorkeling tours, stand-up paddleboarding, kiteboarding, and windsurfing. There's a restaurant and a bar on the property.

Regular rooms and private bungalows are available at ✪ Ventana Bay Resort (tel. 612/114-0222, www.ventanabay.com, US$120). An extra US$25 a day gets you breakfast and lunch. The resort is located farther north in El Sargento, a bit removed from other things, but it has an IKO-certified kiteboarding school on property as well as a bar and restaurant.

Boutique resort Ventana Windsports (tel. 612/114-0065, www.ventanawindsports.com, US$180-250) has 12 accommodations—nine with one bedroom and three with two bedrooms. The property has plenty of lawn and patio common areas as well as a great room for lounging, a massage pagoda, and an outdoor hot tub. The beach restaurant and bar Coyas

Ventana Windsports is a boutique resort in La Ventana.

is a favorite for guests at the hotel as well as outside visitors.

For a quiet and peaceful stay in La Ventana, Casa Verde (tel. 778/679-5242, www.bajacasaverde.com, US$110) has three casitas, three small houses, and four RV spaces with full hookups. Amenities include a common kitchen, *temazcal* sauna, bicycles, kayaks, and SUP boards. Staff can also arrange for private cooks and nannies during your stay.

Located in El Sargento, Down Winder Inn (Calle Ballenato, tel. 612/156-6244, www.downwinderinn. com, US$60) has six rooms in a garden setting. All rooms have a queen-size bed, refrigerator, and coffeemaker. There's a well-stocked communal kitchen and a rooftop perfect for watching sunrises. It offers free shuttle service to windsurfing and kiteboarding beaches.

Ideally located on the beach, Captain Kirk's (Camino de La Ventana Km. 9.1, U.S. tel. 424/339-3080, www.captainkirks.com, US$120) has accommodations ranging from studio casitas to four-bedroom houses. All accommodations have air-conditioning, mini-fridges, wireless Internet, and outdoor patios. Lessons and rentals are available for kiteboarding and windsurfing.

Camping and RV Parks

The main campground in La Ventana, La Ventana Campground (US$7-8), is right in the heart of town on the main beach for kiteboarding and windsurfing. There are restrooms and showers but no hookups.

Campground El Sargento (tel. 612/198-4829, campground elsargento@gmail.com, www.facebook.com/rvparkelsargento) has spots for up to 16 tents and 14 spaces for RVs with hookups for water and sewer. The private beachfront location offers Wi-Fi as well as restrooms with hot water. In addition to casitas and houses for rent, Kurt 'N Marina (tel. 612/114-0010, www.kurtnmarina.com, US$20) offers 10 beachfront RV spots with full hookups.

BAHÍA DE LOS MUERTOS

There are many theories behind the name Bahía de los Muertos (Bay of the Dead). One theory involves a Chinese ship that landed in 1885 and lost 18 crew members; another theory claims that a group of U.S. farmers died of starvation trying to cultivate the land in the 1900s. A third theory says that *muertos* refers to moorings that were buried underwater to anchor barges for the mines in El Triunfo. Regardless of the origin, when the large development project located here came in to build, it found the name off-putting and referred to the resort as Bahía de los Sueños, meaning Bay of Dreams. The Bahía de los Sueños property is currently closed, but many people now call the entire bay Bahía de los Sueños. It's a beautiful and relaxing area, popular with snorkelers.

FOOD

With a stunning seafront setting and satisfying seafood, Restaurant 1535 (the former Giggling Marlin, tel. 612/183-2724, 8am-8pm daily, US$6-9) offers relaxing patio seating overlooking Bahía de los Sueños. The restaurant has outdoor showers for the many snorkelers who come to the area to snorkel and then enjoy a meal.

RANCHO LAS CRUCES

Set on 4,000 private hectares (9,884 acres) of a natural sanctuary with 11 kilometers (6.8 miles) of private beach

Bahía de los Muertos is a calm and remote bay.

coastline, **Rancho las Cruces** (tel. 612/125-5639, www.rancholascruces.com, US$265-295) is an escape that has lured the rich and famous for decades.

Abelardo L. Rodriguez Montijo, the son of a former president of Mexico, who started the resort in 1948, had such success that he went on to open Hotel Palmilla (now the One&Only Palmilla) in Cabo in 1956 as well as the Hacienda Hotel. In the Hollywood heyday of Rancho las Cruces, stars such as Bing Crosby and Desi Arnaz were frequent guests at the ranch, and both of their families have inherited private houses that are on the property.

The ranch is named for the three crosses that Spanish conquistador Hernán Cortés placed on land when he came to the area in 1535. Stone replicas of the three crosses now stand on the property. Guests enjoy exploring the 13 different trails for walks and hikes. Boats are available for charter, and the property has swimming pools, tennis courts, croquet courts, shuffleboard, and badminton. The one thing that you won't find here is televisions, as the idea is to escape from daily life. The white hacienda buildings and arched walkways evoke an old Mexico feel, taking guests back to another era.

Because of its remote location, the resort is all-inclusive, providing three meals a day and an evening snack. It's possible to drive in from La Paz, but inquire about road conditions with the resort before setting out. Many guests arrive by private plane on the private airstrip.

TRANSPORTATION

Private vehicles are required to get to and around this area. Travelers can fly into La Paz's **Manuel Marquez de Leon International Airport (LAP)** (tel. 612/124-6307) and rent a car to drive the approximately 45 minutes to the area. Private shuttles from the La Paz airport cost around US$120.

TODOS SANTOS AND THE WEST CAPE

Just an hour's drive up Mexico 19

from Cabo San Lucas, travelers will find a place where the mega-resorts, nightclubs, and commotion melt away to reveal pristine beaches and undeveloped landscapes.

The West Cape prides itself on being the intimate and serene alternative to Los Cabos.

Once thought of as a side trip from Cabo, the West Cape has now become a popular destination in its own right. Small boutique hotels and B&Bs offer a relaxed alternative to the major resorts of Los Cabos. Deserted beaches and quaint

HIGHLIGHTS

⭐ **TODOS SANTOS HISTORIC CENTER:** Brick and pastel adobe colonial buildings line the streets and town plaza. Wander the picturesque area and check out art galleries, artisanal shops, restaurants, and cafés (page 152).

⭐ **SEA TURTLE RESCUE:** December-April, head to the beach to see hatchlings re-leased. Stay longer to help volunteer in conservation efforts (page 152).

⭐ **SURFING:** The breaks in this region have lured adventurous surfers, from novices to experts, for decades. (page 155).

⭐ **GALLERY-HOPPING IN TODOS SANTOS:** This art-ist town is one of the best spots in Baja to peruse galleries and explore a colorful art scene (page 158).

⭐ **PLAYA LOS CERRITOS:** The most popular beach in the region offers swimmable waters and mild waves for beginner surfers (page 168).

towns replace the Cabo golf courses and rowdy tourist zones.

Surfers, artists, snowbirds, and chic jet-setters all find themselves in the West Cape, either passing through or taking up residence. Many expats have made a home here, and with the prox-imity to the Los Cabos airport, many travelers make their way here as well. While the area is developing rapidly, lo-cals remain hopeful that the region will retain its authentic small-town charm.

The beaches in this area are beau-tiful with white sand shores and dramatic pounding waves that draw surfers from around the world. The currents can be strong and the surf rough, so be aware that most beaches on the West Cape are not for swimming.

Anchoring the region is Todos Santos, a designated *Pueblo Mágico*—only one of three on the entire Baja peninsula. This title was awarded from the Mexican government because of the historical and cultural value the town offers. Todos Santos was noticed by expat artists a number of decades

Todos Santos and the West Cape

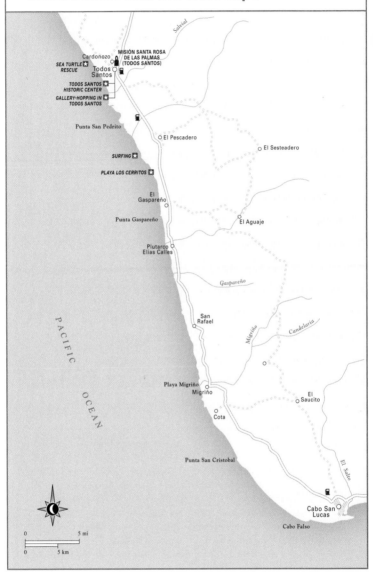

ago, and the art scene remains strong with numerous galleries in addition to the artisanal shops, restaurants, and bars that now reside in the restored colonial buildings throughout town.

To the south of Todos Santos, the small fishing village of El Pescadero has now grown into another tourist area with plenty of hotels and restaurants to accommodate the expanding number of travelers. Most of the action takes place on or around Playa Los Cerritos, one of the best beaches in the region for surfing, swimming, and relaxing.

While the climate for most of the year is pleasantly moderate, August and September are extremely hot and also hurricane season. Many businesses, including some hotels, shut down during this time, so it's best to make arrangements in advance. December-March is the busiest time of year with holidays, the Todos Santos Music Festival, and the film festival.

PLANNING YOUR TIME

As the West Cape is just an hour's drive from Los Cabos, the region can be a day trip for those who are staying in the Cabo area. However, most people come to the West Cape to relax and enjoy the beautiful beaches and the quaint town of Todos Santos, so they stay for at least a long weekend, if not longer. There are plenty of boutique luxury hotels, B&Bs, and eco-lodges to choose from.

There are more things to do in Todos Santos than in El Pescadero. Surfers and beachgoers are often attracted to staying in El Pescadero, while those looking to explore shops, restaurants, bars, and galleries opt to make Todos Santos their base for the region.

If you're interested in exploring the nearby Sierra de la Laguna, plan on spending at least four days up in the mountains.

Todos Santos

Todos Santos is a designated *Pueblo Mágico* (only one of three on the entire Baja peninsula)—a moniker given by the Mexican government for places that have significant offerings in terms of natural beauty, cultural riches, or historical relevance. Travelers only need to spend a few moments in the central historic district to understand why the town was chosen for this special honor. Todos Santos oozes charm with its restored colonial buildings, town plaza, palm-lined streets, and the stunning beaches nearby. The town has become a popular spot for visitors

looking for an escape from the large resorts and glamour of Cabo.

The modern history of the town begins in the 18th century when the Jesuits discovered freshwater springs here and built a *visita* for the La Paz mission. They eventually founded a separate mission in 1733—Misión Santa Rosa de las Palmas. The mission was secularized in 1840, and only a few ruins remain today. In the 19th century, Todos Santos became the sugarcane capital of Baja with eight sugar mills supporting a thriving industry. Most of the springs dried up in the

Todos Santos

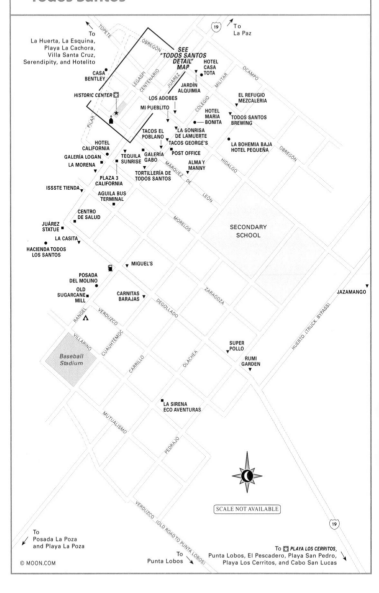

To La Huerta, La Esquina,
Playa La Cachora,
Villa Santa Cruz,
Serendipity, and Hotelito

To
La Paz

19

TOPETE

OBREGÓN

SEE "TODOS SANTOS DETAIL" MAP

CASA BENTLEY

HOTEL CASA TOTA

OCAMPO

HISTORIC CENTER

LEGASPI

CENTENARIO

JUAREZ

JARDÍN ALQUIMIA

MILITAR

EL REFUGIO MEZCALERIA

COLEGIO

LOS ADOBES

MI PUEBLITO

PILAR

HOTEL MARIA BONITA

TODOS SANTOS BREWING

TACOS EL POBLANO

LA SONRISA DE LAMUERTE

TACOS GEORGE'S

LA BOHEMIA BAJA HOTEL PEQUEÑA

HOTEL CALIFORNIA

POST OFFICE

HIDALGO

OBREGÓN

GALERÍA LOGAN

LA MORENA

TEQUILA SUNRISE

GALERÍA GABO

ALMA Y MANNY

MARQUEZ DE LEON

PLAZA 3 CALIFORNIA

TORTILLERÍA DE TODOS SANTOS

ISSSTE TIENDA

AGUILA BUS TERMINAL

CENTRO DE SALUD

MORELOS

SECONDARY SCHOOL

JUÁREZ STATUE

LA CASITA

HACIENDA TODOS LOS SANTOS

MIGUEL'S

JAZAMANGO

POSADA DEL MOLINO

ZARAGOZA

OLD SUGARCANE MILL

CARNITAS BARAJAS

DEGOLLADO

HUERTO (TRUCK BYPASS)

RANGEL

VERDUZCO

VILLARINO

CUAUHTEMOC

Baseball Stadium

SUPER POLLO

CARRILLO

OLACHEA

RUMI GARDEN

LA SIRENA ECO AVENTURAS

MUTUALISMO

PEDRAJO

SCALE NOT AVAILABLE

VERDUZCO (OLD ROAD TO PUNTA LOBOS)

19

To
Posada La Poza
and Playa La Poza

© MOON.COM

To
Punta Lobos

To ⚑ PLAYA LOS CERRITOS,
Punta Lobos, El Pescadero, Playa San Pedro,
Playa Los Cerritos, and Cabo San Lucas

1950s, and the sugarcane industry soon faded out.

The town was bleak for a number of decades until the springs came back to life in 1981 and the freeway was paved in the mid-1980s. A thriving agricultural industry developed (and continues to this day), providing markets and Cabo restaurants with organic produce. American and Canadian artists discovered Todos Santos in the 1980s and helped to revitalize the town, turning it into a chic and bohemian destination for expats and travelers. Today, the art scene is still thriving, and many travelers spend time visiting the numerous art galleries around Todos Santos.

While Todos Santos is considered to be a coastal destination, the center of town is not directly on the beach. Beach communities and some boutique hotels have started to populate the coastline, but most of the action

is in town, about 2 kilometers (1.2 miles) away from the beaches. Surfers will want to head out to the waves, but the beaches in this area are not safe for swimming because of the heavy surf and riptides. It's beautiful to walk along the beach and watch the sunset over the Pacific, but save the swimming for the hotel pool.

Although the plaza is missing the hustle and bustle that most plazas have, it is home to the historic church and old theater. Most of the tourist action in Todos Santos takes place on the surrounding streets. It's pleasant to spend the afternoon walking around the town, admiring the brick and colorful adobe colonial buildings that have now been restored as boutique hotels, art galleries, artisanal shops, cafés, and upscale restaurants. Ecotourism is also important for Todos Santos, and the sea turtle rescue projects are a popular draw for volunteers.

Todos Santos town plaza

Todos Santos Detail

Map labels: CENTENARIO, OBREGON, BANORTE, CENTRO CULTURAL, CAFFÉ TODOS SANTOS, GALERÍA DE TODOS SANTOS & MICHAEL'S AT THE GALLERY, TODOS SANTOS INN/LA COPA, ÉTNICA, TOPETE, TRE GALLINE, GUAYCURA HOTEL, LEGASPI, MANOS MEXICANOS, EZRA KATZ, FONDA EL ZAGUÁN, MEXICO GOURMET, EL TECOLOTE BOOKS, HIDALGO, TALLER 17, POLICE, JUAREZ/MEXICO 19, HISTORIC CENTER, THE VIBE, TEATRO MÁRQUEZ DE LEÓN, CAFÉ SANTA FE, MÁRQUEZ DE LEÓN, MARISOL, IGLESIA NUESTRA SEÑORA DEL PILAR

SCALE NOT AVAILABLE   © MOON.COM

SIGHTS

✪ HISTORIC CENTER

The large town plaza is lined with colonial buildings including the **Teatro Márquez de León, Iglesia Nuestra Señora del Pilar,** and the Café Santa Fe restaurant, housed in one of the largest adobe structures still remaining in town. But unlike in other Mexican towns, the plaza in Todos Santos is not the epicenter of activity. The surrounding streets are much busier, with active businesses and people milling about. A stroll around the streets to the north and east of the plaza will reward travelers with galleries, shops, restaurants, bars, and hotels.

✪ SEA TURTLE RESCUE

Tortugueros Las Playitas (tel. 612/145-0353, U.S. tel. 213/265-9943, www.todostortugueros.org) is a non-profit that helps to restore the Pacific leatherback, a critically endangered sea turtle on the verge of extinction. The organization collects the eggs and places them in its incubation greenhouse, which helps to keep the eggs warm and safe from predators. Once the eggs hatch, the hatchlings are released into the ocean. Hatchling releases happen between November 15 and April in the evenings around sunset at **Las Tunas Sanctuary** (the Tortugueros website and Facebook page will have specific information during hatchling release season). Hatchling releases are open to the public and free of charge for anyone who wants to watch the young sea turtles venture out into the ocean for the first time. Tortugueros Las Playitas accepts volunteers to help with nest relocation, recording data, incubation supervision, and caring for hatchlings. Volunteers are responsible for paying for their own airfare, transportation, accommodations, and meals.

LA POZA

This freshwater lagoon is a bird-watchers' paradise, home to over 100 species of birds. Egrets, herons, gulls, ducks, pelicans, and sandpipers are just some of the birds that can be found at **La Poza.** This picturesque spot features sand dunes on one side of the lagoon, providing a barrier to the ocean, and palm trees on the other side. Stay out of the lagoon, as the waters are deeper than they look and large waves are known to have come crashing over the dunes. The easiest way to get to the lagoon is to follow the signs for Posada La Poza.

PACIFIC LEATHERBACK SEA TURTLES

The leatherback sea turtle is the largest of all living turtles. Its name comes from its unique back, covered only by skin instead of the hard shell other turtles have. Adults can grow up to 2 meters (6.6 feet) in length and weigh up to 907 kilograms (2,000 pounds). It's estimated that they live around 45 years in the wild. The leatherback is the world's most migratory sea turtle and can travel up to 16,000 kilometers (9,940 miles) a year.

Leatherbacks mate at sea, and the females come ashore at night to nest. They dig a hole in the ground and deposit around 80 eggs, filling the nest before returning to sea. Incubation is about 60 days, and once the eggs hatch, the baby sea turtles make their way into the ocean where they must learn to fend for themselves without any help from their parents. Female hatchlings will roam the seas until they reach sexual maturity, when they will return to the same nesting area to produce their own offspring. Male leatherbacks spend the rest of their lives in the ocean without returning to land.

The leatherback population is rapidly declining in many parts of the world. There are only about 2,300 females of the Pacific leatherback sea turtle remaining, making it the most endangered marine turtle subpopulation.

MISIÓN SANTA ROSA DE LAS PALMAS

In 1724 Spanish Jesuit Padre Jaime Bravo founded Todos Santos as a *visita* for the La Paz mission. Because of the freshwater springs and prime location, the *visita* eventually became a full mission under Padre Sigismundo Taraval in 1733. **Misión Santa Rosa de las Palmas** was destroyed the following year during the great revolt of the Pericú natives. A second mission was built and eventually relocated to another spot 0.6 kilometer (1 mile) south in 1825. Its population decreased until the mission was eventually secularized in 1840. The original mission site, just north of town, is now a car repair business (ruins of the mission walls were expanded upon to create the repair shop) and a church that was built in 1970. The **Iglesia Nuestra Señora del Pilar** on the town plaza occupies the second 1825 mission site. Newer construction was added to the original foundation and walls.

BEACHES

The beaches of Todos Santos are stunningly beautiful with white sand, crashing waves, and often complemented by sand dunes and palm trees speckling the landscape. However, the beaches in this area are not for swimming. The strong currents and forceful waves create dangerous situations for swimmers. Beaches are great for sunbathing, taking walks, or enjoying sunsets, but not for a swim. Most of the beaches are accessed by little dirt roads heading west from town. There are no services at the beaches so take umbrellas, water, and food if you plan on spending the day. The following beaches are listed in order from north to south.

Playa La Pastora is a sandy beach popular with surfers because the right point break will be breaking when other surf spots are not. The long stretches of sand are beautiful for taking a walk, but strong waves mean that swimming is not an option here. Because La Pastora is a little more difficult to get to than other beaches in the area, you'll likely have the beach mostly to yourself. Access is via Topete, which turns into Horizonte, and then the coastal road, going north about 3 kilometers (1.8 miles) out of town.

Playa La Cachora is a great beach for whale-watching, walking along the shore, and horseback riding—but not for swimming. This is one of the beaches in the area where the sea turtles come to lay their eggs. From town, take Topete west to La Cachora.

Playa La Poza (Las Pocitas) is known for the freshwater lagoon, La Poza, which is a fantastic spot for birdwatching. Surf fishing can be good here early in the morning. Sunbathing and relaxing for the day are popular activities, made more convenient by the access to the restaurant at nearby Posada La Poza. From town, follow the signs for Posada La Poza.

Punta Lobos is where local fishers depart on their *pangas* for bigger catches out in the Pacific. This can be a great spot to buy fresh fish from their daily catches when they come back into shore in the afternoon. If it's whale season and the fishing is slow, you may be able to arrange with one of the *pangueros* (you'll need to speak Spanish) to take you out whale-watching for a few hours. There's a colony of sea lions near the south point of the beach. For surfers, the point/reef breaks on south swells. Access Punta Lobos by heading south on Vidal in town or from Mexico 19 at kilometer 54.

Playa San Pedro (Playa Las Palmas) is a small and secluded beach accessed by walking through a grove of palm trees. There are rocky points at both ends of the beach providing a protected area in between. If the sea is calm, this can sometimes be a good swimming spot. Hiking and bodysurfing are other popular activities here. There's a small lagoon and an abandoned old ranch from sugarcane days. There are no concessions and the location is remote, so take snacks and a picnic lunch if you plan on staying for the day. To access the beach, look for a small turnoff from

Playa La Pastora

Mexico 19 at kilometer 57 across from the research station. There's a gate that closes at 6pm, so plan to be out by then.

Playa San Pedrito at the north end of Playa Pescadero is popular with body boarders, anglers, and surfers. There's a rocky point at the north end of the beach that produces decent waves on west and north swells. The point is also a good spot for fishing. The turnoff for the beach is just south of the El Pescadero Pemex gas station on Mexico 19 at kilometer 62.

SPORTS AND RECREATION

✪ SURFING

The lure of big breaks and near-empty waves along the West Cape has attracted adventurous surfers to the area for decades, although empty waves are becoming increasingly difficult to find. Todos Santos is an area for experienced surfers who have their own boards and know what they're doing. Beginners will want to head down to El Pescadero where surf lessons and board rentals are readily available at Playa Los Cerritos.

Playa La Pastora has an exposed point break with right and left breaks, but is mostly known for bigger rights on northwest swells. This is a popular spot because it can be breaking when other spots are not. There's a rocky bottom, so this is not a spot for beginners. Access is via Topete, which turns into Horizonte, and then the coastal road, going north about 3 kilometers (1.8 miles) out of town.

To the north of La Pastora on the coastal road, **Punta Márquez** and **Punta Conejo** require some serious off-road exploring to reach. You can camp along the shore if you bring all your own supplies. Make sure to set up on the bluff and not below in the sandy *vado,* where you could be at risk for flash floods. You'll likely find a small community of surfers and families who come to camp here for a few days while enjoying the surf and serene beaches. These spots are also accessible from Bahía Magdalena to the north.

Named for the colony of sea lions, **Punta Lobos** breaks on south swells. Local fishers launch their *pangas* here, and the beach has a rocky point and lighthouse. It can be accessed from Vidal in town or from a turnoff at kilometer 54 on Mexico 19.

Down near El Pescadero, **Playa San Pedrito** is a solid beach break that's best on west and north swells. Between San Pedrito and El Pescadero, around kilometer 59, are consistent right reef and beach breaks. Many paddle out from the sandy beach as there are sea urchins on the reef.

YOGA

Yoga classes are a favorite pastime of many residents and visitors of Todos Santos, and there are a number of options. Some hotels, such as **The Hotelito** (Rancho de la Cachora, tel. 612/145-0099, www.thehotelito.com) and **Villa Santa Cruz** (Camino a la Playitas, tel. 612/143-9230, U.S. tel. 760/230-5557, www.villasantacruzbaja.com), hold classes or can arrange for a private instructor. **Cuatro Vientos** (Calle Horizonte, no tel., www.cuatrovientosbaja.com) is a center for yoga, arts, meditation, and movement. It offers a variety of classes at its studio. **Gypsy Canyon** (www.gypsycanyonbaja.com) also offers yoga classes on a regular basis at its glamping site, located just out of

Cuatro Vientos yoga studio

town. Check the website for the current schedule.

ORGANIZED TOURS

Todos Santos Eco Adventures (tel. 612/145-0189, www.tosea.net) offers a multitude of single-day and multiday excursions to swim with sea lions and whale sharks, venture into the Sierra de la Laguna, go whale-watching, try rock climbing, or take a cultural visit to a local ranch. Some of its trips are around the Todos Santos area, and some of the excursions take you to other locations in Baja Sur for your adventure.

Leading similar adventures for wildlife excursions and water sports is **La Sirena Eco-Adventures** (tel. 612/145-0353, www.lasirenakayaksurf. com) a branch of Tortugueros Las Playitas, which runs the sea turtle rescue. It also has vacation rentals available. **Adventure 19** (Mexico 19 at Colegio Militar, tel. 740/080-0854, www.adventure19.com) has 30 years of experience leading excursions like snorkeling with whale sharks, horseback riding, and fishing, as well as tours into the sierras.

ENTERTAINMENT AND EVENTS

BARS

While there are a number of little bars in town that provide a great option for grabbing a few drinks, there are no nightclubs or swanky lounges in Todos Santos like those found in Cabo. The bar scene here is much more casual and subdued, with most places closing down around 10pm.

A number of hotels have popular bars, such as **La Copa Bar** (Calle Legaspi 33, tel. 612/145-0040, 3pm-11pm daily) at The Todos Santos Inn, where visitors will find a classy saloon-style setting and a nice selection of wine. Over at Hotel California's **La Coronela** (Benito Juárez, tel. 612/145-0525, 9am-10:30pm daily), a decent selection of wines and flavored margaritas grace the menu. You can enjoy the bar inside or sit outside in the courtyard patio. The rooftop bar at Guaycura Hotel, **Sky Lounge** (Calle Legaspi at Topete, tel. 612/175-0800, noon-9pm daily) is a perfect spot to enjoy beautiful sunset views with your cocktail.

If you're really in the mood for margaritas, head across the street from Hotel California to **Tequila's Sunrise Bar & Grill** (Benito Juárez, no tel., 11am-9pm daily). The damiana margarita is a specialty and definitely worth trying. The funky decor features retro-inspired margarita signs and plenty of messages from patrons who have been inspired to leave their mark on the wall with Sharpies.

For a sports bar that serves cold beer and a great burger, don't miss **Shut up Frank's** (Santo Degollado 13, tel. 612/145-0707, 10am-10pm daily). This low-key and friendly spot is popular with both the expat locals and tourists passing through. With plenty of big-screen TVs, it's one of the best places to catch a game in town. Another sports bar, Chill n Grill (Calle Rangel, tel. 612/145-0014) is a local's favorite serving pub food and strong margaritas.

Mezcal lovers won't want to miss El Refugio Mezcaleria (Calle Obregón 12, tel. 612/145-0651, www.elrefugiobaja.com, 5pm-10pm Wed.-Sat.). Serving small-batch mezcals as well as traditional pre-Hispanic Mexican food, this casual spot has indoor seating as well as a large outdoor space.

For live music and mixology cocktails in a quaint garden setting, head to Jardín Alquimia (Álvaro Obregón, tel. 612/233-3320, 6pm-midnight Wed.-Sat.). The intimate setting is the perfect spot for date night or an enjoyable evening with friends. Tapas and wood-fired pizzas are available to nosh on.

The new craft brewery in town, Todos Santos Brewing (Álvaro Obregón between Militar and Rangel, tel. 612/145-2023, www.todossantosbrewing.mx, noon-9pm Wed.-Mon.) has a plethora of housemade craft beers on tap. To wash down your beer, it has a variety of hamburgers available every day as well as a daily food special. The great beer and fun atmosphere have made this a fast favorite of many locals. Trivia, live music, and open mic night take place on a regular basis.

FESTIVALS AND EVENTS

Todos Santos is home to a music festival every January. The organizers have varied over the years, but the festival attracts good musical acts as well as big crowds who come to see them play. Be sure to book your hotel in advance.

The Open Studios Tour (www.todossantosopenstudio.org) takes place over a few days each February where the artists of Todos Santos open up their studios to the public. People can visit with the artists in their studios to get a behind-the-scenes experience about their process. The Festival de Cine (www.todossantoscinefest.com) takes place in March and features films by local and international filmmakers.

SHOPPING

For Mexican crafts and souvenirs, there are a number of shops and artisan stalls around town. Colorful Talavera pottery, wood-frame hammocks, Mexican blankets and ponchos, and silver jewelry are common, as well as other trinkets. The Plaza 3 Californias, an artisan plaza directly across the street from Hotel California, is home to a number of stalls and shops all carrying traditional Mexican handicrafts like leather bags, jewelry, colorful blankets, and metal sculptures. At the end of that block, the store on the corner, Marisol (corner of Leon and Benito Juárez, no tel., 8am-8pm daily), carries a large selection of colorful Talavera pottery, traditional textiles, and other decorative pieces.

If you're looking for a quality Mexican souvenir to take home, try Manos Mexicanos (Topete and Centenario, tel. 612/145-0538, 10am-5pm Mon.-Sat.). The selection includes local crafts, soaps, jewelry, and home decorations as well as handcrafted pottery by artist Rubén Gutierrez.

In a storefront adjoining the hotel, Emporio Hotel California (Juárez between Morelos and Márquez de León, tel. 512/145-0217, 10am-7pm daily) has an eclectic assortment of books, jewelry, clothing, decorative home accessories, and artwork by local artists.

artisanal goods found in the shops in downtown Todos Santos

For a dose of bohemian dresses, chic kaftans, and ethnic jewelry, don't miss Nomad Chic (Juárez and Hidalgo, tel. 612/105-2857, www. nomadchic.mx, 11am-5pm daily). Owner Linda Hamilton stocks contemporary designers not easily found in other stores. She also designs her own line of apparel, jewelry, and accessories, inspired by travels around the world.

If you're looking for colorful, traditional Mexican clothing, head to Étnica (Av. Topete, tel. 612/143-7587, www. etnica-todos-santos.com, 11am-3pm Mon.-Sat.). Hip accessories accompany a selection of embroidered dresses and blouses from all over Mexico.

For a unique gift or souvenir from the region, La Sonrisa de la Muerte (Centro C/Militar and Hidalgo, no tel., www.smuerte.com, 10am-5pm daily) is an art and graphics gallery with handpicked prints from young Mexican artists. In addition to prints, this hip little shop sells items like T-shirts, bags, stickers, and cards.

Bibliophiles will love a trip to El Tecolote Bookstore (Juárez and Hidalgo, 9am-5pm Mon.-Sat., noon-3pm Sun., reduced hours during the summer) with its curated selection of new and used books. The assortment includes fiction, coffee-table books, and Baja-specific titles, as well as maps, DVDs, music, and cards.

Specializing in mezcals, Mexico Gourmet (Calle Hidalgo between Juárez and Centenario, tel. 612/168-3816) has hundreds of options to choose from. Staff have a deep and intimate knowledge of mezcal and offer mezcal tastings in the shop. It also makes its own house mezcal.

TOP EXPERIENCE

✪ ART GALLERIES AND STUDIOS

One of the top galleries in town, and a must-visit for anyone who appreciates art, is Galería de Todos Santos (Juárez, tel. 612/145-0500, www. galeriatodossantos-com.webs.com,

10am-4:30pm Mon.-Sat., 11am-4pm Sun.). The gallery has been carrying a variety of artists and mediums since 1994. The light and airy space features pieces from local and international artists.

Featuring the work of artist Gabo and his son, Gabriel Rodriguez, Gabo Galería (Calle Márquez de León, tel. 612/145-0514, 11am-4:30pm Mon.-Sat.) is popular with those who appreciate abstract art. Gabo is a popular Mexican artist whose work can be seen all over town in various hotels and public spaces.

Artist Jill Logan has her work on display at her gallery Galería Logan (Juárez and Morelos, tel. 612/145-0151, www.jilllogan.com, 11am-4pm Mon.-Sat.). Her colorful and bold paintings are a favorite among tourists and locals.

Galería Logan

Paintings of Baja landscapes and local scenes can be found at gallery Ezra Katz (Mexico 19 at Topete, no tel., www.ezrakatz.com, noon-5pm daily). The eponymous artist is a native Baja Californian who has become a favorite of art collectors.

For a more hands-on approach to the Todos Santos art scene, Todos Artes (tel. 503/219-5918, www. donnabillickart.com/todos-artes) hosts destination art workshops with instruction from guest artists. Various mediums and projects are explored.

FOOD
MEXICAN

For a trifecta of great food, setting, and ambience, head to Los Adobes de Todos Santos (Calle Hidalgo between Juárez and Colegio Militar, tel. 612/145-0203, www. losadobesdetodossantos.com, 11:30am-9pm Mon.-Sat., 11:30am-5pm Sun., US$10-13). Tucked away in a courtyard behind a 100-year-old adobe building, the outdoor dining patio looks over a beautiful and well-manicured cactus garden. Start with one of the traditional soups on the menu, and for your entrée, enjoy a hearty meat or seafood dish prepared in authentic Mexican style.

Good service, delicious traditional Mexican food, and great margaritas (try the damiana flavor) keep patrons going back to ✪ Tequila's Sunrise Bar & Grill (Benito Juárez, no tel., 10am-8pm Mon.-Sat., US$9-15). It's a fun environment with flat-screen TVs and signatures of patrons all over the walls. The shrimp chiles rellenos and the Mexican combination plate are favorites among patrons.

For good fresh food, attentive service, and great prices, head just out of town to La Cocina de Cleo (Calle las Playitas, tel. 612/178-0026, US$6-9). With a fun and casual atmosphere, this family-run restaurant has a diverse menu with offerings from hamburgers to enchiladas. Don't miss the margaritas, as they're rumored to be some of the best in town.

Serving breakfast, lunch, evening tapas, and dinner, La Morena (Benito Juárez, tel. 612/145-0789, 8am-9pm Mon.-Sat., US$6-10) is a comfortable gathering spot for tourists and locals.

La Morena restaurant and bar

The restaurant features indoor seating, a lovely outdoor patio, and a bar. Regular live music adds to the casual and friendly vibe. The menu features fresh salads, paninis, and seafood, with a variety of cocktails, beer, and Baja wines to drink.

For casual *palapa* dining, **Miguel's** (Degollado and Rangel, tel. 613/134-4149, noon-9pm Mon.-Sat., US$6-10) is the place to go for cold beer and tasty authentic Mexican dishes. Surfboards line the ceiling, and the restaurant just recently upgraded from dirt floors. Miguel himself is usually there to wait on customers. The chiles rellenos stuffed with shrimp are a well-deserved favorite dish of anyone who visits. Finish up with the flan for dessert (Miguel's wife makes it).

One of the top chefs in northern Baja, Javier Plascencia has brought casual outdoor *campestre*-style eating to Baja Sur with ✪ **Jazamango** (Calle Naranjos, tel. 612/688-1501, www.jazamango.com, 1pm-9pm Mon.-Sat., 10am-9pm Sun., US$8-14). Using local products and organic ingredients, the food is carefully prepared. Diners will find appetizers like steamed mussels, Kumamoto oysters, and yellowfin tuna. For entrées, traditional dishes like pozole and chiles

rellenos are offered alongside smoked pork belly and wood-grilled lamb. The outdoor dining room overlooks the garden where much of the produce comes from.

The fresh guacamole, nachos, and fish tacos are what keep people coming back for the traditional Mexican cuisine at **Mi Pueblito** (Calle Hidalgo, tel. 612/145-0173, mipueblitobcs@gmail.com, noon-8pm Mon.-Sat., US$6-9). There's inside and patio seating, and most of the staff speak English.

What originally started as a small tamale stand has now been upgraded to an open-air restaurant at **Alma y Manny** (Márquez de León, tel. 612/155-5046, 9am-9pm daily, US$3-6). With a selection of homemade tamales, tacos, chiles rellenos, and traditional Mexican breakfasts, the spot has become a favorite of local Mexicans and expats. The plastic chairs and *palapa* roof create a casual setting for enjoying a deliciously authentic and affordable meal.

SEAFOOD
In a friendly and unassuming setting, **Fonda El Zaguán** (Juárez, tel. 612/145-0485, noon-9pm Mon.-Sat., US$8-11) serves not only fresh fish and seafood but also has some meat and poultry

chef Javier Plascencia's Jazamango restaurant

BEST RESTAURANTS IN TODOS SANTOS AND THE WEST CAPE

○ **TEQUILA'S SUNRISE BAR & GRILL:** Offering traditional Mexican food and good service, this fun spot keeps patrons coming back (page 159).

○ **JAZAMANGO:** Javier Plascencia's new restaurant brings northern Baja's *campestre*-style dining to Baja Sur (page 160).

○ **CAFÉ SANTA FE:** Don't miss the lobster ravioli at this delicious Italian restaurant right on the historic plaza of Todos Santos (page 162).

○ **TRE GALLINE:** Delicious handcrafted pastas and other Italian dishes make for some of the best dining in Todos Santos (page 162).

○ **HORTALIZA HIERBABUENA:** Farm-to-table dining is taken literally at this open-air restaurant situated in the midst of lush vegetable gardens in El Pescadero (page 170).

options on the menu. Main dishes are served with fresh garden vegetables and rice. If you don't want to eat in the dining room, there are sidewalk tables that are perfect for enjoying a glass of Baja wine and people-watching.

Focusing on small plates and fresh ingredients, La Casita Tapas and Wine Bar (Degollado and Calle Militar, tel. 612/145-0192, www. lacasitatapaswinebar.com, noon-10pm Tues.-Sun., US$8-13) is known for sushi and seafood dishes like coconut shrimp. The wine menu includes a good selection of Baja and international wines, and La Casita also serves delicious sangria. This is a great family-friendly restaurant that's a favorite of both locals and visitors.

For a quick and easy lunch, head out to Pacifica Fish Market (Calle Horizonte, tel. 612/117-2426, noon-7pm Tues.-Sat., US$6-8), where you can order fish grilled, blackened, or fried and as a taco, burrito, or plate. The owner, Patrick, was the former sushi chef at La Copa, and daily specials often include sushi rolls.

TACO STANDS

Owner Pepe and his team at Tacos y Mariscos El Sinaloense (Calle Colegio Militar at Obregón, tel. 612/145-1113, 10am-6pm Wed.-Mon., US$2-5) win over crowds with their friendly service and marlin fish tacos. They serve a variety of seafood tacos and ceviches at affordable prices.

For a tasty, cheap, and quick meal, Carnitas Barajas (Santa Degollado and Calle Cuauhtemoc, no tel., 8am-11pm daily, US$2-6) has *carnitas* by the taco, half kilo, and kilo. It also has fish, shrimp, and carne asada tacos as well as *papas rellenas* (stuffed potatoes). The service can be aloof, but the food and price make up for it.

If you're in the mood for fresh ceviche, Mariscos el Compa Chava (Del Huerto, no tel., 10am-7pm daily, US$4-7) is the place to go. In addition to seafood cocktails and ceviche, it has cooked fish and shrimp dishes—all served with homemade sauces in a breezy *palapa* setting.

Tacos George's (Heroico Colegio Militar 85, tel. 612/102-8768, 9am-3pm daily, US$1-2) serves up fish and shrimp tacos and is loved by locals and travelers. Make sure to load up your tacos with all of the fresh toppings.

For meat tacos, head to Tacos El Poblano (Colegio Militar, tel. 612/202-8617, 3pm-11pm Fri.-Wed., US$1-3), which serves asada and al pastor. Tacos, *tortas*, burritos, and *papas rellenas* (stuffed baked potatoes) are all on the menu.

ITALIAN

For decades, a mandatory dining experience in Todos Santos has been ✪ Café Santa Fe (Calle Centenario 4, tel. 612/145-0340, www.cafesantafetodossantos.com, noon-9pm Wed.-Mon., closed Sept. and Oct., US$15-22). Paula and Ezio Colombo opened the restaurant in late 1990, and with Ezio's northern Italian background, they bring uncompromised flavors of Italy to Baja. The food is carefully crafted with produce grown in their own organic garden and fresh fish and meats. The results always seem to exceed expectations. The atmosphere is Italian bistro meets Mexican paradise, with checkered floors and white tablecloths in the open-air dining room looking out onto the tropical *palapa* patio. The service is always great here, and some of the servers, like Carlos, have been working at the restaurant for two decades. Don't visit without trying the fish carpaccio and the lobster ravioli.

Tucked into a lush garden setting, ✪ Tre Galline (Calle Centenario 33, tel. 612/145-0300, 5pm-10pm daily, US$12-15) is another Italian restaurant that's become a favorite for locals and travelers. Owners Magda Valpiani and Angelo Dal Bon came from Italy in 2006 and also run Caffé

Todos Santos. Fresh ingredients are skillfully prepared into dishes such as artisanal pizzas, the daily fresh catch, and homemade pasta dishes.

INTERNATIONAL

On the grounds of The Todos Santos Inn, La Copa Cocina (Calle Legaspi 33, tel. 612/117-2426, www.todossantosinn.com, 5pm-10pm Thurs.-Tues., US$15-20) serves gourmet tacos, sliders, sushi, and other California-inspired tapas. The extensive wine list and beautiful outdoor garden help to create a romantic setting.

For a dining experience accompanied by incredible views, El Mirador (Old Punta Lobos Rd., tel. 612/175-0800, www.guaycura.com, 2pm-10pm Wed.-Mon., US$16) is the place to go. Sunset is the best time to go to really take advantage of the vista offered by this large *palapa* on the beach outside town. The service is average and prices are a bit high, but many people return just for the views.

It doesn't look like much from the outside, but don't let appearances fool you at Rumi Garden (128 Santos Degollado, tel. 612/145-1088, www.rumigarden.com, noon-8pm Wed.-Mon., US$10). Once you get past the monolithic-looking exterior, the inside unfolds into a colorful dining area with a garden and fountain. With authentic dishes like pad thai and shrimp curry made with organic ingredients, this is a favorite spot for locals and tourists.

For a unique twist on fresh Asian fusion cuisine, try Michael's at the Gallery (Juárez, tel. 612/145-0500, 6pm-10pm Fri.-Sat., US$13-16). The ambience is memorable, as the restaurant is located on the veranda of a gallery space. Reservations are required as the restaurant is only open limited hours on Friday and Saturday.

CAFÉS

Serving breakfast, lunch, and dinner, **Caffé Todos Santos** (Calle Centenario 33, tel. 612/145-0300, 7am-10pm Tues.-Sun., US$8-11) is a longtime favorite in town. It's now owned by the proprietors of Tre Galline, so in addition to great pastries and breakfasts, it serves well-made Italian food for lunch and dinner.

In addition to coffee and baked goods, **La Esquina** (tel. 612/145-0851, www.laesquinats.com, 7am-7pm Mon.-Tues., 7am-10pm Wed.-Sat., 9am-2pm Sun., US$4-7) serves breakfast and lunch with healthy food choices like made-to-order sandwiches, soups, and organic salads. This is a popular hangout for locals, and it regularly hosts community events like fundraisers, movie screenings, and live music. There's a farmers market 9am-noon on Wednesday.

If you need to caffeinate while you're strolling around town, head to **Taller 17** (Centenario and Miguel Hidalgo y Costilla, tel. 612/145-2019, 7:30am-7pm Thurs.-Tues.). It makes delicious roasted coffees, and its baked goods are made from scratch daily. Don't miss the scones and cinnamon rolls.

For a sweet treat, **La Paloma** (Colegio Militar, tel. 612/145-0573, US$1-2) is a *paletería* serving homemade ice cream and *paletas* (Mexican popsicles) in a wide variety of flavors.

ACCOMMODATIONS

Many hotels in Todos Santos are seasonal, closing for the hot, humid summers in August and September. Accommodations that remain open during that time may offer cheaper rates, but be sure to ask if they have air-conditioning in the rooms. There are no large resorts here; accommodations consist mostly of B&Bs and boutique hotels with only a few rooms. Reservations should be booked in advance for this region, especially around Christmas and New Year's when the area is extremely popular and room rates go up for a few weeks.

UNDER US$50

Todos Santos finally has a hostel for those looking for budget accommodations. With clean and modern facilities, **Todos Santos Hostel** (Francisco Bojorquer Vidal 112, tel. 646/124-2320, www.todossantoshostel.com, US$35) has shared rooms in addition to campsites and RV spots. Guests enjoy a shared kitchen, Wi-Fi, a patio, and lush gardens.

Hotel Maria Bonita (Militar and Hidalgo, tel. 612/145-0289, US$37) has a good location downtown and is within walking distance to everything. Rooms are very basic but do have air-conditioning, TVs, and Wi-Fi.

US$50-150

With a relaxed and manicured vibe, **Perro Surfero** (Calle Bravo 36, tel. 624/137-7551, www.perrosurfero.com, US$65) caters to younger surfers looking for nice accommodations at an affordable price. There's Wi-Fi, a shared kitchen, a yoga deck, and lots of common spaces for relaxing, such as hammocks or around the firepit.

The rooms are spacious and comfortable at **Serendipity** (Las Tunas, tel. 612/178-0104, www.serendipityventures.com, US$120-160), a hacienda-style bed-and-breakfast. In addition to having a pool, the property runs down to the beach and all rooms have ocean views. It

BEST ACCOMMODATIONS IN TODOS SANTOS AND THE WEST CAPE

✪ **THE HOTELITO:** Beautifully designed, this bright and modern hotel offers cozy accommodations and welcome margaritas by the pool (page 164).

✪ **HOTEL CALIFORNIA:** This popular choice has eclectic decor, comfortable beds, and an on-site restaurant and bar (page 165).

✪ **LA BOHEMIA BAJA HOTEL PEQUEÑO:** Mixing outdoor adventure and comfy lodging, this bed-and-breakfast aims to give guests unforgettable experiences (page 165).

✪ **VILLA SANTA CRUZ:** Every detail is incredibly curated at this intimate and magical B&B on the beach at Todos Santos (page 166).

✪ **RANCHO PESCADERO:** This mini-resort in El Pescadero has become a hip spot for jet-setters looking for a more relaxed alternative to Cabo (page 173).

offers a renowned full to-order breakfast in the mornings. The B&B is 2 kilometers (1.2 miles) outside the town and a short drive to the center.

With eight spacious suites, **The Vibe** (Calle del Pilar, tel. 612/145-0482, www.thevibebb.com, US$95-130) is a bed-and-breakfast in town that provides modern, relaxing accommodations and an attentive staff. Rooms feature kitchenettes, and a healthy breakfast is included in your stay. The B&B is located within walking distance of shops and restaurants in town.

For a stay in a Portuguese-style castle, try **Casa Bentley** (Calle Pilar 99, tel. 612/145-0276, www.casabentleybaja.com, US$110-130). This boutique hotel is set on lush grounds with palm trees and century-old mango trees. The building is made of incredible stonework, featuring multi-level patios, and features a pool fed by waterfall. The location is easy walking distance to the town center.

The Spanish colonial-style **Posada del Molino** (Col San Vicente, tel. 612/169-2095, www.posadadelmolino.com, US$90-110) has an old mill on the premises, left over from the town's sugarcane era. With Mexican-style decor, each studio has a fully equipped kitchenette.

With a design that strikes a balance between cozy and modern, ✪ **The Hotelito** (Rancho de la Cachora, tel. 612/145-0099, www.thehotelito.com, US$135) is a small property with four well-crafted rooms. Owner Jenny Armit has taken care to finish modern rooms with bright paint colors and designer furniture touches. Each has its own private garden. Services include a 48-foot saltwater pool and welcome margaritas. The beach is a 10-minute walk from this property on the edge of town.

Although housed in an old historic building, **Hotel Casa Tota** (Calle Álvaro Obregón, tel. 612/145-0590, www.hotelcasatota.com, US$123-143) features modern rooms with amenities like plasma TVs and room service. There are 15 rooms, a roof deck, swimming pool, and hot tub. There's

Hotel Casa Tota

an on-site store where the hotel sells its own blends of tequila and mezcal.

US$150-250

The fact that it wasn't actually the inspiration for the famous Eagles song (although many rumors claim that it was) doesn't seem to diminish the popularity of ✪ **Hotel California** (Benito Juárez between Morelos and Márquez de León, tel. 612/145-0525, www. hotelcaliforniabaja.com, US$150-185). It has 11 rooms with down comforters, air-conditioning, and patios. Eclectic decorations and artwork come from around the world. Founded in 1947, the hotel has a lock on the town of Todos Santos with its **La Coronela** restaurant and bar and **Emporio** gallery and store. The landmark is home

mariachi statues on the roof of Hotel California

to the annual music festival and remains a stop for many tourists passing through town, whether they come to dine, drink, shop, or stay.

With three guesthouses and four luxury suites, **Hacienda Todos los Santos** (Benito Juárez, tel. 612/145-0547, www.tshacienda.com, US$130-190) also boasts beautiful lush grounds and a nice pool area. The modern rooms are luxuriously appointed with comfortable beds, high ceilings, and large bathrooms. Breakfast is included in your stay, and the property has a great location a few blocks away from the center of town.

The historic brick building that now houses **The Todos Santos Inn** (Calle Legaspi 33, tel. 612/145-0040, www.todossantosinn.com, US$145-225) was once the home of a sugar baron in the mid-19th century during the town's sugar mill days. The hotel offers terrace rooms, junior suites, and garden suites. All rooms come with free breakfast. The popular **La Copa Cocina** restaurant offers enchanting outdoor dining in the courtyard and also has an accompanying wine bar.

With the mission of creating an unforgettable experience by way of accommodation and facilitating exploration is ✪ **La Bohemia Baja Hotel Pequeño** (Calle Rangel 108, tel. 612/145-0759, www. labohemiabaja.com, US$146-183). Owners Erin and Andrew Wheelwright are the perfect hosts and create a welcoming atmosphere for all their guests. The well-curated bed-and-breakfast has six rooms with whitewashed walls and traditional Mexican textiles and decorations. Gardens and hammocks help guests relax during their stay, and there's a main *palapa* for breakfast in the morning, cocktails in

the pool at Villa Santa Cruz

the evening, and social gatherings. The hotel serves as a delightful base camp for getting out to explore Todos Sandos and the surrounding sierras. The owners can help arrange explorations like hiking to waterfalls, surf lessons, whale-watching, and cycling. A new sister property, Gypsy Canyon (www.gypsycanyonbaja. com), is a glamping spot featuring luxury tents located just out of town in a cactus grove near the beach. The same attention to detail and chic ambience is brought to the experience where they've combined the comfort of staying in a hotel with the raw nature of Baja. Gypsy Canyon is currently only available for private groups and events.

One of the few accommodations actually located on the beach in Todos Santos is the magical bed-and-breakfast ✪ Villa Santa Cruz (Camino a la Playitas, tel. 612/143-9230, U.S. tel. 760/230-5557, www. villasantacruzbaja.com, US$195-250). Americans Matt and Jessica

Canepa opened the B&B in 2011 and overlooked no detail in building the property from the ground up. While you're enjoying your welcome margarita, you'll get a tour of the exquisite villa and grounds. Decorated with authentic wood and wrought-iron Mexican furniture and accented with colorful artisan pieces, the villa looks like something out of a movie (the floating glass staircase is uniquely superb). The pool is perfectly heated to 87 degrees and comes complete with a large hot tub, lots of comfortable chaise lounges, and a hammock. There's a large *palapa*, replete with a comfy sleeping loft, that sits up on the sand dunes overlooking the magnificent, and fairly empty, beach. The famous La Pastora surf spot is a 10-minute walk south from here. There are beach towels, coolers, beach chairs, and sunscreen available for guest use. There's also a cask of tequila (first shot is on the house) as well as wine and beer (all available on the honor system). At night, tiki torches illuminate the outdoor areas and candles are lit throughout the villa, giving everything an ethereal glow. You can enjoy the hot tub under a blanket of stars and the sound of crashing waves in the background, or there are fire pits set up on the roof for enjoyment as well. Sleep with the French doors open to enjoy the lulling sound of crashing waves throughout the night. In the morning, you'll awake to find a basket of hot coffee and tea outside the door, which you can leisurely enjoy on your balcony before heading downstairs for a full breakfast served in the outdoor dining area.

Guests at Guaycura (Calle Legaspi at Topete, tel. 612/175-0800, www.guaycura.com, US$175-228) get to enjoy the central location of the hotel in town and also have access to Guaycura's El Faro Beach Club, outside town on the beach, with a swimming pool and the El Mirador restaurant. There's a shuttle that will take guests from the hotel in town to the beach club. The hotel in town has 14 elegantly decorated rooms and a rooftop bar that has great views at sunset time.

Located directly on the lagoon, Posada La Poza (Col. La Poza, tel. 612/145-0400, toll-free U.S. tel. 855/552-7692, www.hotelposadalapozatodossantos.com, US$195-235) has eight boutique suites that are well appointed with air-conditioning, orthopedic mattresses, and high-quality linens. To augment its lagoon location, binoculars and bird books are available in all rooms, and it's a great spot for bird-watching. There's a heated saltwater pool and hot tub for guests to enjoy. Spa services are available, and El Gusto restaurant is located right on the property.

OVER US$250

Located south of town on Punta Lobos beach, Hotel San Cristóbal (Mexico 19 Km. 54, tel. 612/175-1530, www.sancristobalbaja.com, US$230-400) is a 32-room beachfront property. Rooms are situated around a central pool and offer an indoor/outdoor experience, overlooking the beach and Sierra de la Laguna mountains. A restaurant is also on the property.

INFORMATION AND SERVICES

There's a gas station in town at the intersection of Degollado and Militar. There are Bancomer and Banorte branches for withdrawing money from ATMs. The town has small markets but no large grocery stores. There's no official tourist office in Todos Santos, but most hotels and businesses are willing to give recommendations and answer questions.

While there are no large hospitals in the area, the Centro de Salud (tel. 612/145-0095) is located at Degollado and Juárez and is open 24/7. Call 911 for any emergencies.

TRANSPORTATION
GETTING THERE

The nearest airport is in Los Cabos, an hour's drive from the West Cape. Most travelers fly into Los Cabos and rent a car at the airport to drive north up Mexico 19 to get to the West Cape. There's a new toll road bypass from the airport to north of Cabo San Lucas, so drivers can easily skip the traffic and congestion of both San José del Cabo and Cabo San Lucas.

There's a gas station in Todos Santos as well as one in El Pescadero. Outside of the two towns, there are no gas stations or services for cars in the West Cape. Most major car repair and services will need to be done in Los Cabos.

Aguila (toll-free Mex. tel. 800/026-8931, www.autobusesaguila.com) and Autobuses de la Baja California (ABC, tel. 664/104-7400, www.abc.com.mx) buses have service directly to Todos Santos from Cabo San Lucas and other cities in Baja. Both companies run buses from La Paz and Cabo to Todos Santos every hour (US$10), and the ride takes about an hour from either destination. A 10-minute bus ride between El Pescadero and Todos Santos (US$1.50) also runs every hour.

EcoBaja (tel. 624/144-3066, www.ecobajatours.com) has a shuttle service that runs from Todos Santos to downtown Cabo San Lucas or Los Cabos International Airport for US$20.

GETTING AROUND

There is no local bus service in town. The central historic district is very compact, and the best way to explore it is on foot. There are very few taxis in Todos Santos, so if you plan on exploring the region, it's best to have your own vehicle or rent a car when you fly into Los Cabos.

El Pescadero

The beach community of El Pescadero, 13 kilometers (8.1 miles) south of Todos Santos, used to be a small remote fishing and agricultural village. The area has grown rapidly over the past number of years and now supports an assortment of boutique hotels, eco-lodgings, and even a mini-resort. There is a handful of restaurants and bars, as well as a Pemex gas station. The actual town of Pescadero is on the eastern side of Mexico 19, but most of the hotels and attractions for tourists are to the west, down near the beaches.

Bordered by the Sierra de la Laguna to the east and the Pacific to the west, the area boasts a number of surf breaks that have helped bolster its popularity with bohemian types. Most of the action in Pescadero centers around Playa Los Cerritos. The beach is popular for beginning surfing and boogie boarding, and is one of the few spots in the West Cape safe for swimming. In the

past decade, many new hotels and restaurants have opened up near Cerritos, catering to surfers and savvy travelers looking for a more tranquil alternative to Cabo.

BEACHES

✪ PLAYA LOS CERRITOS

For years, Playa Los Cerritos was referred to as one of the best beaches in Baja. Word got out, and the once tranquil beach is now constantly buzzing with surfers, tourists, vendors, and a growing number of beachfront developments. Although the beach has changed, it remains a favorite for many Baja travelers. The waves are great for beginner surfers, and it's one of the few beaches on the West Cape safe for swimming as well. It's also a great spot for sunsets. Access to the beach (without having to pay for parking) is now only available in two areas on the far north and south sides of the beach.

SPORTS AND RECREATION

SURFING

Playa Los Cerritos is a popular spot for beginner surfers because of the beach breaks, sandy bottom, and easy fun waves. There's a break at the point that more experienced surfers will enjoy. Farther south of El Pescadero, at kilometer 73, is **Punta Gaspareño**, a right point break that breaks on west or northwest swells.

Surfers of any level will want to check out **Mario's Surf School** (tel. 612/130-3319, www.mariosurfschool. com). Mario has over 10 years of experience as a surf instructor and is great about showing the ropes to beginners or taking out more experienced surfers on excursions to some of the more advanced breaks in the region. Private lessons start at US$60 per hour. Look for their blue Mario's Surf School umbrella on Playa Los Cerritos.

Costa Azul Surf Shop (tel. 624/142-2771, www.costa-azul.com. mx, 8am-6pm Mon.-Sat., 9am-5pm Sun.) is also located on Playa Los Cerritos and offers surf lessons for US$150 for two hours as well as surf excursions for all levels. It has surfboard rentals for US$20 a day and also rents paddleboards, skim boards, body boards, and snorkeling equipment. The shop sells surf wear, accessories, and clothing.

Cerritos Beach Club & Surf (tel. 624/124-6315, www.cerritosbcs.com) also rents surfboards on Playa Los Cerritos.

YOGA

Near the main entrance to Playa Los Cerritos, **Baja-Zen** (tel. 612/142-5038, www.baja-zen.com) yoga studio and retreat center has a beautiful facility, offers daily public yoga classes, and can also arrange for private classes. It has simple but nice accommodations for those participating in a yoga retreat.

El Pescadero

Surfers, swimmers, and sunbathers enjoy Playa Los Cerritos.

FOOD

On the dirt road out to Rancho Pescadero resort, visitors will find ✪ Hortaliza Hierbabuena (tel. 612/149-2568, www.hierbabuena restaurante.com, 1pm-9pm Wed.-Mon., US$10-14), where farm-to-table dining comes alive at its finest. The open-air restaurant is surrounded by lush vegetable gardens that supply the restaurant with fresh produce. The menu changes with what's in season and growing in the garden. It's known for its wood-fired pizzas, and other entrées, like flank steak, fresh fish of the day, and baked eggplant, are all made from ingredients grown on the property and locally sourced. There's a separate bar area where drinks like the "Sandiatini" (vodka, watermelon juice, and mint) and the "Baja Surprise" (hibiscus liqueur, citrus juices, tequila) are served, as well as a wide variety of freshly squeezed juices. If you want to take home some of the fresh flavors, the restaurant sells bundles of vegetables and herbs picked from the gardens.

The large roadside *palapa* at Jungle Pescadero (Mexico 19 Km. 69, tel. 612/226-5811, noon-8pm Wed.-Sun., US$8-11) is a popular local hangout serving margaritas in mason jars. For food it offers shrimp in a variety of styles and fish fillets. There's a corn hole game and fire pit on-site. With a kids' menu and a playground, this is a great spot for families.

With a casual setting, enjoyable

Hortaliza Hierbabuena restaurant

atmosphere, and friendly service, Barracuda Cantina (Cerritos beach, tel. 612/157-5354, noon-8pm Thurs.-Tues., US$2-6) is a glorified beach taco stand where diners enjoy their tacos and ceviche with specialty craft cocktails and cold beers. The owners work hard to treat their customers to great food and a fun vibe.

Another casual food spot in Pescadero is Carnitas Machin Puro Michoacan (Mexico 19, tel. 612/214-9748, 7am-4pm daily, US$1-3). Located right off the highway, it serves *carnitas* by the taco or by the kilo along with all the fixings. It's the perfect fast, simple, and cheap meal.

Don't let the sports bar setting turn you off from Shaka's Delicious Wood Cantina y Galeria (Mexico 19 Km. 65, tel. 624/137-3746, US$8-10). The large open-air *palapa* restaurant serves up delicious Mexican and seafood dishes (don't miss the shrimp) and makes great cocktails. Happy hour features a 2-for-1 special.

For unique Asian-inspired seafood creations, Carlito's Place (just east of Mexico 19, tel. 612/137-9419, 1pm-9pm Tues.-Sun., US$12-18) is so popular that people drive up from Cabo just to dine here. The prices can be expensive, but those who love sushi and fresh seafood say that it's worth it. The setting is serene, with outdoor dining under a large *palapa* roof and lush surroundings. If Carlito himself is around, try the chef's choice with Carlito making custom dishes for your enjoyment.

You'll have to pay a fee to even enter the parking lot of Cerritos Beach Club & Surf (tel. 624/129-6315, www.cerritosbcs.com, 8am-6pm daily, US$12-24, entrance fee $30). Located right in the middle of the action on Playa Los Cerritos, the restaurant makes the most of a prime beach location and often has live music. Many complain that it's become a tourist trap with mediocre food and expensive prices (even by U.S. standards), but it remains a popular spot with tourists because of the setting. It stays open for breakfast, lunch, and dinner.

The rooftop restaurant and bar Free Souls (Freesouls Street, tel. 624/191-4666, info@thefreesoulsproject.com, 12:30pm-10pm Wed.-Mon., US$9-15) has captivated patrons with its cool vibe. The menu has a wide range of items, but a solid choice is the Mediterranean-style pizzas cooked in a wood-burning oven. The rooftop has great views at sunset, and a saltwater infinity-edge swimming pool looks out onto the beach and Pacific. Expect U.S. prices on drinks and food here.

With good strong coffee and tasty baked goods, Baja Beans (Mexico 19 Km. 19, tel. 612/130-3391, www.bajabeanscoffee.com, 7am-6pm daily) has made quite a splash since opening in 2011. This combo bakery, café, and roasting company has plenty of outdoor seating in the large garden. It's a popular gathering spot for locals and visitors, and even more so on Sunday mornings when there's a large market with music and handicrafts.

ACCOMMODATIONS

Many of the accommodations in this area are centered on Playa Los Cerritos. There are also a number of vacation rentals in the area that can offer lodgings ranging from individual rooms and casitas to large houses. Budget accommodations are increasingly difficult to find as more and more resorts and higher-end inns are making inroads.

UNDER US$50

Choose from one of the casitas or bring your own tent for camping at Pescadero Surf Camp (Mexico 19 Km. 64, tel. 612/134-0480, www. pescaderosurf.com, US$10-45). There's a pool with a swim-up bar (BYOB), as well as a large outdoor kitchen and barbecue area. Located about 3 kilometers (2 miles) from the beach, it's a bit too far to walk to the ocean, but with the affordable price, this is a great budget option for the area. It offers boogie board and surfboard rentals as well as surf lessons for all levels.

US$50-150

A short walking distance to Cerritos beach, Olas de Cerritos (Mexico 19 Km. 66, tel. 612/159-0396, US$70) offers the use of beach chairs, umbrellas, boogie boards, and surfboards to guests. The small eight-room hotel has a nice pool and a communal kitchen and *palapa* area. A cold breakfast and coffee are served every morning, and pots and pans are available for those guests who wish to cook their own breakfast.

With a beautiful beachfront location, Cerritos Surf Town (Mexico 19 Km. 69, tel. 624/129-6494, www. cerritossurftown.com, US$120) also has a pool with a swim-up bar and a restaurant on the property. All the accommodations are stand-alone structures and range from a studio suite to a two-bedroom villa. There is currently no air-conditioning in the rooms, and Wi-Fi is only available in the pool area.

Brought to you by the same owners as Pescadero Surf Camp is Cerritos Beach Hotel, Desert Moon (tel. 811/911-9300, www. cerritosbeachhotel.com, US$150). Just steps away from Playa Los Cerritos, the hotel is popular with surfers and beachgoers. The modern, minimal rooms are all well appointed with kitchens and have beach views. There's a restaurant on-site serving dishes like pizza and wings, and there's also a pool with a poolside bar.

US$150-250

If you don't mind roughing it a bit in exchange for location and views, Mayan Village Resort (Mexico 19 Km. 67, U.S. tel. 858/551-8852, US$185) offers beachfront eco-*cabañas*. Each *cabaña* is an individual *palapa* structure right on Playa Los Cerritos. Bathrooms are shared (separate for men and women), and there's no wireless Internet.

Located right on Playa Los Cerritos but south of most of the activity and crowds is the Cerritos Beach Inn (Mexico 19 Km. 68, tel. 612/168-2619, www.cerritosbeachinn.com, US$125-250). This property features a swimming pool, rooftop deck, and outdoor cantina. With high-end finishes and a variety of amenities, this is one of the nicest properties in the area. Oceanfront rooms cost double the price of desert/mountain view rooms.

OVER US$250

Looming over the cliff of Punta Pescadero on the north side of Playa Los Cerritos is Hacienda Cerritos (Mexico 19 Km. 65, tel. 612/104-2878, www.haciendacerritos.com, US$350). This boutique hotel has fewer than 12 rooms, all set in the large mansion

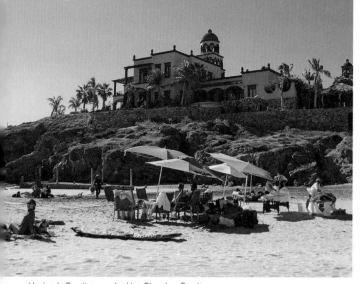
Hacienda Cerritos overlooking Playa Los Cerritos

with pools and incredible ocean views surrounding. The property has fallen into some disrepair after damage from Hurricane Odile in 2014 that was not fixed. Wireless access is available only in common areas. The hotel bar, which has beautiful ocean views, particularly at sunset, is open to the public, so you don't have to stay at the Hacienda to enjoy a margarita with a vista of the Pacific.

Currently closed for renovations until 2020, ✪ Rancho Pescadero (Mexico 19 Km. 62, U.S. tel. 910/300-8891, www.ranchopescadero.com, US$275-450) is a boutique resort with chic and luxurious amenities and a relaxed vibe, located north of Cerritos on Playa Pescadero. It is expanding to reopen with 95 rooms and suites. Situated on 30 acres of beach and farmland, the renovated hotel will feature an oceanfront restaurant, lagoon pool, a new spa, expanded yoga studios, and 12 oceanfront villas each with a private plunge pool.

SERVICES

El Pescadero is home to the only gas station and OXXO convenience store between Cabo and Todos Santos. They are conveniently located on Mexico 19 in the actual town of El Pescadero. Buses stop across the highway from the gas station. Ask at your hotel for tourist information and local recommendations.

TRANSPORTATION
GETTING THERE

El Pescadero is 65 kilometers (40 miles) and just under an hour's drive north of Cabo San Lucas on Mexico 19.

Aguila (toll-free Mex. tel. 800/026-8931, www.autobusesaguila.com) and Autobuses de la Baja California (ABC, tel. 664/104-7400, www.abc.com.mx) have service directly to El Pescadero from Cabo San Lucas and other cities in Baja. Both companies have buses from La Paz and Cabo to El Pescadero every hour (US$10), and

beach *palapas* at Rancho Pescadero

the ride takes about an hour from either destination. The 10-minute bus ride between El Pescadero and Todos Santos (US$1.50) also runs every hour.

The West Cape

The stretch between El Pescadero and Cabo is filled with beautiful undeveloped landscapes and empty beaches, making for a scenic drive. Adventurous travelers looking for access to the empty beaches can find unmarked turnoffs along Mexico 19. Signals of pending development are popping up in the form of real estate signs littering the landscape and the rumors that the locals will tell you. For now, enjoy the relatively empty beaches and the peaceful views of the Pacific. The area is remote, and there are no accommodations and very few services here. Most travelers stay in El

GETTING AROUND

There are no bus services within El Pescadero, so travelers will need to walk or rely on the limited taxi service.

Pescadero or Todos Santos and explore this area on day trips.

There are no gas stations or services for cars in the West Cape.

TURTLE RESCUE

About 20 kilometers (12.4 miles) northwest of Cabo San Lucas is the coastal village of San Cristóbal where visitors will find the sea turtle rescue nonprofit **Asupmatoma AC** (tel. 624/143-0269). It offers people the chance to camp for the night and participate in either collecting and relocating newly laid turtle eggs or releasing hatchlings into the ocean

(US$6 pp). Egg relocation happens between July 15 and September 15, and hatchling releases take place between September 15 and December 15. Those who just want to participate in the turtle hatchling release without spending the night are able to do so as well (US$3 adults, US$2 children 10 and under).

PLAYA MIGRIÑO

The beautiful shore at Playa Migriño is a great spot for whale-watching and catching the sunset. While the beach is not for swimming, surfers may be interested in the right point and hollow beach breaks that receive lots of swell. Unfortunately the peace and quiet of the location is often disrupted by ATV tours coming through. There are unmarked turnoffs on the west side of Mexico 19 at both kilometer 94 and kilometer 97.

The turnoff at kilometer 94 requires a high-clearance vehicle. The beach is about 2 kilometers (1.2 miles) from the highway.

LA CANDELARIA

In the foothills of the Sierra de la Laguna is the small ranching oasis town of La Candelaria. Because ATV tours have been coming up to the town in recent years, it's become known as a spot to purchase pottery from local residents. There's not much of a town in La Candelaria, and you have to know how to get there and what to look for once you arrive, so the best way to access La Candelaria is with a guide on an ATV tour, such as with Cactus ATV Tours (tel. 334/170-8171, www.cactusatvtours.com) and Amigos Cabo Moto (tel. 624/143-0808, www.amigosactivities.com).

For those who want to drive to La

Playa Migriño

Candelaria on their own, there is access from Cabo San Lucas on a dirt road called Camino a la Candelaria just to the east of the small Cabo San Lucas airport. For true off-road enthusiasts with good high-clearance, four-wheel-drive vehicles, there is a way to get to La Candelaria through the riverbed at Playa Migriño. The route is unmarked and extremely sandy and rocky. It should not be attempted in the rainy season.

SIERRA DE LA LAGUNA

The mountains of the Sierra de la Laguna biosphere reserve can be accessed from either the East Cape or the West Cape. The approach depends on the final destination. Most tours and guided hikes depart from the West Cape, while the East Cape makes a better base for self-guided day trips and treks. The sierras are filled with lush canyons, waterfalls, and plenty of opportunities for single-day or multiday hikes. While the namesake lake of the Sierra de la Laguna has dried up and is now a meadow, a trip to this area is a beautiful adventure to a rarely explored region. It's one of the popular spots in the range accessed from the West Cape. Treks to the *laguna* of the Sierra de la Laguna can be made through multiday hikes from Todos Santos. Todos Santos Eco Adventures (tel. 612/145-0189, www.tosea.net) offers guided hikes and treks with pack animals.

SPORTS AND RECREATION

ATV TOURS

Both with convenient highway locations on Mexico 19, Cactus ATV Tours (tel. 334/170-8171, www.cactusatvtours.com) and Amigos Cabo Moto (Mexico 19 Km. 106, tel. 624/143-0808, www.amigosactivities.com, 9am-7pm daily) offer ATV and horseback riding adventures to various destinations around the region.

BACKGROUND

The Landscape

GEOGRAPHY

The entire Baja peninsula is 1,300 kilometers (810 miles) long, from Tijuana in the north to Cabo San Lucas at the southern tip. As the northwestern region of Mexico, the Baja peninsula is separated from mainland Mexico by the Golfo de California (Gulf of California), more commonly referred to as the Mar de Cortés (Sea of Cortez).

HURRICANES

Hurricane season runs June-November, with August-October being the most intense months. If you are traveling in the region when a tropical storm or hurricane hits, obey all evacuation orders and avoid driving on washed-out roads or through *vados* as flash floods can be likely. U.S. and Canadian citizens should follow directions from their consulates. U.S. citizens should register with STEP (https://step.state.gov/step) before traveling outside the United States to receive emails and notifications in the case of an emergency. The **National Hurricane Center** (www.nhc.noaa.gov) has more information on forecasts and preparation for a hurricane.

The Pacific Ocean borders the western side of the Baja peninsula.

There are four main desert areas that make up 65 percent of the peninsula—the San Felipe Desert, the Central Coast Desert, the Vizcaíno Desert, and the Magdalena Plain Desert. There are 23 mountain ranges on the peninsula with the highest peak being Picacho del Diablo at 3,095 meters (10,154 feet) in the Sierra de San Pedro Mártir.

CLIMATE

While the climate varies by region and season, what attracts most travelers to Baja California is the warm, sunny weather. The southern part of the peninsula is the warmest, drawing snowbirds in the winter. Summers in Baja Sur can be extremely hot and humid, especially along the Sea of Cortez. The Pacific side of the peninsula generally has much cooler temperatures. In the late summer and early fall, tropical storms (called *chubascos*) and hurricanes can hit southern Baja, bringing high winds and heavy rains.

ENVIRONMENTAL ISSUES

Most of the Baja peninsula remains undeveloped due to the desert and mountain terrain and a lack of fresh water. But recent years have seen rapid growth in the development around the Los Cabos area for tourism as well as real estate. This development is starting to spread north up to both the West Cape and the East Cape. Cabo Pulmo has often been a place of contention between developers and environmentalists over the years, with concern for protecting the natural coral reef. In recent years, the danger of mining developments in the Sierra de la Laguna have threatened to contaminate the springs of the mountain range, which provide water to many of the towns on the East Cape.

PLANTS

There are over 4,000 plant species and subspecies on the peninsula with over 600 species endemic to Baja. For the most descriptive information on the flora of Baja California, pick up a copy of the *Baja California Plant Field Guide,* by Jon P. Rebman and Norman C. Roberts. The animal life is just as diverse with over 100 types of mammals inhabiting the peninsula, two dozen of which are considered to be endemic.

CACTI

There are 120 species of cactus in Baja, and many of them flower after rains, which can paint the desert with a vibrant splash of color for a few weeks. The most dominant, and perhaps most recognizable, cactus of the Baja landscape is the *cardón,* or elephant cactus. It's also the largest cactus and can reach heights of up to 20 meters (66 feet), and can weigh up to 10 tons. Some of the older plants are believed to be over 200 years old. Other common types of cacti found on the peninsula include varieties of the barrel cactus, cholla, and *nopal* (prickly pear). The *nopal* is an edible cactus and commonly found on menus around the region.

AGAVES

There are over 20 species of agave growing on the peninsula. Many are edible, so the agaves have always been a source of food, drink, and fiber. Agaves live many decades before they flower, earning them the name "century plant" (although flowering actually happens between years 30 and 60). The flower stalk emerges from the cluster of basal stems.

a donkey next to a *cardón* cactus

TREES

Trees found along the peninsula are often very specific to their regions. There are seven different varieties of palm trees in the oases farther south on the peninsula. This includes the date palm, which was brought over

cactus in bloom

from Europe by the Jesuit missionaries to be cultivated.

ANIMALS

LAND MAMMALS
There are more than 100 types of mammals on the peninsula, with over 20 endemic species. Coyotes, mountain lions, foxes, bobcats, and raccoons are fairly prevalent. The desert bighorn sheep and the endangered peninsular pronghorn (*berrendo*) are among the endangered species on the peninsula.

MARINE MAMMALS
Blue whales, pilot whales, humpback whales, and orca can all be spotted along the peninsula. The gray whales migrate to the Pacific side of the peninsula in the winter to mate and birth their young. Dolphins are prolific in the Pacific Ocean and Sea of Cortez. California sea lions can be found living in colonies around islands in the Sea of Cortez.

FISH
To the delight of anglers and divers, thousands of species of fish ply the waters of both the Pacific Ocean and the Sea of Cortez. Yellowtail, marlin, amberjack, corvina, roosterfish, dorado, wahoo, bluefin tuna, halibut, snapper, and sea bass are just some of the species that lure anglers who come to fish the prolific waters. There are a number of tropical fish, eels, and rays, including the Pacific manta rays that can have wingspans of up to 7 meters (23 feet).

Shellfish including shrimp, clams, oysters, mussels, scallops, and lobster are all found in large numbers, making them popular dishes at restaurants and food carts. There are over 60 types of sharks around the peninsula, including the whale shark, which can be found increasingly in the warm waters of the Sea of Cortez in areas like La Paz.

BIRDS
With over 400 species of birds, Baja can be a birders' paradise. Coastal birds such as pelicans, blue-footed boobies, frigate birds, egrets, and gulls are commonly spotted. Inland lakes and streams are home to freshwater birds such as ducks, geese, herons, sandpipers, teals, and storks. In the desert, falcons, hawks, owls, hummingbirds, sparrows, roadrunners, and turkey vultures can be sighted. Mountain birds like eagles, red-tailed hawks, pheasants, woodpeckers, and wrens are common to the Sierras.

pelicans

REPTILES AND AMPHIBIANS
Sea Turtles
There are five types of sea turtles found in Baja: the leatherback, green, hawksbill, western ridley, and loggerhead. All are endangered, and it's illegal to hunt them or their eggs. There are a number of conservation groups in Baja Sur helping to protect the sea turtles and promote their reproduction.

Snakes

Of the 35 snakes (*serpientes*) on the peninsula, about half are nonvenomous (*culebras*) and the other half are poisonous (*víboras*). There are 18 species of rattlesnakes, including the Baja California rattler, red diamondback, and western diamondback.

History

INDIGENOUS HISTORY

Historians agree that there have been people living on the Baja California peninsula for over 11,000 years. In the north were several groups belonging to the Yuman language family: the Kiliwa, Paipai, Kumiai, Cucupá, and Quechan. The Cochimí inhabited the central and southern part of the peninsula. The groups were adaptive to their environments and led mostly hunter-gatherer lifestyles. The Guachimis came from the north and were the people who created most of the impressive Sierra de la Guadalupe cave paintings.

SPANISH EXPLORATION

California existed as a myth for Europeans long before it was finally discovered by explorers in the early 16th century. Following Hernán Cortés's conquest of mainland Mexico, he sent three ships to explore Baja California in 1532. The peninsula was believed to be an island at this time. The ships of that first expedition disappeared without a trace. Cortés sent a follow-up expedition in 1533 that landed in La Paz, but most of the men in the expedition were killed by the indigenous people. In 1539, another expedition sponsored by Cortés was led by Captain Francisco de Ulloa and explored the entire perimeter of the Sea of Cortez as well as the Pacific Coast up to Isla Cedros. It was Ulloa who is credited with naming the Mar de Cortés.

THE MISSION ERA

The Jesuits were the first missionaries to inhabit the peninsula. Padre Juan Maria Salvatierra established the first mission in all of Alta Baja California at Loreto in 1697. The Franciscans and the Dominicans came after the Jesuits to settle the peninsula. In total, there were 27 missions as well as supporting *visitas* (visiting stations) founded on Baja. Uprisings by the indigenous people were very common, the most famous being the Pericú rebellion in 1734, which ended in extensive damage, the destruction of four missions, and the death of two padres. The history of each mission and the GPS points of the current sites (or ruins) can be found in David Kier's book, *Baja California Land of Missions*.

INDEPENDENCE FROM SPAIN

At the end of the 18th century, the Age of Enlightenment and liberal revolutions sparked the movement for independence from Spain. The revolt against the Spanish crown began on September 16, 1810, when Miguel Hidalgo shouted the *Grito de Dolores,* the cry for revolution, from the mainland city of Dolores,

Guanajuato. September 16 is still considered Mexicans' independence day, and the reigning president reenacts the *grito* every year on the evening of September 15. It took more than a decade, but Mexico officially gained its freedom from Spain in 1821 after the Mexican War of Independence.

THE MEXICAN-AMERICAN WAR

The Mexican-American War (1846-1848) had a major impact on Baja California. President James K. Polk believed the United States had a "manifest destiny" to spread across the continent from the Atlantic to the Pacific Ocean. In 1844 Polk made an offer to Mexico to purchase the lands between the Nueces River and Rio Grande (in what is now Texas). The offer was rejected and U.S. forces invaded Mexico, starting a string of battles that would lead to the Mexican-American War and end with Mexico losing one-third of its territory. In the Treaty of Guadalupe Hidalgo ending the war, Mexico gave into the United States and received US$15 million for the land that is now California, Nevada, Utah, and parts of Colorado, Arizona, New Mexico, and Wyoming. In the original draft of the treaty, Baja California was included in the land to be sold to the United States, but it was eventually left to Mexico because of its proximity to Sonora.

THE MEXICAN REVOLUTION

Because of Baja's remote location in relation to the rest of Mexico, the peninsula was somewhat insulated from political turmoil that took place in Mexico in the 19th century. But Baja California played an important part in the Mexican Revolution (1910-1920), which radically changed government and culture in Mexico. The revolution set out to end the dictatorship of President Porfirio Díaz, called for democracy, and demanded the return of lands taken unfairly from Mexican villages. Led by Francisco Madero and aided by Pancho Villa and Emiliano Zapata, rebel armies of workers and peasants rose up to fight against Díaz and his dictatorship. Baja California played a key role in the revolution in the Magonista Rebellion of 1911. This early uprising was organized by the Partido Liberal Mexicano (PLM) against the presidency of dictator Porfirio Díaz. The rebel army took control of both Mexicali and Tijuana. The success of the uprising encouraged rebel troops in other regions to join in the fight of the revolution.

The Mexican Constitution of 1917 is largely looked upon as the end of the Mexican Revolution even though a few more years of instability followed. The constitution returned lands to the peasants in the form of cooperatively owned *ejidos,* which are still in effect today.

STATEHOOD

Northern Baja California became the 29th state of Mexico in 1952. With its sparse fishing villages and small towns, Baja California Sur remained a territory, unable to meet the population requirements to become a Mexican state. When the Transpeninsular Highway (Mexico 1) was finally completed in 1974, it opened up commerce and tourism to the southern part of the peninsula, and Baja California Sur became a state later that year.

Government and Economy

ORGANIZATION

The capital of Baja California Sur is La Paz. There are five municipalities: La Paz, Los Cabos, Mulegé, Loreto, and Comondú. Baja California Sur was officially accepted as a state of Mexico in 1974 after the Transpeninsular Highway was completed.

POLITICAL SYSTEM

There are 31 states in Mexico that form a representative democracy. There are three branches to the government: executive, legislative, and judicial. Mexican presidents serve a six-year term with no reelection. The legislature is comprised of two houses, the Senate and the Chamber of Deputies.

The three main political parties in Mexico are: Partido Acción Nacional (PAN), Mexico's conservative political party; Partido Revolucionario Institucional (PRI), Mexico's centrist political party; and Partido de la Revolución Democrática (PRD), Mexico's leftist political party.

ECONOMY

Tourism is one of the driving factors in Baja's economy. Regions such as Los Cabos heavily rely on tourism from the United States and Canada. Baja's other industries include fishing, agriculture, and manufacturing at *maquiladoras* in the northern border regions. The North American Free Trade Agreement (NAFTA) went into effect in 1994 and opened the door for large car and electronics manufacturers to develop factories in northern Baja and easily import the items produced into the United States. Because of the close ties with the United States, the economy of Baja California is closely tied with that of its northern neighbor.

Economic inequality is a large problem in Mexico. The whole Baja California peninsula is in the higher wage zone for the country, but the minimum is still low, starting at US$5 per day for unskilled workers.

People and Culture

The population of the Baja peninsula is around four million, with most inhabitants living in the northern state of Baja California, and more specifically in the cities of Tijuana and Mexicali. Most of the rest of the peninsula remains sparsely populated. There are very few true indigenous people left on the peninsula today, and most Baja residents are a mix of Spanish and Indian cultures as well as descendants from Europe and Asia. In more recent decades, the peninsula has become home to a growing number of U.S. and Canadian retiree expats.

RELIGION

The Spanish missionaries first brought Catholicism to the peninsula, and it remains the dominant religion. Catholic holidays hold the same importance (or more) than

JANUARY

- New Year's Day, January 1, is a national holiday.

- Día de los Reyes (Day of the Kings), January 6, is a Catholic holiday honoring the three kings who brought gifts to baby Jesus. The day is celebrated with a round cake called a *rosca de reyes,* inside which is hidden a plastic figurine of baby Jesus. Whoever receives the baby Jesus in their piece of cake has to make tamales for friends and family on Día de la Candelaria.

FEBRUARY

- Día de la Candelaria, February 2, is a religious holiday celebrating the Virgen of La Candelaria. Whoever received the figurine of baby Jesus on Día de los Reyes traditionally hosts a tamale party for friends and family.

- Constitution Day, February 5, is a national holiday.

MARCH

- Birthday of Benito Juárez, March 21, is a national holiday.

APRIL

- Semana Santa (Holy Week) is the week before Easter and a popular time for Mexican nationals to take their vacation.

- National Children's Day, April 30, is an observed holiday.

MAY

- Labor Day, May 1, is a national holiday.

SEPTEMBER

- Mexican Independence Day, September 16, is a national holiday celebrating Mexico's independence from Spain.

NOVEMBER

- Día de los Muertos, November 1-2, is All Saints' Day, celebrating those who have passed away.

- Revolution Day, November 20, is a national holiday.

DECEMBER

- Día de Nuestra Señora de Guadalupe (Day of the Virgin of Guadalupe), December 12, is a feast day for this patron saint.

- Las Posadas, December 16-January 6, are traditionally religious processions reenacting Mary and Joseph trying to find accommodations before the birth of Jesus. Today, they have become a time for holiday parties.

- Navidad (Christmas Day), December 25, is a national holiday.

secular national holidays. Missions and churches are prevalent everywhere on the peninsula, and although church and state are separate, Catholicism plays a large part in Mexican culture. One of the most important figures in Mexican Catholicism is the Virgin of Guadalupe, or Our Lady of Guadalupe, a title for the Virgin Mary associated with an apparition at the Basilica of Our Lady of Guadalupe in Mexico City. Representations of the Virgin of Guadalupe are prevalent throughout the peninsula.

LANGUAGE

Latin American Spanish is the primary language spoken in Baja California. Mexicans who work in the tourism industry in large cities do speak at least some English. All travelers heading to Baja should learn at least a few basic greetings and phrases, which will go a long way in providing a better travel experience.

VISUAL ARTS

Baja California Sur has a lively art scene in cities like San José del Cabo and Todos Santos, where the expat community has attracted foreign and local artists who have opened galleries.

MUSIC

Mexico has a vibrant tradition of music. Mariachi music is probably the first thing that comes to mind for most people, and mariachi groups can be found throughout the peninsula, especially in the larger, more touristy towns. The ensemble usually consists of a trumpet, violin, guitar, and *vihuela* (five-string guitar), and performers are distinguished by their silver-studded *charro* suits. Another popular type of music in Baja is Norteño. Norteño music is mostly easily identified for its use of the accordion and polka-like sound. European migrants brought the accordion, along with the waltz and polka, to northern Mexico (hence the designation Norteño) in the late 19th century.

DANCE

The folk dancing of Mexico, the *ballet folklórico,* can be seen in various places along the peninsula. The highly choreographed dance includes both men and women and is characterized by lively music and bold movements. The women wear colorful traditional Mexican dresses with ruffled skirts that they hold while they dance, which are an integral part of the spectacle.

ESSENTIALS

Transportation

GETTING THERE

AIR

Most travelers arriving in Los Cabos come by plane. The commercial **Los Cabos International Airport** (SJD, tel. 624/146-5111, www.sjdloscabosairport.com) is near San José del Cabo. Direct flights are available from the United States, Canada, and other areas of Mexico.

La Paz has its own international airport, Manuel Marquez de Leon International Airport (LAP) (tel. 612/124-6307), 12 kilometers (7.5 miles) south of La Paz. There are currently no direct flights from the United States, but Calafia, Aeromexico, and Volaris have direct flights from Tijuana and other cities in Baja.

It can be cheaper to fly to the airports in Baja California Sur from the Tijuana International Airport (General Abelardo L. Rodriguez International Airport, TIJ, 664/607-8200, www.tijuana-airport.com) rather than from the United States, and thanks to a new pedestrian bridge that connects San Diego to Tijuana's Rodriguez airport, this is now easy to do. Ticketed passengers can park their cars in short- or long-term parking lots in San Diego and walk across the Cross Border Xpress (www.crossborderxpress.com) pedestrian bridge to take them directly to the Tijuana airport. The cost is US$16 one-way.

CAR

Most travelers choose to explore Baja by car—whether flying into an airport and renting a car or driving their own into Mexico. Mexico recognizes U.S. and Canadian driver's licenses, so an international license is not required.

Car Rental

There are car rental companies in La Paz, Los Barriles, Todos Santos, San José del Cabo, and Cabo San Lucas. Larger cities, especially those with airports, generally have more options and cheaper rates.

Some car rental companies in San Diego will allow you to take the rental car to Mexico, but make sure in advance. Understand that you'll need

to purchase Mexican auto insurance through them, which will be an additional charge. If renting a car in Baja, be aware that the insurance is not included in the rate at which you rent the car.

Mexican Auto Insurance

Mexican auto insurance is required by law when driving in Mexico. Even if you have U.S. insurance that covers you in Mexico, this is not sufficient, and you must additionally get a Mexican insurance policy. This is because Mexico does not recognize U.S. insurance and requires that you be financially responsible for any physical and bodily injuries caused by an accident. Mexican auto insurance policies are available for short trips by the day or can be purchased to cover you for the year. Liability-only policies are the minimum required by the law and will cover damages you may cause to other property or people; it costs US$12 a day. Full coverage additionally covers damages to your own vehicle. While the law does not require full coverage, it's always recommended. Full coverage can run US$30-50 a day. With many car rental companies, this added insurance will not be included in your initial quote, which can come as quite a surprise when picking up your rental car. With the insurance added in, expect to pay around US$300-350 a week for a rental car.

A handful of Mexican auto insurance vendors are on the U.S. side of border towns, but it's better to get a policy in advance with a reputable company. A number of options are available. Discover Baja Travel Club (3264 Governor Dr., San Diego, U.S. tel. 619/275-4225, toll-free U.S. tel. 800/727-2252, www.discoverbaja.com) has been in business for over 25 years.

Daily or yearly policies are available online, or you can call or visit the San Diego office.

Temporary Vehicle Importation Permits

Temporary Vehicle Importation Permits are not required for driving in Baja California, but if you are planning on crossing over to mainland Mexico, they are mandatory. Your car can be impounded permanently if you are caught driving in mainland Mexico without the permit. Temporary vehicle import permits can be obtained at the border crossings between the United States and Mexico or in La Paz at the Pichilingue ferry terminal.

SEA

If you have your own boat and are crossing into Baja by sea, there are port captain offices in Cabo San Lucas, San José del Cabo, and La Paz. You must complete a crew list document and get FMMs at your first port of entry for all passengers on the vessel.

Ferry

Passenger and car ferry service is available to Baja from mainland Mexico. Baja Ferries (tel. 612/123-6397, toll-free Mex. tel. 800/337-7437, www.bajaferries.com) is the most popular option with two routes from the mainland—one from Mazatlán and the other from Topolobampo, both arriving in La Paz.

Cruise Ship

There are a number of cruise ship lines that stop in Cabo San Lucas including Princess (www.princess.com), Carnival (www.carnival.com), and Norwegian (www.ncl.com). Most of these cruises depart from Southern California and last about seven days.

Note that Cabo is a tender port, so cruise ships will anchor in the bay and use shuttle boats called tenders to bring passengers to shore. For this reason, most cruise lines that offer two days in port still require passengers to be back on board in the early evening and then return to port the next morning because the ship heads back out to sea at night.

GETTING AROUND
CAR

Most of the highway in Baja consists of the two-lane Mexico 1, with little to no shoulder and inconsistent road conditions. Drive slowly and safely, and you'll have a wonderful time exploring.

Driving Precautions

It's extremely important to only drive during the daylight in Baja. Driving at night is dangerous for a number of reasons. There are no streetlights on the highway, and cows and other animals come to sleep on the warm asphalt at night, causing many accidents for unsuspecting drivers. It's not uncommon for cars in Mexico to not have functioning brake lights, blinkers, or headlights, which can also be dangerous. It's important to keep all this in mind when planning your road trip in the winter, as the days are shorter, giving you less drive time.

It's important to never speed when driving in Baja. *Topes* (speed bumps) and *vados* (dips where the river crosses the road) are often unmarked, and road conditions can deteriorate without any notice, causing a number of potholes in the road. There are no shoulders on the road for many parts of Mexico 1, which is another good reason to take it slow.

You'll encounter many trucks along

Mexico 1. They'll often help you out with passing by putting on their left blinker to tell you when it's clear for you to pass. But be careful to read the situation correctly so as not to misunderstand their signal as an indication that they will be passing or making a left-hand turn themselves.

Off-Highway Travel

Although Mexico 1 has been paved all the way to Cabo since 1974, much of Baja driving still consists of traveling on dirt roads. The condition of the unpaved roads can vary greatly and change quickly, so it's always best to ask around locally about road conditions before taking an off-highway adventure, especially after recent rains. Mexican auto insurance will cover travel on dirt roads (the road must lead to a destination), but will not cover you when off-roading.

Kilometer Markings

The major highways in Baja use kilometer markings. People use these kilometer markings when giving distances and directions. You'll find that many businesses use their kilometer marking as their address.

In Baja Sur, Cabo San Lucas is kilometer marking 0 on Mexico 1, and the kilometers count up as you head north to La Paz. Mexico 19's kilometer marking 0 is at the junction with Mexico 1 (south of La Paz), and kilometers count upward as you head south to Cabo San Lucas.

Road Signs

All speed limits are posted in kilometers. Many Baja road signs are accompanied by symbols, allowing even non-Spanish speakers to understand. Here are some common phrases seen on road signs:

- *Alto:* Stop
- *Tope:* Speed Bump
- *Vado:* Dip
- *Ceda el Paso:* Yield
- *Despacio:* Slow
- *Entrada:* Entrance
- *Salida:* Exit
- *Curva Peligrosa:* Dangerous Curve
- *Desviación:* Detour
- *No Tire Basura:* Don't Throw Trash
- *Conserve Su Derecha:* Keep to the Right
- *No Rebase:* No Passing
- *Un Solo Carril:* Single Lane Ahead
- *Conceda Cambio de Luces:* Dim Your Lights
- *No Deje Piedras Sobre el Pavimento:* Don't Leave Rocks on the Road
- *Este Camino No Es De Alta Velocidad:* Not a High-Speed Road

Fuel

Mexico's gas industry has been state-owned and operated since 1938, but just opened up to deregulation in 2016. The ubiquitous Pemex (Petroleos Mexicanos) gas stations, which were once the only stations on the peninsula, are now joined by other brands of gas stations, and the prices that were once fairly fixed now vary from station to station.

There are two types of regular gas, Magna (87 octane) with the green handle, and Premium (93 octane) with the red handle. Diesel will be available at a separate pump with a black handle.

The price for gas is always shown at the pump. When you pull up to the station, you'll need to let them know how much gas you want and of what type. It's normal to refer to the grade of gas by the color of the handle. *Lleno con verde* (full with green) is a common request when pulling up to the pump.

Gas stations in Mexico are full

service, so the attendant will pump the gas for you. They will often clean your window as well. You should give them a few pesos (US$0.50) as a tip for the service. Even though stations are full service, it's always a good idea to get out and watch them at the pump to ensure that the attendant isn't trying to take advantage of you. Make sure that the pump is zeroed out before they pump gas, and don't let them top off your tank.

It's always a good idea to fill up on gas before leaving large cities as gas stations can be few and far between in more rural areas. As Mexico is on the metric system, gas is sold by the liter. It's always best to pay in pesos for gas, as doing the peso to dollar conversion can get tricky on top of trying to figure out liters to gallons. It's becoming more common for gas stations on the peninsula to accept foreign credit cards, but you should never rely on this. It's always best to have pesos ready to pay for your gas.

Traffic Offenses

In general, the same rules apply in Mexico as do in the United States. You must wear your seat belt, license and registration must be current, no speeding, no drinking and driving, no cell phone usage while driving, and you must have at least liability coverage for Mexican auto insurance. The fines for these infractions vary from region to region but can be very expensive (the ticket for parking illegally in a designated handicap spot in Los Cabos is US$450).

In large cities that you're unfamiliar with, it can be challenging to navigate the busy areas of town, especially knowing when to stop at intersections, as stop signs can often be difficult to see. One-way streets are often not marked well, which can lead to confusion. It's also important to know that in urban areas you must stop for pedestrians in crosswalks.

If you're pulled over by a police officer, remember to be polite and courteous. In southern Baja, you will need to follow the police officer to the local station to pay the fine. If the officer is asking you to pay on the spot, he is illegally asking you for a *mordida,* or bribe. Giving him the bribe is illegal on your behalf and can get you into big trouble. It also perpetuates a cycle of police officers targeting foreigners in the hopes of getting some cash. Don't do it.

Roadside Assistance

The Angeles Verdes (Green Angels) have come to the rescue of many Baja road-trippers who experience a breakdown or troubles on the road. The green trucks are sponsored by the Secretary of Tourism and can assist if you get into an accident, have a flat tire, run out of gas, or break down. They offer free labor, service, and towing. Gas and spare parts are available for a charge. The service of the Green Angels is free, but tips are appreciated.

The Green Angels patrol the roads on a regular basis. If you break down, pull over to the side and lift your hood to signal that you need help. If you have cell phone service, you can call 078, which will get you the 24/7 bilingual tourist assistance, who will send roadside assistance.

Military Checkpoints

Road-trippers will encounter a number of military checkpoints on Mexico 1 throughout the peninsula. The soldiers will be dressed in full army fatigues with large guns and may seem intimidating at first, but they are there to keep you safe and are just checking that you aren't transporting drugs or arms. They will likely ask you where you are coming from and where you are going. They may ask to look through your vehicle. Tell them that you are on *vacaciones* (vacation). It's best to be polite and respectful, and you'll be on your way in no time.

Maps

If you can get a copy of the currently out-of-print *Baja California Almanac* (www.baja-almanac.com), this is the only map you'll need for a road trip on the peninsula. The *Baja Almanac* is considered the ultimate map for Baja and by far the most detailed and accurate navigation tool. Even older editions will still be useful. If you are planning to mostly stay on highways and larger roads, any regular foldout map for Baja will be sufficient.

BUS

There are a number of businesses that provide bus service between the towns on the peninsula. Autobuses de la Baja California (ABC, tel. 664/104-7400, www.abc.com.mx) and Aguila (toll-free Mex. tel. 800/026-8931, www.autobusesaguila.com) are two large companies with routes between most cities on the peninsula. Buses tend to be large and modern, with air-conditioning and comfortable seats. It's generally not necessary to make a reservation in advance, but it's a good idea to stop by the bus depot a day or so ahead of time to check out the schedule and current fares. It takes about 30 hours to travel the full peninsula between Tijuana and Cabo on a bus.

TAXI

Taxis can be found around larger cities, especially in the central tourist areas, at taxi stands, and at larger hotels. There are no meters in taxis in Baja, so always negotiate the fare with the driver before getting in the taxi. The ridesharing app Uber (www.uber.com) is now available in La Paz and Los Cabos (the service area includes Cabo San Lucas, the corridor, and San José del Cabo).

MOTORCYCLE

More and more riders are being lured by the adventure of cruising on their motorcycle down the Baja peninsula. Specifically motorcycle mechanics are less common than auto mechanics, so it's wise to be self-sufficient in this aspect. There are a number of guided motorcycle trips on the peninsula if you don't want to travel alone. Adventure Rider Motorcycle Forum (www.advrider.com) has some of the best information about riding on the peninsula.

BICYCLE

Bicycling along Baja's Mexico 1 is a dangerous feat that should not be attempted by any cyclists who are not experts. The lack of shoulders and guardrails on the windy highway coupled with the fact that there are large trucks and many drivers that speed make for a dangerous situation for any cyclist. The Baja Divide (www.bajadivide.com) is a new self-guided route that links 2,000 miles of dirt roads from Tecate to Cabo for cyclists looking to explore the Baja peninsula without having to take the harrowing highway option.

Visas and Officialdom

PASSPORTS AND VISAS

As of 2009, a passport is required for travel in Baja. If you are crossing in and out of Mexico by land, you can use a passport card. If traveling by air, a passport book is required.

There is a lot of confusion about the visa situation for U.S. and Canadian travelers headed into Mexico. A visa is not required for U.S. and Canadian citizens. However, a *forma migratoria múltiple* (FMM) tourist permit is mandatory for all non-Mexican citizens traveling in Baja. Many people will refer to the FMM as a visa, which causes an extreme amount of confusion about the issue. An FMM is required for all U.S. and Canadian citizens every time they enter Baja, regardless of where they will be going and how long they will be staying. The previous exceptions for trips under 72 hours and/or within the border zone no longer apply. For trips seven days or less, there is no charge for the FMM.

Visas are required for citizens traveling to Mexico from certain countries. For a full list, see www.gob.mx.

FMM TOURIST PERMITS

All U.S. and Canadian citizens are required to have a *forma migratoria múltiple* (FMM) tourist permit every time they enter Baja. The previous exceptions for trips under 72 hours and/or within the border zone no longer apply. To be clear, the FMM tourist permit is not a visa, although many people refer to it as a visa, creating much confusion about the topic.

If crossing by land, travelers must stop at the border to complete the FMM form, pay the US$30 fee, and then have the form stamped with the date of entry. You must present your passport book or passport card when getting your FMM. FMM tourist permits are valid for up to 180 days. If you will be spending seven days or less in Baja, free FMM tourist permits are available as well.

Travelers arriving in Baja by commercial flight from outside Mexico will have the cost of their FMM included in their plane ticket and will be provided with all of the paperwork to clear when arriving in Baja at the airport. Travelers crossing by sea into Baja must stop at the port captain's office to have their FMM stamped. If you will be entering Baja by boat and will not be stopping on land, but will be in Mexican waters, you must get a nautical FMM, which is a separate process. For more information go to www.gob.mx.

EMBASSIES AND CONSULATES

There is a Mexican Consulate (1549 India St., San Diego, tel. 619/231-8414, info@consulmexsd.org, 8am-6pm Mon.-Fri.) in San Diego that can assist with visas, permanent and temporary residency for Mexico, special import permits, and questions about Mexican customs.

There is a U.S. Consular Agency in San José del Cabo that can help with passport and visa services, provide assistance for U.S. citizens arrested in Mexico, register births and deaths of U.S. citizens, and perform notarials.

Canada has a Consular Agency in Cabo San Lucas.

U.S. Consular Agency – San José del Cabo

Tiendas de Palmilla, Mexico 1 Km. 27.5, Local B221
San José del Cabo, Baja California Sur, C.P. 23406
tel. 664/748-0129
9am-2pm Mon.-Thurs.
After-hours emergencies: toll-free Mex. tel. 800/681-9374
ConAgencyLosCabos@state.gov
http://mx.usembassy.gov

Canadian Consular Agency – Cabo San Lucas

Plaza San Lucas
Mexico 1 Km. 0.5, Local 82
Col. El Tezal 23454 Cabo San Lucas, Baja California Sur
tel. 624/142-4333
9:30am-12:30pm Mon.-Fri.
lcabo@international.gc.ca

CUSTOMS

ENTERING MEXICO

Travelers crossing into Mexico are allowed to bring items for personal use, as well as up to US$75 of new merchandise (per adult) duty free when crossing by land. If crossing by air, US$300 of new merchandise is permitted duty free. Adults may bring up to three liters of liquor or beer and up to six liters of wine. You may carry up to US$10,000 cash without paying duty.

Many people find themselves wanting to bring items to donate to orphanages and other charitable causes in Baja. However, bringing large amounts of used clothing and other items will be subject to paying duty. Firearms are illegal in Mexico and may only be possessed with a proper permit for hunting.

RETURNING TO THE UNITED STATES

Travelers may bring up to US$800 worth of new merchandise into the United States from Mexico every 30 days without paying a duty. Adults may bring back one liter of alcohol and 200 cigarettes. Some foods are allowed into the United States from Mexico; however, most fruits, vegetables, nuts, and meat products are prohibited. The specific list changes often, so check with www.cbp.gov for a complete run-down.

Recreation

HIKING AND BACKPACKING

Baja is a peninsula that has captured the hearts of many hikers and explorers. One thing that's common throughout is the lack of well-marked trails, if there are any trails at all. Mexico Maps (www.mexicomaps. com) has topographic maps available for the entire peninsula.

You will need to be prepared for self-sufficient camping, and please be respectful by carrying out all your trash and abiding by low-impact camping principles. Make sure to bring plenty of water and a first-aid kit, in addition to the usual hiking and camping essentials.

FISHING

Sportfishing is popular all over the peninsula, and anglers come for the thrill of catching yellowtail, dorado, tuna, roosterfish, and more. Mexican fishing licenses are required when fishing on the water. Everyone who is on board a boat with tackle, whether or not they are fishing, must have a fishing license. They are available by the day, week, month, or year. You can obtain a fishing permit in advance through the **Mexico Department of Fisheries (PESCA)** (2550 5th Ave. 101, San Diego, tel. 619/233-4324) in San Diego or through **Discover Baja Travel Club** (www.discoverbaja.com). If you are paying to take a fishing charter, they will often take care of the fishing permit for you, but be sure to ask in advance. Fishing permits are not required if you are fishing from shore.

BOATING

Recreational boating is an enjoyable way to experience Baja and grants access to remote beaches and places that other travelers can't easily get to. **Temporary Import Permits** (TIPs) for boats are now required for Baja. The permits are good for 10 years. You can start the process online at www.gob.mx/banjercito.

There are port captain offices in Cabo San Lucas, San José del Cabo, and La Paz. You must complete a crew list document and get FMMs at your first port of entry for all passengers on the vessel. If you will be entering Mexican waters for sportfishing, but not making landfall, you must obtain a **nautical FMM** (www.gob.mx).

KAYAKING

Most kayaking in Baja takes place on the Sea of Cortez, where the waters are crystal clear in certain areas and calmer than the Pacific. La Paz is a popular area for sea kayakers because of the shallow bays and islands to explore.

Kayaking on the Pacific side of the peninsula is for more experienced kayakers. In larger towns like La Paz, kayaks are available for rent, but many serious kayakers bring their own kayaks so that they can explore more freely in areas where there are no rentals.

SURFING

Baja California Sur is full of surf breaks on the Pacific side of the peninsula. There are various breaks in Los Cabos, as well as on the West Cape around Todos Santos. Surf shops, rentals, and lessons can be found in Cabo San Lucas, San José del Cabo, Todos Santos, and El Pescadero. Most surfers who are looking to surf in more remote areas bring their own boards and are prepared for self-sustained camping.

windsurfing near La Paz

WINDSURFING AND KITEBOARDING

Kiteboarding and windsurfing season on the peninsula is November-March. La Ventana south of La Paz and Los Barriles on the East Cape are two of the most popular spots for windsurfing and kiteboarding. A large community has built up around the sport in these two areas, and there are a number of companies that give lessons and have rentals available in both locations.

DIVING AND SNORKELING

The peninsula has a diverse marinelife, which makes for interesting snorkeling and diving in both the waters of the Pacific and the Sea of Cortez. On the southern Sea of Cortez side of the peninsula, the waters are much warmer, and tropical conditions can be found for diving and snorkeling. La Paz, Cabo Pulmo, and the Los Cabos region are the most popular dive and snorkel areas in Baja California Sur. The living coral reef at Cabo Pulmo makes it a particularly unique destination for diving.

Food and Accommodations

FOOD

FOOD AND WATER SAFETY

The most frequently asked question among first-time Baja travelers is "Is it safe to drink the water?" The tap water in Mexico contains different bacteria than that found in the water in the United States, and for this reason can cause upset stomachs for travelers. It's safe to drink the water and ice that is served at large restaurants and hotels in big tourist cities, as they use purified water. You should brush your teeth with bottled water to be safe. When in remoter areas, always ask for bottled water.

As when traveling in any developing country, it's a good idea to carry some Imodium with you. Most towns in Baja have pharmacies where they can give you something like Lomotil over the counter if needed.

WHERE TO EAT

Los Cabos, Todos Santos, and La Paz have a number of nice restaurants, many echoing the ingenuity and creativity coming out of northern Baja, where a culinary movement is drawing foodies from around the world.

Throughout the peninsula, fresh seafood, rich traditional Mexican dishes, and savory *antojitos* like tacos and tamales are the staples. Don't miss picking up a bag of fresh tortillas, either *harina* (flour) or *maíz* (corn), whenever you pass a *tortillería*.

WHAT TO EAT
Street Food (*Antojitos*)

Antojitos (little whims) are traditional Mexican fast-food dishes such as tacos, *tortas,* tamales, tostadas, and quesadillas. You can find these served on menus at many casual sit-down restaurants (either à la carte or served as a

SEAFOOD GUIDE

- *almejas:* clams
- *atún:* tuna
- *camarón:* shrimp
- *cangrejo:* crab
- *caracol:* sea snail
- *erizo:* sea urchin
- *jurel:* yellowtail
- *langosta:* lobster
- *mejillones:* mussels
- *ostiones:* oysters
- *pargo:* red snapper
- *pescado:* fish
- *tiburón:* shark

fresh-caught fish

meal with rice and beans on the side) and also at street food carts.

Seafood

Because the peninsula is surrounded by water, *mariscos* are practically a dietary staple in Baja. You can enjoy seafood at all different price ranges and settings. At street carts and cheap *mariscos* stands, you'll find items like fish tacos, ceviche (raw fish "cooked" in lime juice), and *cocteles de mariscos* (seafood cocktails where the seafood is served chilled in a tomato-based broth). A favorite among locals are *almejas gratinadas* (clams au gratin), where the clam is topped with cheese and served on the grill. At sit-down restaurants, you'll find items like *pescado del día* (fish of the day), *camarón* (shrimp), *langosta* (lobster), and *pulpo* (octopus).

Meat

Carne is a large part of Mexican food, whether served by itself or as part of a dish. You'll find *pollo* (chicken), *puerco* (pork), and *res* (beef) on many menus as well as less-traditional meats like *chiva* (goat) and *borrego* (lamb).

Salsas

No meal in Mexico is complete without adding some kind of salsa. Many restaurants and food stands make their own, adding to the unique flavors of the food. Pico de gallo (also called *salsa fresca* or *salsa bandera*) is a combination of chopped tomatoes, onions, cilantro, and jalapeño. *Crema* (a thinned sour cream), guacamole, and other salsas are common as well. If you don't like hot flavors, ask how hot the salsas are before trying them; you don't want to be caught off-guard by a habanero salsa!

LA CUENTA, POR FAVOR

Mexicans consider it rude to bring the check to the table before it's asked for. They would never dream of kicking you out in order to turn tables. When you eat at a restaurant in Mexico, you are welcomed with a warm hospitality that invites you to come eat, drink, relax, and enjoy. Many foreigners may be frustrated with this at first, but most come to enjoy it. When you're ready for the check, you'll have to ask for it: *la cuenta, por favor.*

Beverages

A standard selection of sodas can be found around the peninsula. Coca-Cola here is made with cane sugar instead of corn syrup, giving it a different taste and making it somewhat of a sought-after beverage over the years. *Aguas frescas* (literally fresh waters) are infused waters, served around Mexico. The most traditional flavors are *jamaica* (hibiscus), *horchata* (rice milk), and *tamarindo* (tamarind), although hip restaurants will serve other refreshing and creative flavors. *Limonada* is Mexico's version of lemonade. It is made with simple syrup and *limones,* which are limes in Mexico. You can order it *natural,* made with still water, or *mineral* with sparkling water.

Alcoholic Beverages

Even those uninitiated with Mexico are likely familiar with the margarita and tequila. Mexico makes a number of good beers, and Tecate, Dos Equis, and Pacífico can be found all along the peninsula. Baja's wine region, the Valle de Guadalupe, has helped wine become more popular around Mexico, and you'll see wines from the region on the menus of nicer restaurants throughout the peninsula.

ACCOMMODATIONS

There are a wide variety of accommodations found on the peninsula. The options depend on your destination and personal preference.

CAMPING AND RV PARKS

There are plenty of places to camp on the peninsula, ranging from isolated sites with no services to fancy RV parks with full hookups. There's a large community of snowbird RVers who spend their winters in Baja California Sur to take advantage of the warm weather.

MOTELS

Budget motels are found all over the peninsula, and in some places are the only option for accommodations. It's common at many of the affordable motels and hotels for them to ask for a deposit of a few hundred pesos as collateral for the TV remote control.

BED-AND-BREAKFASTS AND BOUTIQUE HOTELS

There are more and more boutique hotels and B&Bs opening up on the peninsula. In southern Baja, travelers can find these more intimate accommodations in La Paz, Todos Santos, San José del Cabo, and Cabo San Lucas.

RESORTS

For those who love resorts and luxury, Los Cabos is the place to go. There are no resorts in Baja outside of the Los Cabos area, even though there are a number of establishments that may have the word "resort" included in their name.

VACACTION RENTALS

VACATION RENTALS

Vacation rentals abound all along the peninsula, and these can be a good option for travelers planning to stay for an extended period of time or for locations where there are very few options in terms of hotels or motels. It can also be convenient to have access to a full kitchen to avoid having to eat all meals out at restaurants. **Vacation Rentals by Owner** (VRBO, www.vrbo.com) and **Airbnb** (www.airbnb.com) both have rentals along the peninsula.

Conduct and Customs

TIME

Many foreigners may experience frustration with the fact that things happen at a much slower pace in Baja than at home. It's not abnormal for service to be slower than you are used to and for everything in general to take longer. Punctuality among friends may fall to the wayside in Mexico, but you should be on time for any business-related matters. Most professionals are aware of foreigners' adherence to punctuality and put in the extra effort to be prompt.

POLITE INTERACTIONS

Mexican people are far more polite and less direct than stereotypical U.S. citizens. They always exchange niceties and ask about your well-being and your family before getting to the matter at hand. You should begin all conversations with at least a polite *Hola, buenos días* (or *buenas tardes,* depending on time of day) before delving into matters.

A cultural difference that foreigners may find frustrating is that Mexicans have a hard time delivering bad news or saying "no." They often consider it rude and will skirt the issue, which can lead to much confusion and irritation. Mexicans will rarely give you a "no" for an RSVP; they are far more likely to say "yes" and then not show up, as they consider this to be more acceptable than declining from the beginning. Likewise, if you are waiting on something they don't have, the common response is that they will have it *mañana,* tomorrow. Many foreigners have learned to accept the fact that in Mexico *mañana* doesn't necessarily mean tomorrow, it just means not today.

If you sense that you are not getting a direct answer, it's best to rephrase the question or to ask again in a different manner, to make sure that you are getting the whole story.

TIPPING

You should tip a few pesos to the attendants at the gas station, the baggers at the grocery store, and parking lot attendants. At restaurants, 10 percent is standard, and you should give 15 percent for a fancy fine dining experience. Just a few pesos will be sufficient as a tip at taco stands and food carts.

Health and Safety

MEDICAL ASSISTANCE AND EMERGENCY EVACUATION

Travelers will find knowledgeable doctors and modern medical facilities in nearly every sizable town in Baja. Large modern hospitals operate in larger cities, and clinics and Red Cross facilities are available in smaller towns.

There are a number of companies that provide emergency evacuation from Baja. Medical Air Services Association (MASA, toll-free U.S. tel. 800/423-3226, www.masamts. com) and Aeromedevac (toll-free Mex. tel. 800/832-5087, toll-free U.S. tel. 800/462-0911, www.aeromedevac. com) are two such services. It's always a good idea to purchase extra travel insurance when traveling to help cover any medical payments or emergency evacuation.

SUNBURN AND DEHYDRATION

The Baja sun can be intense and is prone to catching travelers off-guard. Sunburns and dehydration are common afflictions for unsuspecting tourists who have spent too much time out in the sun and heat. Sunscreen and hats should be worn outside. Always make sure you have plenty of drinking water and are staying well hydrated.

STINGS AND BITES

Stingrays and jellyfish are often the culprits for any stings in the ocean. Although the stings may hurt, they are not life-threatening. When entering the water from the shore, always do the "stingray shuffle" to frighten off any unsuspecting rays hiding under the sand. Seek medical attention for any allergic reactions.

On land, scorpions are common throughout the peninsula. They like to hide in cool, dark places like under rocks or in piles of wood. Always shake out towels, blankets, clothing, and shoes that have been outside and may have become a hiding spot for scorpions. A scorpion sting is painful, but rarely dangerous for adults. If your child is stung, seek medical attention.

CRIME

Mexico has been in the news the past decade for drug cartel-related violence. The violence, which was never targeted at tourists, has significantly declined in recent years. That said, it's always a good idea when traveling to be aware of your surroundings and to avoid drawing attention to yourself. Expensive electronics and flashy jewelry should stay at home. Don't leave items in your car that could be a target for petty theft.

EMERGENCY PHONE NUMBERS AND RESOURCES

These numbers can be dialed from any cell phone or landline in order to reach emergency services in Baja:

- **911:** All of Mexico uses 911 as their emergency phone number.

- **078:** Tourist assistance hotline. Travelers can call from anywhere in Baja California Sur to get 24/7 bilingual assistance, from roadside assistance to emergency services or travel information.

- **074:** Roadside assistance

Travel Tips

WHAT TO PACK

If it's your first time road-tripping down the peninsula, here are a few items to bring along:

Electronics: A GPS unit will be your most valuable tool for navigating the peninsula. Street names and addresses don't exist in many areas, so using GPS coordinates is often the most reliable way to find your destination. There are stretches of the peninsula where you won't get music on the radio, so an auxiliary cable and portable music player are a good idea. Camera and cell phone are a must for most Baja travelers. Expensive larger electronic items like laptops should be left at home unless you absolutely need them. The more you bring along, the more you need to keep track of, and most hotels on the peninsula don't have safes. Mexico uses the same outlets as the United States and Canada, so you don't need to bring along a converter for your chargers.

Toiletries and First Aid: Don't forget items like sunscreen, aloe vera, bug spray, and hand sanitizer in addition to your usual toiletry items. Most Baja hotels do not provide toiletries like shampoo, conditioner, or lotion, so you should bring your own from home. Hair dryers are another item not usually provided by hotels, so you should bring one from home if you need one for daily use. Pack a small first-aid kit with Neosporin and Band-Aids. You can get the generic version of most over-the-counter medications and items at any pharmacy on the peninsula, but if there's a specific medication or product you like to have on hand, bring it from home. Most Baja travelers carry Pepto-Bismol and Imodium A-D to help soothe an upset stomach. An extra roll of toilet paper is always valuable to have on hand for pit stops and because many gas station and public restrooms will not provide it.

Personal Items: Bring sturdy footwear for hiking and sandals for the beach. Water shoes can come in handy for hikes where you'll be crossing streams and for swimming in natural pools or rivers. Swimsuits, sunhats, sunglasses, and beach towels are necessary for beach time. Pack clothing that can be layered for hot days and cool nights. Leave expensive jewelry at home. Bring along plenty of reading material as English books and magazines can be difficult to find and expensive.

Sports Equipment: The equipment you bring with you depends on your interests and the size of your vehicle. Most sports enthusiasts secure gear on the top of their car with sturdy straps. You'll be able to rent equipment like kayaks, surfboards, stand-up paddleboards, bicycles, fishing rods, snorkels, and scuba gear in more developed towns. Many road-trippers bring along their own coolers, beach chairs, and umbrellas. Camping equipment will all need to be brought with you.

Vehicle: Be sure to have a standard emergency road kit, tow straps, flashlight, jack, and spare tire at the very minimum. Duct tape and a tire repair kit can help if you're in a desperate situation. It's always a good idea to carry a gas can and extra water.

MONEY

The Mexican currency is the peso, abbreviated MXN or sometimes MN. It uses the same symbol as the U.S. dollar ($), which can cause some confusion at times. Establishments in Mexico are legally required to post their prices in pesos, but you'll sometimes find, at tourist-centered restaurants and some hotels, that the prices are listed in U.S. dollars. Mexico has a 16% IVA (sales tax) that is also supposed to be included in the listed price of items, but sometimes isn't.

DOLLARS OR PESOS?

While U.S. dollars are accepted in some tourist areas of Baja, it's always advisable to pay with pesos so that you get the best exchange rate. There are a number of exchange houses in large cities, but these days most travelers get cash out of the ATMs in Baja for the best exchange rate. Be aware that you'll pay a fee at the ATM and will possibly pay another fee with your bank in the United States, depending on how your bank operates with foreign transaction fees.

Foreign credit cards are commonly accepted in larger cities in the Los Cabos region, but it's always best to have enough cash on you in case businesses don't take cards or the machine is not working (which is common). There are many small towns in the middle of the peninsula where credit cards are not accepted and there are no ATMs, so you'll need to have cash. Always remember to call your bank ahead of time to let them know you will be using your debit or credit card in Mexico, so that they can put a travel alert on your account. Travelers checks are not widely accepted, so it's best to have credit cards or cash.

Bargaining is accepted, and expected, in markets and at street stalls. Start by asking how much the item costs (*¿Cuanto cuesta?*) and then counteroffer with a lower price (go down to about half of the initial asking price). You can go back and forth from there until you settle on a mutually acceptable price. Always be polite and kind while bargaining. Never insult the merchandise or the vendor in an attempt to get a lower price. For brick-and-mortar stores, the set price will likely be posted.

COMMUNICATIONS

PHONES AND CELL PHONES

Because of the growing numbers of cross-border travelers and citizens, many of the large U.S. phone carriers have plans that will give you data, minutes, and texting in Baja. Always make sure to call your carrier to learn about your options before traveling. There will be places on the peninsula where no cell phone service is available.

Phone numbers in Baja follow the same format as numbers in the United States, with a three-digit area code followed by a seven-digit number. There's no standard format for hyphenating the phone numbers in Mexico, so they may at times look different than presented in this book. The area code for Mexico is 52. For dialing a Mexican phone number from the United States, you will need to dial 011-52 before the area code and phone number.

INTERNET ACCESS

Many hotels along the peninsula now offer wireless access. The service is not guaranteed and the signal is not always strong enough to extend everywhere around a property. But it's usually sufficient for light Internet use and will be available at least in the lobby area. More restaurants are also offering wireless Internet, especially in larger cities. Internet cafés are few and far between along the peninsula because of the prevalence of wireless Internet access.

WEIGHTS AND MEASURES

Mexico is on the metric system for weights, volumes, temperature, and distances. Driving directions and speed limits are given in kilometers. Gas is sold in liters, and temperature is measured in degrees Celsius.

TIME ZONE

The state of Baja California (Norte) is on Pacific Standard Time, while Baja California Sur is an hour ahead on Mountain Time. Daylight saving time takes effect in the two states at slightly different times, usually a few weeks apart, just to add to the confusion.

ACCESS FOR TRAVELERS WITH DISABILITIES

Baja California is a region that can be difficult to explore independently for visitors with disabilities. Uneven sidewalks (if there are sidewalks at all), stairs without ramps, and dirt roads and floors can make getting around in a wheelchair nearly impossible in most areas. Buses and shuttles are generally not wheelchair accessible. Check in advance with your hotel to ask about accessibility and to make any special advance arrangements. Large resorts in the Cabo region will be the most likely to have wheelchair access and the ability to accommodate travelers with disabilities.

There are very few provisions in Baja for blind or hearing-impaired travelers.

TRAVELING WITH CHILDREN

Baja is a great place to travel with children, and there are plenty of activities for kids of all ages and interests. Many hotel rooms along the peninsula are equipped with multiple beds to suit families. There are a few adults-only resorts in Cabo, and some of the exclusive boutique accommodations in places like Todos Santos many not accept children, so it's best to check ahead.

TRAVELING WITH PETS

Many road-trippers travel with their dogs as there are a number of motels and campsites that are pet-friendly in Baja. You should carry current vaccinations and registration for your dog. Mexico requires that travelers have a "certificate of health" from a veterinarian dated within 72 hours of entering Mexico.

TRAVELING ALONE

Solo travelers heading to the southern cape region shouldn't have any hesitation in doing so. Driving the peninsula alone or heading to remote areas requires a firm grasp of the Spanish language and sufficient automotive skills in case of a breakdown. Many solo travelers who are driving down the peninsula look for other travelers to caravan with.

SENIOR TRAVELERS

A large number of senior travelers are attracted to Baja California because of the warm weather and affordable prices. Retired snowbirds arrive in Baja California Sur each winter to enjoy the sunny days and laid-back quality of life. There are a growing number of retired expats all over the peninsula who have made Baja their full-time or part-time home.

GAY AND LESBIAN TRAVELERS

LGBT travelers should have no problems traveling in Baja. Larger cities like La Paz and Los Cabos will have more options for nightlife and entertainment.

Tourist Information

TOURIST OFFICES

Most large cities in Baja have at least one tourist office where travelers can speak to someone in English and gather brochures and information about the region. The **Baja California Sur website** (www.visitbajasur.travel) has helpful information.

TRAVEL CLUBS

Whether you are a first-time tourist or a seasoned Baja traveler, there are a number of advantages to joining a Baja-specific travel club. They offer up-to-date information, travel discounts, services and assistance, and premium Mexican auto insurance. **Discover Baja Travel Club** (3264 Governor Dr., San Diego, U.S. tel. 619/275-4225, toll-free U.S. tel. 800/727-2252, www.discoverbaja.com, US$39/year) is conveniently located

in San Diego, where you can stop in to get your auto insurance, prepaid FMM tourist permit, fishing license, and Baja books and maps, before heading south.

MAPS

The **Got Baja?** (www.gotbaja.mx) series of maps are available for a number of cities in Baja California Sur, like Cabo, La Paz, and Todos Santos. The free maps can be found around the city and are helpful for identifying sights, restaurants, bars, and hotels. For driving the peninsula, the currently out-of-print *Baja California Almanac* (www.baja-almanac.com) is considered the ultimate map of Baja and by far the most detailed and accurate navigation tool. Even older editions are still useful.

RESOURCES

Glossary

abarrotes: groceries

aduana: customs

aguas termales: hot springs

alberca: swimming pool

antojitos: literally "little whims," casual Mexican dishes like tacos or *tortas*

bahía: bay

BCN: the state of Baja California (Norte)

BCS: the state of Baja California Sur

calle: street

callejón: alley

campestre: literally "country," used to refer to outdoor country restaurants

cañon: canyon

cardón: a large cactus native to northwestern Mexico

caseta: tollbooth or guard shack

cervecería: brewery

cerveza: beer

colectivo: taxi van that picks up several passengers at a time, operating like a small bus

efectivo: cash

ejido: communally held land

farmacia: pharmacy

federales: nickname for the federal police

FMM *(forma migratoria múltiple):* tourist permit required for non-Mexican citizens traveling in Baja

Green Angels: a group providing free roadside assistance

gringo: a foreigner in a Spanish-speaking country who is not Latino or Hispanic

INM (Instituto Nacional de Migración): unit of the Mexican government that controls migration

malecón: waterfront promenade

mariscos: seafood

mercado: market

mordida: literally "bite," a bribe

palapa: structure with a thatched roof

PAN (Partido Acción Nacional): Mexico's conservative political party

panga: aluminum fishing boat

Pemex: the government-regulated gas stations in Mexico

playa: beach

PRD (Partido de la Revolución Democrática): Mexico's leftist political party

PRI (Partido Revolucionario Institucional): Mexico's centrist political party

punta: point

SAT (Servicio de Administración Tributaria): unit of Mexican government that controls customs

SECTUR (Secretaria de Turismo): Secretary of Tourism

tienda: store

tinaja: pool or spring

tope: speed bump

ultramarine: mini market/liquor store

vino: wine

ABBREVIATIONS

Av.: Avenida

Blvd.: Boulevard

Col.: Colonia

Km.: Kilometer

s/n: *sin número* (without number, used for addresses without building numbers)

Spanish Phrasebook

Spanish commonly uses 30 letters—the familiar English 26, plus four straightforward additions: ch, ll, ñ, and rr, which are explained in "Consonants," below.

PRONUNCIATION

Once you learn them, Spanish pronunciation rules—in contrast to English—don't change. Spanish vowels generally sound softer than in English. (*Note:* The capitalized syllables below receive stronger accents.)

VOWELS

a like ah, as in "hah": *agua* AH-gooah (water), *pan* PAHN (bread), and *casa* CAH-sah (house)

e like ay, as in "may:" *mesa* MAY-sah (table), *tela* TAY-lah (cloth), and *de* DAY (of, from)

i like ee, as in "need": *diez* dee-AYZ (ten), *comida* ko-MEE-dah (meal), and *fin* FEEN (end)

o like oh, as in "go": *peso* PAY-soh (weight), *ocho* OH-choh (eight), and *poco* POH-koh (a bit)

u like oo, as in "cool": *uno* OO-noh (one), *cuarto* KOOAHR-toh (room), and *usted* oos-TAYD (you); when it follows a "q" the u is silent; when it follows an "h" or has an umlaut, it's pronounced like "w"

CONSONANTS

b, d, f, k, l, m, n, p, q, s, t, v, w, x, y, z, and ch pronounced almost as in English; **h** occurs, but is silent—not pronounced at all

c like k as in "keep": *cuarto* KOOAR-toh (room), Tepic tay-PEEK (capital of Nayarit state); when it precedes "e" or "i," pronounce c like s, as in "sit": *cerveza* sayr-VAY-sah (beer), *encima* ayn-SEE-mah (atop)

g like g as in "gift" when it precedes "a," "o," "u," or a consonant: *gato* GAH-toh (cat), *hago* AH-goh (I do, make); otherwise, pronounce **g** like h as in "hat": *giro* HEE-roh (money order), *gente* HAYN-tay (people)

j like h, as in "has": *Jueves* HOOAY-vays (Thursday), *mejor* may-HOR (better)

ll like y, as in "yes": *toalla* toh-AH-yah (towel), *ellos* AY-yohs (they, them)

ñ like ny, as in "canyon": *año* AH-nyo (year), *señor* SAY-nyor (Mr., sir)

r is lightly trilled, with tongue at the roof of your mouth like a very light English d, as in "ready": *pero* PAY-doh (but), *tres* TDAYS (three), *cuatro* KOOAH-tdoh (four)

rr like a Spanish r, but with much more emphasis and trill. Let your tongue flap. Practice with *burro* (donkey), *carretera* (highway), and Carrillo (proper name), then really let go with *ferrocarril* (railroad)

Note: The single small but common exception to all of the above is the pronunciation of Spanish **y** when it's being used as the Spanish word for "and," as in "Ron y Kathy." In such case, pronounce it like the English ee, as in "keep": Ron "ee" Kathy (Ron and Kathy).

ACCENT

The rule for accent, the relative stress given to syllables within a given word, is straightforward. If a word ends in a vowel, an n, or an s, accent the next-to-last syllable; if not, accent the last syllable.

Pronounce *gracias* GRAH-seeahs (thank you), *orden* OHR-dayn (order), and *carretera* kah-ray-TAY-rah (highway) with stress on the next-to-last syllable.

Otherwise, accent the last syllable: *venir* vay-NEER (to come), *ferrocarril* fay-roh-cah-REEL (railroad), and *edad* ay-DAHD (age).

Exceptions to the accent rule are always marked with an accent sign: (á, é, í, ó, or ú), such as *teléfono* tay-LAY-foh-noh (telephone), *jabón* hah-BON (soap), and *rápido* RAH-pee-doh (rapid).

BASIC AND COURTEOUS EXPRESSIONS

Most Spanish-speaking people consider formalities important. Whenever approaching anyone for information or some other reason, do not forget the appropriate salutation—good morning, good evening, etc. Standing alone, the greeting *hola* (hello) can sound brusque.

Hello. *Hola.*
Good morning. *Buenos días.*
Good afternoon. *Buenas tardes.*
Good evening. *Buenas noches.*
How are you? *¿Cómo está usted?*
Very well, thank you. *Muy bien, gracias.*
Okay; good. *Bien.*
Not okay; bad. *Mal or feo.*
So-so. *Más o menos.*
And you? *¿Y usted?*
Thank you. *Gracias.*
Thank you very much. *Muchas gracias.*
You're very kind. *Muy amable.*
You're welcome. *De nada.*
Goodbye. *Adios.*
See you later. *Hasta luego.*
please *por favor*
yes *sí*
no *no*
I don't know. *No sé.*
Just a moment, please. *Momentito, por favor.*
Excuse me, please (when you're trying to get attention). *Disculpe* or *Con permiso.*

Excuse me (when you've made a mistake). *Lo siento.*
Pleased to meet you. *Mucho gusto.*
What is your name? *¿Cómo se llama usted?*
Do you speak English? *¿Habla usted inglés?*
Is English spoken here? (Does anyone here speak English?) *¿Se habla inglés?*
I don't speak Spanish well. *No hablo bien el español.*
I don't understand. *No entiendo.*
How do you say . . . in Spanish? *¿Cómo se dice… en español?*
My name is . . . *Me llamo…*
Would you like . . . *¿Quisiera usted…*
Let's go to . . . *Vamos a…*

TERMS OF ADDRESS

When in doubt, use the formal *usted* (you) as a form of address.

I *yo*
you (formal) *usted*
you (familiar) *tu*
he/him *él*
she/her *ella*
we/us *nosotros*
you (plural) *ustedes*
they/them *ellos* (all males or mixed gender); *ellas* (all females)
Mr., sir *señor*
Mrs., madam *señora*
miss, young lady *señorita*
wife *esposa*
husband *esposo*
friend *amigo* (male); *amiga* (female)
sweetheart *novio* (male); *novia* (female)
son; daughter *hijo; hija*
brother; sister *hermano; hermana*
father; mother *padre; madre*
grandfather; grandmother *abuelo; abuela*

TRANSPORTATION

Where is . . . ? *¿Dónde está . . . ?*
How far is it to . . . ? *¿A cuánto está . . . ?*
from . . . to . . . *de . . . a . . .*
How many blocks? *¿Cuántas cuadras?*
Where (Which) is the way
   to . . . ? *¿Dónde está el camino a . . . ?*
the bus station *la terminal de
   autobuses*
the bus stop *la parada de autobuses*
Where is this bus going? *¿Adónde va
   este autobús?*
the taxi stand *la parada de taxis*
the train station *la estación de
   ferrocarril*
the boat *el barco*
the launch *lancha; tiburonera*
the dock *el muelle*
the airport *el aeropuerto*
I'd like a ticket to . . . *Quisiera un
   boleto a . . .*
first (second) class *primera (segunda)
   clase*
roundtrip *ida y vuelta*
reservation *reservación*
baggage *equipaje*
Stop here, please. *Pare aquí, por favor.*
the entrance *la entrada*
the exit *la salida*
the ticket office *la oficina de boletos*
(very) near; far *(muy) cerca; lejos*
to; toward *a*
by; through *por*
from *de*
the right *la derecha*
the left *la izquierda*
straight ahead *derecho; directo*
in front *en frente*
beside *al lado*
behind *atrás*
the corner *la esquina*
the stoplight *la semáforo*
a turn *una vuelta*
right here *aquí*
somewhere around here *por acá*
right there *allí*
somewhere around there *por allá*

road *el camino*
street; boulevard *calle; bulevar*
block *la cuadra*
highway *carretera*
kilometer *kilómetro*
bridge; toll *puente; cuota*
address *dirección*
north; south *norte; sur*
east; west *oriente (este); poniente (oeste)*

FOOD

I'm hungry. *Tengo hambre.*
I'm thirsty. *Tengo sed.*
menu *carta; menú*
order *orden*
glass *vaso*
fork *tenedor*
knife *cuchillo*
spoon *cuchara*
napkin *servilleta*
soft drink *refresco*
coffee *café*
tea *té*
drinking water *agua pura; agua
   potable*
bottled carbonated water *agua
   mineral*
bottled uncarbonated water *agua
   sin gas*
beer *cerveza*
wine *vino*
milk *leche*
juice *jugo*
cream *crema*
sugar *azúcar*
cheese *queso*
snack *antojo; botana*
breakfast *desayuno*
lunch *almuerzo*
daily lunch special *comida corrida (or
   el menú del día depending on region)*
dinner *comida (often eaten in late
   afternoon); cena (a late-night snack)*
the check *la cuenta*
eggs *huevos*
bread *pan*
salad *ensalada*

fruit *fruta*
mango *mango*
watermelon *sandía*
papaya *papaya*
banana *plátano*
apple *manzana*
orange *naranja*
lime *limón*
fish *pescado*
shellfish *mariscos*
shrimp *camarones*
meat (without) *(sin) carne*
chicken *pollo*
pork *puerco*
beef; steak *res; bistec*
bacon; ham *tocino; jamón*
fried *frito*
roasted *asada*
barbecue; barbecued *barbacoa; al carbon*

ACCOMMODATIONS

hotel *hotel*
Is there a room? *¿Hay cuarto?*
May I (may we) see it? *¿Puedo (podemos) verlo?*
What is the rate? *¿Cuál es el precio?*
Is that your best rate? *¿Es su mejor precio?*
Is there something cheaper? *¿Hay algo más económico?*
a single room *un cuarto sencillo*
a double room *un cuarto doble*
double bed *cama matrimonial*
twin beds *camas gemelas*
with private bath *con baño*
hot water *agua caliente*
shower *ducha*
towels *toallas*
soap *jabón*
toilet paper *papel higiénico*
blanket *frazada; manta*
sheets *sábanas*
air-conditioned *aire acondicionado*
fan *abanico; ventilador*
key *llave*
manager *gerente*

SHOPPING

money *dinero*
money-exchange bureau *casa de cambio*
I would like to exchange traveler's checks. *Quisiera cambiar cheques de viajero.*
What is the exchange rate? *¿Cuál es el tipo de cambio?*
How much is the commission? *¿Cuánto cuesta la comisión?*
Do you accept credit cards? *¿Aceptan tarjetas de crédito?*
money order *giro*
How much does it cost? *¿Cuánto cuesta?*
What is your final price? *¿Cuál es su último precio?*
expensive *caro*
cheap *barato; económico*
more *más*
less *menos*
a little *un poco*
too much *demasiado*

HEALTH

Help me please. *Ayúdeme por favor.*
I am ill. *Estoy enfermo.*
Call a doctor. *Llame un doctor.*
Take me to . . . *Lléveme a . . .*
hospital *hospital; sanatorio*
drugstore *farmacia*
pain *dolor*
fever *fiebre*
headache *dolor de cabeza*
stomach ache *dolor de estómago*
burn *quemadura*
cramp *calambre*
nausea *náusea*
vomiting *vomitar*
medicine *medicina*
antibiotic *antibiótico*
pill; tablet *pastilla*
aspirin *aspirina*
ointment; cream *pomada; crema*
bandage *venda*

cotton *algodón*

sanitary napkins *use brand name,*
   e.g., Kotex

birth control pills *pastillas*
   anticonceptivas

contraceptive foam *espuma*
   anticonceptiva

condoms *preservativos; condones*

toothbrush *cepilla dental*

dental floss *hilo dental*

toothpaste *crema dental*

dentist *dentista*

toothache *dolor de muelas*

POST OFFICE AND COMMUNICATIONS

long-distance telephone *teléfono*
   larga distancia

I would like to call . . . *Quisiera llamar*
   a . . .

collect *por cobrar*

station to station *a quien contesta*

person to person *persona a persona*

credit card *tarjeta de crédito*

post office *correo*

general delivery *lista de correo*

letter *carta*

stamp *estampilla, timbre*

postcard *tarjeta*

aerogram *aerograma*

air mail *correo aereo*

registered *registrado*

money order *giro*

package; box *paquete; caja*

string; tape *cuerda; cinta*

AT THE BORDER

border *frontera*

customs *aduana*

immigration *migración*

tourist card *tarjeta de turista*

inspection *inspección; revisión*

passport *pasaporte*

profession *profesión*

marital status *estado civil*

single *soltero*

married; divorced *casado; divorciado*

widowed *viudado*

insurance *seguros*

title *título*

driver's license *licencia de manejar*

AT THE GAS STATION

gas station *gasolinera*

gasoline *gasolina*

unleaded *sin plomo*

full, please *lleno, por favor*

tire *llanta*

tire repair shop *vulcanizadora*

air *aire*

water *agua*

oil (change) *aceite (cambio)*

grease *grasa*

My . . . doesn't work. *Mi . . . no sirve.*

battery *batería*

radiator *radiador*

alternator *alternador*

generator *generador*

tow truck *grúa*

repair shop *taller mecánico*

tune-up *afinación*

auto parts store *refaccionería*

VERBS

Verbs are the key to getting along in Spanish. They employ mostly predictable forms and come in three classes, which end in *ar, er,* and *ir,* respectively:

to buy *comprar*

I buy, you (he, she, it) buys *compro,*
   compra

we buy, you (they) buy *compramos,*
   compran

to eat *comer*

I eat, you (he, she, it) eats *como,*
   come

we eat, you (they) eat *comemos,*
   comen

to climb *subir*

I climb, you (he, she, it) climbs *subo,*
   sube

we climb, you (they) climb *subimos,*
   suben

Here are more (with irregularities indicated):

to do or make *hacer* (regular except for *hago*, I do or make)

to go *ir* (very irregular: *voy, va, vamos, van*)

to go (walk) *andar*

to love *amar*

to work *trabajar*

to want *desear, querer*

to need *necesitar*

to read *leer*

to write *escribir*

to repair *reparar*

to stop *parar*

to get off (the bus) *bajar*

to arrive *llegar*

to stay (remain) *quedar*

to stay (lodge) *hospedar*

to leave *salir* (regular except for *salgo*, I leave)

to look at *mirar*

to look for *buscar*

to give *dar* (regular except for *doy*, I give)

to carry *llevar*

to have *tener* (irregular but important: *tengo, tiene, tenemos, tienen*)

to come *venir* (similarly irregular: *vengo, viene, venimos, vienen*)

Spanish has two forms of "to be":

to be *estar* (regular except for *estoy*, I am)

to be *ser* (very irregular: *soy, es, somos, son*)

Use *estar* when speaking of location or a temporary state of being: "I am at home." *"Estoy en casa."* "I'm sick." *"Estoy enfermo."* Use *ser* for a permanent state of being: "I am a doctor." *"Soy doctora."*

NUMBERS

zero *cero*

one *uno*

two *dos*

three *tres*

four *cuatro*

five *cinco*

six *seis*

seven *siete*

eight *ocho*

nine *nueve*

10 *diez*

11 *once*

12 *doce*

13 *trece*

14 *catorce*

15 *quince*

16 *dieciseis*

17 *diecisiete*

18 *dieciocho*

19 *diecinueve*

20 *veinte*

21 *veinte y uno* or *veintiuno*

30 *treinta*

40 *cuarenta*

50 *cincuenta*

60 *sesenta*

70 *setenta*

80 *ochenta*

90 *noventa*

100 *ciento*

101 *ciento y uno* or *cientiuno*

200 *doscientos*

500 *quinientos*

1,000 *mil*

10,000 *diez mil*

100,000 *cien mil*

1,000,000 *millón*

one half *medio*

one third *un tercio*

one fourth *un cuarto*

TIME

What time is it? *¿Qué hora es?*

It's one o'clock. *Es la una.*

It's three in the afternoon. *Son las tres de la tarde.*

It's 4 a.m. *Son las cuatro de la mañana.*

six-thirty *seis y media*

a quarter till eleven *un cuarto para las once*

a quarter past five *las cinco y cuarto*
an hour *una hora*

DAYS AND MONTHS
Monday *lunes*
Tuesday *martes*
Wednesday *miércoles*
Thursday *jueves*
Friday *viernes*
Saturday *sábado*
Sunday *domingo*
today *hoy*
tomorrow *mañana*
yesterday *ayer*
January *enero*
February *febrero*
March *marzo*
April *abril*
May *mayo*
June *junio*
July *julio*
August *agosto*
September *septiembre*
October *octubre*
November *noviembre*
December *diciembre*
a week *una semana*
a month *un mes*
after *después*
before *antes*

(Courtesy of Bruce Whipperman, author of *Moon Pacific Mexico*.)

Suggested Reading

TRAVELOGUES

Berger, Bruce. *Almost an Island: Travels in Baja California.* Tucson: University of Arizona Press, 1998. With his rich and descriptive writing, Berger recounts his three decades spent traveling in Baja California.

Hazard, Ann. *Agave Sunsets: Treasured Tales of Baja.* San Diego: Sunbelt Publications, 2002. This collection of spirited Baja tales will introduce you to colorful characters and erase barriers between Mexican and gringo cultures.

Hill, Herman, and Silliman, Roger. *Baja's Hidden Gold: Treasure Along the Mission Trail,* 2nd ed. Oaxaca: Carpe Diem Publishing, 2014. A collection of the stories of Herman Hill, a prospector, dreamer, and adventurer seeking gold in Baja California.

Mackintosh, Graham. *Into a Desert Place.* New York: W.W. Norton & Co., 1995. One of the most widely read Baja books chronicling the journey of a British self-described "couch potato" who walks the entire coastline of the Baja peninsula.

Steinbeck, John. *The Log from the Sea of Cortez.* New York: Penguin USA, Viking, 1951. This classic book recounts Steinbeck's journey by boat into the Sea of Cortez with marine biologist Ed Ricketts.

HISTORY AND CULTURE

Crosby, Harry W. *The Cave Paintings of Baja California: Discovering the Great Murals of an Unknown People.* San Diego: Sunbelt Publications, 1998. Crosby is viewed as the ultimate authority on the rock art of

Baja California, and this book provides detailed descriptions and color photographs of most of the sites.

Kier, David. *Baja California Land of Missions*. El Cajon, CA: M&E Books, 2016. This comprehensive guide covering the history and information about all of the Spanish missions in Baja California is an invaluable tool for any Baja traveler.

Niemann, Greg. *Baja Legends*. San Diego: Sunbelt Publications, 2002. The useful book explains some of the most prominent Baja establishments, personalities, and legends region by region.

NATURAL HISTORY AND FIELD GUIDES

Hupp, Betty, and Malone, Marilyn. *The Edge of the Sea of Cortez*. Tucson: Operculum, LLC, 2008. For beachcombers who love exploring tidepools, this guide will help with identifying shells, sea creatures, and birds found along the shore.

Rebman, Jon P., and Roberts, Norman C. *Baja California Plant Field Guide,* 3rd ed. San Diego: Sunbelt Publications, 2012. This must-have field guide is the definitive book for identifying Baja's diverse flora.

Swartz, Steven L. *Lagoon Time: A Guide to Gray Whales and the Natural History of San Ignacio Lagoon*. San Diego: Sunbelt Publications, 2014. This firsthand account looks into the natural history of Laguna San Ignacio and provides a guide to gray whale behavior.

SPORTS AND RECREATION

Church, Mike and Terry. *Traveler's Guide to Camping Mexico's Baja*, 6th ed. Rolling Homes Press, 2017. This indispensable guide gives all of the most accurate information for all the campsites and RV parks on the peninsula.

Parise, Mike. *The Surfer's Guide to Baja*. Surf Press Publishers, 2012. This guide gives detailed directions and maps to the best surf spots along the peninsula.

Internet Resources

Many establishments in Baja now have websites or at least Facebook pages where you can find information about hours and location. For general Baja travel, there are a number of online forums and even Facebook groups, but always double-check the information that you find, as it's not always accurate. The websites below have reliable and accurate information about travel in Baja.

Baja California Sur State Tourism
www.visitbajasur.travel
The state tourism website for Baja California Sur gives specific and helpful information about hotels, sights, and activities for each region.

Baja Insider
www.bajainsider.com
This comprehensive website covers valuable information for Baja residents and visitors.

Discover Baja
www.discoverbaja.com
Not only do they offer Mexican auto insurance, but this website is a wealth of information about travel regulations and the best places to go and best things to do in Baja.

Gobierno de México (Government of Mexico)
www.gob.mx
On the Mexican government website, users can find tools and services such as obtaining temporary importation permits for boats and vehicles going to mainland Mexico, and FMM tourist permits.

INAH
http://inah.gob.mx
INAH is responsible for protecting Baja's cultural sites like rock art and the Spanish missions.

Los Cabos Tourism
http://visitloscabos.travel
The Los Cabos tourism website has helpful information about hotels and events.

Smart Traveler Enrollment Program (STEP)
https://step.state.gov
The U.S. Department of State runs the Smart Traveler Enrollment Program (STEP) as a free service that allows U.S. citizens traveling abroad to enroll their trip with the nearest U.S. embassy or consulate.

U.S. Customs and Border Protection
www.cbp.gov
Has customs information about items allowed back into the United States from Mexico.

U.S. Embassy
https://mx.usembassy.gov
The website for the U.S. embassy in Mexico City has information about services for U.S. citizens.

ONLINE NEWSLETTERS
Discover Baja (www.discoverbaja.com) has a monthly online newsletter with helpful travel information and quality articles about all areas of Baja. Travelers can go to the website to sign up for the email list.

For events and news for specific regions, The Baja Western Onion (http://bajawesternonion.com) focuses on Todos Santos and the West Cape; The Ventana View (www.theventanaview.com) promotes events and news around La Ventana; and The Baja Pony Express (www.thebajaponyexpress.com) covers updates about the East Cape area.

Index

List of Maps

Photo Credits

MAP SYMBOLS

════	Expressway	○	City/Town	✈	Airport	⚲	Golf Course
─────	Primary Road	◉	State Capital	✈	Airfield	P	Parking Area
··········	Secondary Road	◉	National Capital	▲	Mountain	⚏	Archaeological Site
- - - -	Unpaved Road	★	Point of Interest	✦	Unique Natural Feature	⛪	Church
- - - -	Trail	•	Accommodation		Waterfall	⛽	Gas Station
··············	Ferry	▾	Restaurant/Bar	⚑	Park		Glacier
━━━━	Railroad	■	Other Location	⛳	Trailhead		Mangrove
═══	Pedestrian Walkway	△	Campground	�skiing	Skiing Area		Reef
‑‑‑‑‑‑	Stairs						Swamp

CONVERSION TABLES

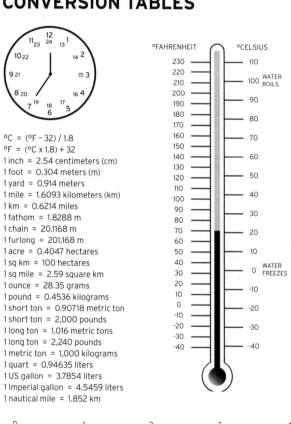

°C = (°F – 32) / 1.8
°F = (°C x 1.8) + 32
1 inch = 2.54 centimeters (cm)
1 foot = 0.304 meters (m)
1 yard = 0.914 meters
1 mile = 1.6093 kilometers (km)
1 km = 0.6214 miles
1 fathom = 1.8288 m
1 chain = 20.1168 m
1 furlong = 201.168 m
1 acre = 0.4047 hectares
1 sq km = 100 hectares
1 sq mile = 2.59 square km
1 ounce = 28.35 grams
1 pound = 0.4536 kilograms
1 short ton = 0.90718 metric ton
1 short ton = 2,000 pounds
1 long ton = 1.016 metric tons
1 long ton = 2,240 pounds
1 metric ton = 1,000 kilograms
1 quart = 0.94635 liters
1 US gallon = 3.7854 liters
1 Imperial gallon = 4.5459 liters
1 nautical mile = 1.852 km

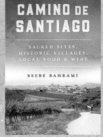

MOON LOS CABOS
Avalon Travel
Hachette Book Group
1700 Fourth Street
Berkeley, CA 94710, USA
www.moon.com

Editor and Series Manager: Kathryn Ettinger
Acquiring Editor: Grace Fujimoto
Copy Editor: Ann Seifert
Graphics and Production Coordinator: Lucie Ericksen
Cover Design: Faceout Studios, Charles Brock
Interior Design: Domini Dragoone
Moon Logo: Tim McGrath
Map Editor: Albert Angulo
Cartographers: Austin Erhardt and Andrew Dolan
Indexer: Greg Jewett

ISBN-13: 978-1-64049-105-2

Printing History
1st Edition — 1995
11th Edition — November 2019
5 4 3 2 1